online : adventures of an
information sleuth

Finding Reliable Information Online

Finding Reliable Information Online

Adventures of an Information Sleuth

Leslie F. Stebbins

ROWMAN & LITTLEFIELD
Lanham • Boulder • New York • London

Published by Rowman & Littlefield
A wholly owned subsidiary of The Rowman & Littlefield Publishing Group, Inc.
4501 Forbes Boulevard, Suite 200, Lanham, Maryland 20706
www.rowman.com

Unit A, Whitacre Mews, 26-34 Stannary Street, London SE11 4AB

British Library Cataloguing in Publication Information Available

Library of Congress Cataloging-in-Publication Data

Stebbins, Leslie F., 1958-
Finding reliable information online : adventures of an information sleuth / Leslie F. Stebbins.
pages cm
Includes bibliographical references and index.
ISBN 978-1-4422-5392-6 (cloth : alk. paper) — ISBN 978-1-4422-5393-3 (pbk. : alk. paper) — ISBN 978-1-4422-5394-0 (ebook)
1. Internet searching. 2. Electronic information resource searching. 3. Computer network resources—Evaluation. 4. Information behavior. I. Title.
ZA4230.S74 2015
025.0425—dc23
2015016987

∞ ™ The paper used in this publication meets the minimum requirements of American National Standard for Information Sciences Permanence of Paper for Printed Library Materials, ANSI/NISO Z39.48-1992.

Printed in the United States of America

Contents

Foreword

The question that lies at the heart of this book—the question of how to find reliable information—is not a new question, but it is a question with new urgency due to developments in the information ecosystem that have occurred since the appearance and widespread adoption of the Internet. It is also an extremely important question, as the consequences of relying on unreliable information cut across several important life domains and range from unpleasant to severe. For example, relying on "misinformation" can lead to financial fraud or missed opportunities for professional gain, social embarrassment, and in the case of health or medical information, using faulty, incomplete, or inaccurate information may literally be a matter of life or death.

There are several reasons for why the problem of finding reliable information is both more pressing and more complicated than ever before. Probably the most significant change in the information environment over the last two decades is that the Internet opened access to an unprecedented amount of information for public consumption. Digital network technologies lowered many hurdles to information provision, including the cost and complexity of producing and disseminating information for a wide audience, such that more than any other time in human history, information today is provided by a wider range of sources that can readily deliver information to large audiences located across the globe. This (r)evolution in information production has resulted in an incomprehensibly vast online information repository. Although exciting, the massive amount of information available today complicates the problem of locating reliable information both psychologically (How to deal with the information overload?) and in actual practice (Where to begin vetting the sea of information?).

The proliferation of information also means that much of what is available online is not subject to filtering through professional gatekeepers. Under conditions of information "scarcity," it is possible for gatekeepers to filter much of the information available, and gatekeepers have professional incentive to uphold quality standards when doing so. However, the Internet presents an environment of information abundance that makes traditional models of gatekeeper oversight and quality control untenable due to the sheer volume of information that has to be vetted. As a result, a good deal of information available online may be prone to being poorly organized, outdated, incomplete, or inaccurate. At the same time, many traditional information intermediaries, including opinion leaders, experts, and information arbiters such as travel agents and journalists, have disappeared either because of or concurrent with the introduction of the Internet. This forces individuals to evaluate a vast amount of information online on their own.

Traditional strategies for information evaluation may also be unavailable in the new media environment. Some have noted, for example, that online information is often missing standard authority indicators such as author identity or reputation, and yet research shows that source information is often the primary basis upon which credibility judgments rest. In some cases, source information is masked intentionally, yet in other cases, information about the source is provided, but difficult to interpret, such as when information is coproduced, repurposed from one site, channel, or application to another, or when information or news from multiple sources is displayed on an aggregated website that may itself be perceived as the source. These problems create uncertainty regarding who is responsible for information, the source's motive for providing the information, and, thus, whether users should rely on it.

Understanding whether some piece of information they found online is reliable is further complicated by the fact that users often have to consider many potential "layers" of the information simultaneously in their evaluation. Wikipedia presents a nice case in point. Evaluating the reliability of information in Wikipedia involves judgments made at the *website* level (is Wikipedia a credible source of information?), at the informational *content* level (is a specific entry within Wikipedia credible?), or regarding the information's *author(s)* (are specific contributors to Wikipedia credible?). Evaluations made at each of these layers can work in concert or may be at odds with one another, making the complexity of credibility judgments even more pronounced compared to most traditional information repositories. Research has confirmed this complexity, as studies show that evaluations of the source and content of online information interact in intricate ways to affect users' credibility judgments.

Adding to this complexity is the rise in "user-generated content" online, which is both a needed and important focus of this book. User-generated content such as reviews, testimonials, blogs, wikis, social Q&A sites, chats, pins, and the like has prompted a number of concerns with regard to the reliability of such sources and the information they create. Although user-generated information offers exciting promise and useful information, the so-called unfiltered social Web can result in the proliferation of information that is erroneous or biased, and it can be difficult to undo damage caused by the spread of this information. In addition, it is difficult to know whether information sources in these venues are who or what they claim to be and thus are impartial, and whether the information they provide is original or has been repurposed or altered. Moreover, and as Leslie Stebbins so nicely explains in this book, user-generated mechanisms only work to produce reliable information under very particular circumstances, and although these conditions are sometimes present in some social media venues, they are often missing. Group processes, including for example, groupthink and bandwagon effects, are ripe to operate in these environments as well, and are well known to produce biased and incomplete information.

The issues described above inevitably lead one to wonder: What is an information seeker to do to successfully navigate the sea of information available today? In this book, Leslie Stebbins provides an answer to this question that is as entertaining as it is informative, and offers a guide for anyone who ventures online in search of information that they can trust—which pretty much means all of us. Drawing from her experiences as a research librarian, educator, and everyday information consumer, Stebbins tackles the many thorny issues involved in finding reliable information with a highly engaging style, cleverly addressing common pitfalls and misperceptions on the part of information consumers, and showing how to avoid them. She focuses on what are arguably some of the most relevant types of information to a wide range of online information seekers, including finding credible health, travel, scholarly, and scientific information, as well as how to judge the reliability of restaurant and other kinds of service or product reviews. Moreover, the guidelines she offers to help users locate reliable information can be generalized to many other types of information as well.

The book also highlights important distinctions between slow versus fast thinking when it comes to information evaluation, the deep versus the shallow web, and sheds light on underused but highly valuable online resources including Google Scholar, Alexa.com, Worldcat, and others that will propel information consumers beyond their typical go-to sources—such as Google, Wikipedia, TripAdvisor—which are so popular, and yet can be quite problematic in terms of providing reliable information. She does this with eye-opening examples and anecdotes that challenge readers to rethink their suppositions as well as their approach to finding reliable information.

Throughout the book, Stebbins masterfully weaves the vast research literature pertaining to information processing and evaluation. As a leading researcher, educator, and policy consultant for over fifteen years on the topic of information credibility evaluation, and having published extensively on these issues during that time, I can say that this is one of the most valuable—and unique—aspects of the book. The six strategies for information evaluation Stebbins offers are both situated in, and supported by, a great deal of scientific research that she makes accessible and interesting to readers. (I wish I had the same talent!) Perhaps most important, they are also easy for anyone to apply as they search for information online, unlike the many typical "checklist" approaches that require a level of fact checking that is so effortful for information seekers as to render them useless in actual practice. With her six strategies, Stebbins instead offers information seekers a mindset and set of supporting tools that they can employ readily to help locate reliable information across a wide array of information types and platforms.

As Stebbins adroitly observes, sometimes having reliable information doesn't matter. But when it does, this book provides a timely and useful guide for information seekers—as well as the educators and librarians that support them—that they can rely on to help find reliable information online.

Miriam J. Metzger, Ph.D.
Professor, Department of Communication
University of California, Santa Barbara

Dr. Metzger is author of two volumes (*Digital Media, Youth, and Credibility* and *Kids & Credibility: An Empirical Examination of Youth, Digital Media Use, and Information Credibility*, both published by MIT Press) and over thirty articles, chapters, and essays on the credibility of digital information among both adults and children.

Acknowledgments

I have a confession to make: this book is largely the work of others. In many respects I am only a compiler and synthesizer. My biggest debt of gratitude goes to all the researchers, scholars, "big thinkers," and writers who are pondering and studying how we find information, make decisions about using it, and judge whether specific pieces of information are reliable. I spent two years reading much of the research in these areas in order to build the structure of my book and the six strategies from the ground up. The list of writers and thinkers is much too long to list here—all of them are cited in my endnotes—but I wanted to specifically thank David Carr, Miriam Metzger, Andrew Flanagin, Howard Gardner, Daniel Kahneman, Alison Head, Jaron Lanier, Marc Meola, David M. Levy, James Surowiecki, and Howard Rheingold.

I am also grateful for the enthusiasm and support of my editor, Charles Harmon, as well as the wonderful staff at Rowman & Littlefield, including Robert Hayunga, Darren Williams, and Jared Hughes. For their early support and valuable feedback I would also like to thank Steven L. Mitchell from Prometheus Books and Erica Wetter from Routledge. In addition I would like to thank Mark Warschauer from the University of California, Irvine, an early and instrumental reviewer who helped set me on course, as well as the three blind peer reviewers who spent hours providing feedback on early chapter drafts. Thanks also to Trudi E. Jacobson at the University at Albany SUNY and to my close friend Sally Wyman at Boston College for useful feedback and encouragement on early drafts.

For helping me wade through the worlds of food and travel I want to especially thank my guides Robert Reid from *National Geographic*; Catharine Hamm, the travel editor at the *Los Angeles Times*; Jenn Leo, a *Los Angeles Times* blogger; Wendy Perrin, master of all things travel; Anna

Roth, the food and drink editor of *SF Weekly*; and Allie Pape, the editor of *Eater San Francisco*. I would also like to thank the dozens of food and travel bloggers and reviewers who were so willing to email and talk with me about their impressions and experiences.

An enormous thank you to Sue Woodson from Johns Hopkins and Anne E. Leonard from New York City College of Technology for spending many hours reading a draft of the completed manuscript and providing many useful comments, ideas, and suggestions. Also, a huge thank you to my good friend Leslie Damon for her extremely comprehensive feedback and comments, and thank you to Miriam Metzger for her support and for writing the foreword.

The biggest thank you is to my husband, Tom Blumenthal, for his support and for serving uncomplainingly as my editor of first resort and my filter. Thank you for preventing me from embarrassing myself—to the degree that that is possible—you will probably suggest I edit out this line as well. And lastly, a big thank you to Anna and Will, our children, for their support and encouragement.

Introduction

I just think that people seem less and less concerned about where their information comes from at a time when I think they should be more and more concerned about it.

—David Carr

My teenage son comes down for breakfast and reports that Adam Sandler has Ebola. He saw it trending on Facebook.

I sigh inwardly and ask if he has looked at the source of the information. He says yes: CNN.com. [1]

Actor Adam Sandler under hospitalized care after contracting symptoms of the Ebola Virus

CNN.COM | BY BY GREG BOTELHO, CNN

Example of a hacked news site where information appears to come from CNN .com.

While educators used to teach a checklist of skills—*currency, relevance, authority, accuracy, purpose*—we have moved way past that now. Finding reliable information online is beyond challenging. The process has to start with *where* you choose to look for information. This book is based on a conceptual approach to finding and evaluating information based on the understanding that research is a creative, reflective, iterative, and most of all a messy process. [2]

Google works magically for some types of information seeking, but in other cases it leads us to information that is unreliable and in some cases costly or even dangerous. The enormous amount of user-generated content combined with powerful commercial interests clamoring for attention calls for more savvy and nuanced strategies for tracking down reliable information. [3] These strategies are essential in an age when we are bombarded with information and every answer feels like only a Google search away. This doesn't mean we need to abandon our Google habit altogether, it just means we need to be strategic in how we search, and understand what types of questions cannot be answered with a simple Google search.

Finding Reliable Information Online uses stories to illustrate strategies for finding and evaluating different types of information. Health, vacation planning, restaurant and product reviews, workplace needs, and scientific claims serve as examples to demonstrate the different purposes of a piece of information: as a commodity, as a means of education, as a means to influence, and as a means of negotiating and understanding the world. [4]

The stories serve as a way to explore many questions about how we can judge the credibility of a piece of information. What percentage of Yelp restaurant reviews are fake? Can we learn to spot these fake reviews? What does a 5-star rating really mean? Are WebMD and Mayo Clinic comparable and trustworthy health information sites? When can we trust the "wisdom of the crowd" and when should we seek out an expert? When can an amateur give us good advice? Do professional critics still play a role? What's the difference between a blog and a newspaper site? Is there a difference? When do we need to use scholarly research to solve an information need? Can we trust what we read in *National Geographic*?

CHAPTER OVERVIEWS

Each chapter investigates a research question from its initial formulation to the final analysis of the best sources that can provide credible and reliable information to answer the question.

Chapter 1 investigates a seemingly simple health question about red wine and longevity. Over 80 percent of people in the United States who search the Web search for health information, and a significant majority of searchers report that they have used the information found online to make a decision about their own health or the way they cared for someone else.[5] Because research on health topics is so popular, thousands of pages of content are generated daily to attract viewers. Much of the content churned out is unreliable, but some is incredibly useful and credible. This chapter looks closely at user-generated Q&A sites, popular sites such as WebMD, scholarly sites like PubMed, and commonly used sites such as Wikipedia. It also looks at the search process itself and how biases we bring to the table can greatly influence our search results. The chapter also delves deeply into the scholarly research process in health and medicine and unpacks both the challenges and opportunities in finding and evaluating the latest research studies.

Chapter 2 focuses on restaurant reviews within the larger arena of user-generated and professional reviews for products, movies, the theater, and books. This chapter traces the origins of restaurant reviews and picks apart the differences between a professional critic, a blogger, or a crowdsourced review site such as Yelp. Along the way concepts are introduced related to the psychology of search such as our overconfidence in our ability to spot fake reviews, our bias toward thinking a top hit in Google confers a high reliability score, and the problem of source amnesia. Examining when crowdsourced information can be useful, and uncovering issues with rating systems such as positive data skew; herding behavior; and selection bias are explored in order to understand how to evaluate online restaurant information. This chapter also looks at the different types of knowledge that define expertise and whether professional training is essential to conferring expert status. The ethics of different types of reviewers are examined and the transformed world of restaurant criticism is analyzed.

Chapter 3 investigates a work question from the CEO of a successful start-up company that is designing a new office building and wants to know if an open-plan office design will increase productivity. The process begins with a simple Google search and then digs heavily into social science research. The concept of the Deep Web is explained and a contextual approach to research is conducted. Research is messy and a certain amount of poking around is needed to uncover reliable information. Formulating a search query and understanding the notion of "satisficing," confirmation bias, our strong need for closure, and other heuristics—shortcuts—are explored along with the perils of echo chambers. Developing a need for healthy skepticism without becoming cynical, and avoiding "fast thinking" and our tendency to substitute an easier question to avoid doing the work of answering a more challenging question are examined.[6] The chapter illustrates the need to evaluate arguments based on evidence rather than getting swept up in the easy fix.

This chapter also looks more closely at research processes within the social sciences, including the invisible college, the idea of scholarship as an ongoing conversation, the role of research review articles, and techniques and shortcuts for digesting the contents of a research article and evaluating its worth and importance. Patience, persistence, and resilience are needed to fully understand the research on a complex subject. This chapter also looks closely at how to comprehensively research authority: both publishing body and author.

Chapter 4 explores the challenge of planning a vacation and deciding what information is reliable in an area where marketing sites dominate. User-generated rating and review systems are unpacked to understand how they should be interpreted and the current research on popular travel sites such as TripAdvisor and Airbnb is explored. The rise of the collaborative sharing economy and its counterpart the "pseudo sharing economy" are also investigated.

Figuring out which sites best match your "travel tribe" and the pros and cons of relying on amateur travel bloggers, professional travel writers, and traditional travel guidebooks are compared. What is expertise in the world of travel? If someone travels a lot are they an expert? What is a parachute artist? Is Google good at selecting the most reliable travel information? This chapter explores bounce rates, negative search engine optimization attacks, and whether it is sometimes ethical to write a fake review. Should travel bloggers disclose free trips? How good are people at spotting false or biased information online?

Chapter 5 delves deeply into the problematic link between science journalism and scientific research in looking at the question of whether dogs possess some rudimentary form of empathy. The chapter also illustrates the use of many of the heuristics we use when we search for information: reputation, bandwagon, consistency, persuasive intent, and other shortcuts are examined. These heuristics are a double-edged sword because, on the one hand, they can reduce the amount of cognitive effort used in decision making. On the other hand, using heuristics can also lead to systematic biases or errors in judgment.[7]

The scientific research process and the way that this clashes with the demands of journalism are reviewed and Q&A sites, White Papers, and magazines such as _National Geographic_ and _Discovery_——that tend to come up first in Google searches—are analyzed to see if they contain reliable science information. Research on the different roles of science blogs and their use in the research process and in communicating science information to the public is also explored. The parallel universe of scientific research that is separate from journalism, the challenges from the lack of open access journals, and the hyping of science by journalists, university press offices, and even the researchers themselves is examined in terms of the roles these play in finding reliable science information. Finally, tracking, filtering, and evaluating the research on a single science topic is demonstrated to uncover the current state of the research on dogs and empathy.

MORE, FASTER, BETTER?

What started as an exciting experiment—all the world's information at our finger tips—is evolving into a complex information environment where competing interests vie for our attention. We used to consume our information after it had been filtered for us: by publishers, editors, booksellers, libraries, and others. While there are significant downsides to having an elite group decide what we see and don't see, we have gone to the other extreme. The gatekeepers are gone, the gates have been flung open, and those with the most strategic marketing plans and search engine optimization strategies are often the ones that win our attention. Who do we want in charge of answering our information queries and giving us advice?

There is a groundswell of thinkers sounding alarms about the dangers of our shoddy information diet, our loss of focus, and our inability to take time for contemplative thinking and long-form reading and analysis.[8] We celebrate our ability to participate in creating content and we enjoy the vast access we now have to information without questioning the quality and reliability of what we are consuming. There is a great deal of well-founded joy in the wisdom and promise of user-generated crowdsourced content. Crowdsourced projects—such as Galaxy Zoo, where amateurs help classify millions of galaxies, or grassroots flu-tracking by smart phone app—are expanding our research capabilities. But sometimes we conflate all the positive uses of user-generated data with activities where user data is not useful for generating reliable information or is being gamed by commercial interests. Jaron Lanier has said: "there is an odd lack of curiosity about the limits of crowd wisdom."[9]

Professor David M. Levy talks about how American society is succumbing to an ethic of "more-faster-better" and is losing the ability for reflection. Levy notes that while there is great value in the variety of information online, people are feeling:

> *overloaded, overwhelmed, and oppressed by the amount of information they find themselves sifting through; by the fragmentary nature of the info–bits they are consuming and their own fragmented states of mind.* "[10]

In terms of information "more" is often not "faster" or "better." Ironically, the more information available on a topic the less likely we are able to find the most reliable sources.

Writer Leon Wieseltier laments the constant disruption from disintermediated pieces of information and the focus on content creation that values quantity over quality:

> *Journalistic institutions slowly transform themselves into silent sweatshops in which words cannot wait for thoughts, and first responses are promoted into best responses, and patience is a professional liability. As the frequency of expression grows, the force of expression diminishes: Digital expectations of alacrity and terseness confer the highest prestige upon the twittering cacophony of one-liners and promotional announcements.* [11]

The push to constantly churn out new "content" at the expense of creating valuable knowledge is probably the biggest threat to this wonderful opportunity we have of harnessing the Web as a tool for knowledge sharing and education. Instead we have pharmaceutical companies directly providing us with health advice by coming up first in Google searches, and gaming platforms giving us relationship or travel advice in order to pull in new customers.

Psychologist Daniel Kahneman encourages us to engage in more "Slow Thinking." He argues that our brains use two systems to process information. *Thinking Fast* involves instantly fitting what we see into our preconceived notions of how the world works, whereas *Thinking Slow* involves making a conscious effort to question the information we are viewing. [12] Taking Kahneman's work one step further: We need to slow down and question how we search for information and where we look for it. We need to become more proactive in our selection of sources.

Media expert Dominique Brossard has conducted research showing that many of us are getting sucked into a self-reinforcing information spiral in which *how* we search for a topic subsequently influences the algorithms that a search provider like Google uses to weigh and retrieve content. Brossard questions whether we are moving toward a communication process in which knowledge that people acquire is greatly influenced by what links search engines pull up and how they direct traffic to us. Rather than expanding our information universe, search engines and Facebook feeds may be narrowing our options. [13]

AVOIDING THE DROOL BUCKET

In the Air Force the expression "drool bucket" is used to describe the massive amounts of data provided to pilots who experience such overload that they find themselves lost and staring unblinkingly into massive data systems. While multiple data sources greatly enhance tactical capabilities for pilots, too much data results in an overload that causes this channelized attention that is one of the most common human factors in flight accidents.[14] The military is currently studying ways to increase the capacity of pilots to focus on important information, while at the same time improving and limiting the flow of data that is provided to these pilots in order to avoid the "drool bucket" phenomenon.

With Twitter, Facebook feeds, and the cacophonous collection of videos, news, blogs, apps, and entertainment services surrounding us we are prime candidates for drool bucket syndrome as well—unless we become more engaged in how we search for information and where we look. Google has come a long way toward effectively delivering search results that are targeted to our requests, but unlike the military that controls and chooses which data goes into the feed a pilot views, Google searches are combing through billions of pages of data, much of it data from sources we would not voluntarily select. At the same time, Google is not able to get to billions of web pages beyond the shallow web including many scholarly databases and journal articles.[15]

We are at a crucial tipping point in the evolution of search engines, and in particular in the evolution of Google, Bing, and Yahoo! Every day Google is searched more than *3.5 billion* times. Google is not able to keep on top of the search engine optimization marketers that are gaming the system, and Google itself is engaging in questionable practices by manipulating search results for commercial gain by pointing to Google-owned sites first.[16] Many factors contribute to why we get the results we get when searching Google or other search engines. Hitting the top five in the search list sometimes has little correlation with quality and credibility, though research has shown that many people equate link order with reliability.[17]

As we become more reliant on the Web for everyday-life information, as well as for our research and workplace needs, it is essential that we develop ways to home in on the most useful and trustworthy information, rather than letting other interests control the information that we find. In this book we peek under the hood and kick the tires of such well-known players as Wikipedia and Answers.com. Sites like Wikipedia have become a mainstay for those searching for information via Google, but the early hubris of the Wikipedia community is falling away to reveal a bureaucratic and increasingly small number of predominantly male editors who are heavily controlling "all the world's knowledge," while the quality of that information declines.[18] At the same time, the stakes are so high for sites like TripAdvisor and Yelp— with millions of dollars in play—that questionable marketing tactics are now being used to compete effectively for our increasingly short attention spans.

In a study on the information competencies of recent college graduates in the workplace, employers indicated that their newly hired students were adept at quickly finding an answer, but lacked the skills needed to find the *best* answers to solve problems in the workplace; they lacked persistence and patience and relied on information found on initial search screens rather than moving beyond Google and using more sophisticated strategies.[19] This book seeks to address this issue.

AND THIS IS YOUR BRAIN ON INFORMATION

New research on the brain suggests that we are increasingly depending on external sources like the Web to serve as an extension of our brain.[20] A recent study on memory from Harvard and Columbia confirms this phenomenon and demonstrates that having easy access to information on the Internet results in people retaining fewer facts, but instead remembering how to find those facts.[21] Not surprisingly, people have adapted to the smart phone in their pocket by no longer trying to remember an address or the hours their favorite coffee shop is open, because they know with a few taps they can retrieve this information.

Scientists suggest that this move toward reaching outside of our brains is inevitable, and what we should focus on is not whether we *should* be doing this, but on ways to improve this brain-Internet connection. One area of focus should be making sure that the information we reach out and use is reliable. Using the Web to augment our brains is fantastic, but not if what we reach out and retrieve is biased or of poor quality. Finding coffee shop hours and basic factual information about the world around us has become straightforward—one tap on a smartphone—but researching more complex questions often cannot be approached with a simple Google search if we want a credible answer.

It would be wonderful to think of the Web as an extremely sophisticated system that could retrieve the highest quality information for every question asked, but basic questions like "how do I get a strawberry jam stain out of my shirt?" are very different from research questions like "Is wind power a threat to birds?" or consumer questions like "What are the least expensive hotels in safe areas of Bangkok?" We are reasonably good at judging the information we get in person from people we know, we weight information with varying degrees of reliability based on who it comes from. We are far less experienced at judging the validity and authority of disintermediated information and too prone to be satisfied with a quick answer. Our vast social networks also provide us with product recommendations and information, but in many cases these "likes" may have hidden motives such as giving five stars to a cousin's sushi restaurant without ever having eaten there.

THE SIX STRATEGIES

The six strategies for finding reliable information are not just another check-list to pop through when reading a piece of information. The strategies start *before* the search question is even defined, well before the piece of information is viewed. By developing a deeper understanding of how information is created, constructed, and packaged; how search engines and websites function; and the many different types and purposes of information available, we can approach search armed with the knowledge needed to strategically uncover the most trustworthy information about a topic.

The six strategies are:

1. Start at the Source

This seemingly simple but complex idea involves conceptually changing the focus of the search: To hunt for a *source* for the information first and *then* the information itself. By taking control of the sources viewed, half the job of evaluation is completed up front, before even reading a piece of information. This conceptual approach is indebted to the work of Marc Meola and his radical notion of "chucking the checklist," as well as the many librarians involved in the new "Framework for Information Literacy for Higher Education."[22] Searching *is* strategic and this new framework has driven the development of this book:

> *Information searching is often nonlinear and iterative, requiring the evaluation of a broad range of information sources and the mental flexibility to pursue alternate avenues as new understanding is developed.*[23]

Starting at the source might involve a simple decision such as starting the search with Google Scholar instead of Google, or making a few tweaks in how a search query is constructed, but it sometimes involves a lengthier and more sophisticated strategy.

2. The Psychology of Search

This strategy focuses on the other side of the search equation: the psychological baggage *we* bring to the search. We have a tremendous impact on our search results: the potential for bias in how we ask questions, how easily we are satisfied or willing to settle, the influence of "name" brands and reputations, and social factors that influence our choices. In investigating the psychology of search we look at the search habits of Supreme Court Justices, the information decision-making strategies of burglars deciding which houses to rob, and why tourists using TripAdvisor thought they were going to a resort and ended up at a homeless shelter. The psychology of search draws on the work of Metzger and Flanagin, who have investigated the "heuristics"—shortcuts—we rely on when searching for and evaluating information, as well as the work of Daniel Kahneman on *Thinking, Fast and Slow,* and many other researchers who investigate how people search for and evaluate information. The psychology of search also includes the ways we can develop metacognitive habits—thinking about how we are thinking—in order to adjust our search behavior.

3. Expert, Amateur, Crowd

This strategy involves making a conscious decision as to when to use an expert and when an amateur or crowdsourced wisdom can be valuable. Some researchers suggest that there is a paradigm shift taking place in how we define credibility as we weigh expectations about expertise, accuracy, and absence of bias with the desire for interactivity, transparency, and identification. [24] There are not always easy answers: For high-stakes searches often a combination of types of information is desirable, but there are also times when expertise provides richer, more complex, and more reliable information. This strategy looks closely at the definition of an expert in different arenas: restaurant and travel information, health advice, scientific research, and workplace information needs. The Association of College and Research Libraries Framework underlines the idea that authority can be fluid: for a medical decision we may want a doctor, but for dating advice a peer might be the superior source. At the same time, Howard Gardner's recent work provides an anchor and inspiration in an information world that has been turned upside down:

> best antidote to the attack on truth is understanding the methods that expert people use to determine the truth. . . . you have to understand the methods that human beings have developed over hundreds if not thousands of years, of separating the truth from the chaff . . . And I think it can be done. Indeed, I'd even go further. . . . I think at this point in human history . . . if you're willing to work at it, if you're willing to be skeptical without being cynical, the chances of establishing what's really true are greater than ever before. [25]

4. Context, Motivation, and Bias

Context relates to everything surrounding the information, including the context of the search you are embarking on: Bar bet? Research paper? And context also includes determining the purpose of a piece of information, understanding how it was constructed, whether it was vetted, edited, peer reviewed, published, and commented on. By figuring out context we can better understand the motivation and potential bias of a piece of information.

Many of us rely on a few trusted sources for many of our information needs, but we need to be both flexible and skeptical and adjust our strategies according to the importance of a particular search. Sometimes we want to take charge and control the context ourselves: if we are researching bee colony collapse we might want to go onto a biology or science database such as PLOS.org, rather than rely on what comes up first on Google: a four-paragraph article from *Forbes* suggesting a simple cause of colony collapse and surrounded by advertisements.

5. Comparison and Corroboration

In scholarly research there is an ingrained process of basing new research on previous findings. Research is not conducted in a vacuum. When carrying out a comprehensive literature review on a health, social science, or science topic, comparison and corroboration are built into the process. But for many everyday-life searches we pop in and look for a quick answer. If we pop in to an extremely trustworthy source and the information topic is a low-stakes issue, we may need to use only a bare-bones comparison and corroboration process. But even confirming a simple piece of information can be challenging because so much information is rebroadcast and regurgitated across the Web. The comparison process needs to involve using independent resources and the corroboration process involves unpacking the factual claims and confirming that they hold up.

6. Going Deep, or Not

Searching for information is an iterative process fraught with continual choices: where to look, how far to go, how many sources to read, what types of sources to go after. Taking a piece of information and uncovering the backstory—*and every piece of information has a backstory*—can be a lengthy process. How was it created? Who is this author? What is the purpose? Do others agree? What is it based on?

An important component of the search process is recognizing when a quick piece of information will suffice and when it is going to be a long night. A simple bar bet can turn into a "Who killed JFK?" type of search, and what appears at first glance to be a complex science search can sometimes lead easily to the perfect review article at the top of a Google Scholar results list. Stay open, bend your knees, *be flexible*.

The American Library Association recently stated that:

> *Increasingly, information comes to individuals in unfiltered formats, raising questions about its authenticity, validity, and reliability . . . The uncertain quality and expanding quantity of information pose large challenges for society. The sheer abundance of information will not in itself create a more in-*

formed citizenry without a complementary cluster of abilities necessary to use information effectively. [26]

This book is about developing that *cluster of abilities* needed to find reliable information online. Thinking strategically and controlling *where* you look for information and how you evaluate it are pieces of a much larger ongoing challenge for how we build the Web in the years to come. There is no reason why shoe stores, doctors, restaurants, libraries, and schools cannot coexist on the Web, but we need to have better markers of quality and reliability. We need to know when we are in a shoe store and when we are in a library when we are online. We need many new tools, beyond the six strategies discussed in this book, to help filter and curate the Web. Crowd-sourcing "likes" is not a sufficient strategy.

NOTES

1. A Facebook user shared this on his Facebook feed and then described how to hack the text and photos on a news outlet's site and then share the results so that the image and text link back to the official site, even though once you go to the official site the hacked story and image do not exist. In this case the site hacked was CNN.com.

2. "The Framework for Information Literacy for Higher Education," Draft 3, Association of College and Research Libraries, November 2014, http://acrl.ala.org/ilstandards/wp-content/uploads/2014/11/Framework-for-IL-for-HE-draft-3.pdf.

3. This book uses the word "reliable" to mean trustworthy, true, valid, authentic, and accurate. It is used to apply to all types of information: factual and subjective, to the degree that that is possible. For a good discussion of the differences between words such as credibility, accuracy, trust, and authority, see Andrew Flanagin and Miriam Metzger, "The Credibility of Volunteered Geographic Information," *GeoJournal* 72 (2008), doi: 10.1007/s10708-008-9188-y.

4. Framework for Information Literacy for Higher Education, Association of College and Research Libraries, February 2015, http://www.ala.org/acrl/standards/ilframework.

5. Susannah Fox, "Health Topics Report," Pew Internet and American Life Project, February 2011, http://www.pewinternet.org/Reports/2011/HealthTopics/Summary-of-Findings.aspx.

6. Daniel Kahneman, *Thinking, Fast and Slow* (New York: Farrar, Straus & Giroux, 2011).

7. Katarzyna Materska, "Information Heuristics of Information Literate People," 2014 (Preprint), http://eprints.rclis.org/23919/.

8. Clay Johnson, *The Information Diet: A Case for Conscious Consumption* (Sebastopal, CA: O'Reilly, 2012); Jaron Lanier, *You Are Not a Gadget: A Manifesto* (New York: Vintage Books, 2011); David Levy, "More Better Faster: Governance in an Age of Overload, Busyness, and Speed," *First Monday* 7 (2006), http://firstmonday.org/ojs/index.php/fm/article/view/1618/1533.

9. Lanier, *You Are Not a Gadget*.

10. Levy, "More Better Faster."

11. Leon Wieseltier, "Among the Disrupted," *New York Time Book Review*, January 7, 2015, http://www.nytimes.com/2015/01/18/books/review/among-the-disrupted.html?_r=0.

12. Kahneman, *Thinking, Fast and Slow*.

13. Dominique Brossard and Dietram A. Scheufele, "Science, New Media, and the Public," *Science* 339, no. 6114 (2013); Amy Mitchell, "State of the News Media 2014," Pew Research Journalism Project, March 26, 2014, http://www.journalism.org/2014/03/26/state-of-the-news-media-2014-overview/; Claire Cain Miller, "Why BuzzFeed Is Trying to Shift Its Strategy," *New York Times,* August 12, 2014; Vindu Goel and Ravi Somaiya, "With New App, Facebook

Aims to Make Its Users' Feeds Newsier," *New York Times,* February 3 2014, http://www.nytimes.com/2014/02/04/technology/with-new-app-facebook-aims-to-make-its-users-feeds-newsier.html.

14. Thom Shanker and Matt Richtel, "In New Military, Data Overload Can Be Deadly," *New York Times,* January 17, 2011, http://www.nytimes.com/2011/01/17/technology/17brain.html?pagewanted=all&_r=0#.

15. Goshen College, "The Invisible Web," http://libraryguides.goshen.edu/beyond_googling.

16. Amir Efrati, "Rivals Say Google Plays Favorites: Search Giant Displays Its Own Health, Shopping, Local Content Ahead of Links to Competing Sites," *Wall Street Journal,* December 12, 2010, http://online.wsj.com/news/articles/SB10001424052748704058704576015630188568972.

17. Eszter, HargittaI, Lindsay Fullerton, Ericka Menchen-Trevino, and Kristin Yates Thomas, "Trust Online: Young Adults' Evaluation of Web Content," *International Journal of Communication* 4 (April 2010), http://ijoc.org/index.php/ijoc/article/view/636.

18. Tom Simonite, "The Decline of Wikipedia," *MIT Technology Review,* October 22, 2013, http://www.technologyreview.com/featuredstory/520446/the-decline-of-wikipedia.

19. Alison J. Head, *How College Graduates Solve Information Problems Once They Join the Workplace,* Project Information Literacy Research Report, the Passage Studies, Institute of Museum and Library Services and the Berkman Center for Internet and Society at Harvard, October 16, 2012, http://projectinfolit.org/pdfs/PIL_fall2012_workplaceStudy_FullReport.pdf.

20. Carl Zimmer, "How Google Is Making Us Smarter: Humans Are 'Natural-Born Cyborgs,' and the Internet Is Our Giant 'Extended Mind,'" *Discover Magazine,* February 2009.

21. Betsy Sparrow, Jenny Liu, and Daniel M. Wegner, "Google Effects on Memory: Cognitive Consequences of Having Information at Our Fingertips," *ScienceExpress Report,* 2011, http://www.wjh.harvard.edu/~wegner/pdfs/science.1207745.full.pdf.

22. Marc Meola, "Chucking the Checklist: A Contextual Approach to Teaching Undergraduates Web-Site Evaluation," *Portal: Libraries and the Academy* 4 2004. For a review of approaches, see Birger Hjorland, "Methods for Evaluating Information Sources: An Annotated Catalogue," *Journal of Information Science* 38 (June 2012), doi: 10.1177/016555151439178.

23. "Framework for Information Literacy for Higher Education."

24. Brian Carroll and R. Randolph Richardson, "Identification, Transparency, Interactivity: Towards a New Paradigm for Credibility for Single-Voice Blogs," *International Journal of Interactive Communication Systems and Technologies* 1, no. 1 (January 2011), doi: 10.4018/ijicst.2011010102.

25. "Howard Gardner on Truth, Beauty, and Goodness," July 2, 2011, http://video.pbs.org/video/2034568996/.

26. Association of College and Research Libraries, Information Literacy Competency Standards, 2000, http://www.ala.org/acrl/standards/informationliteracycompetency.

Chapter One

Drinking: An Information Story

Finding Reliable Health Information

Embrace the "messiness" of research.
—The Framework for Information Literacy for Higher Education (2014)

When Sarah McCloud, aged twenty-seven, entered the Weymouth Bank wearing a baseball cap and New England Patriots sweatshirt, she had done her homework. Or at least she thought she had. Before robbing the bank she made two disastrous mistakes in her research. That morning she had searched Google and asked several questions, including:

What happens to someone when they rob a bank?

What happens to someone when they rob a house?

Her two mistakes? She asked the wrong questions and she used Google. Had she focused her questions on how likely it would be that she might be *caught* robbing a bank, and had she tapped into the FBI national bank robbery statistics easily available from many news sites, she would have discovered that more than three-quarters of all bank robbers are apprehended, whereas less than 10 percent of people who rob houses are caught. (Embezzlement is an even better deal with a minuscule chance of getting caught and low odds of serving time if caught.)[1]

McCloud, like most bank robbers, was apprehended. The police used her Google searches as evidence against her. Had McCloud been a better researcher she might have pursued a crime that involved less risk and a higher

1

probability of success, but like most people who search Google her results were limited by the questions she asked and by the failure of Google to identify the most useful information.

Most people rely on Google when looking for a quick information fix, and many people treat Google like a Magic 8 Ball, therapist, lawyer, or trusted friend. The number of people that seek relationship advice using Google is so large that a whole slew of websites—such as MarriageBuilders.com and LinksToLove.com—has grown up around providing relationship advice, combined with advertisements, in order to cash in on this high demand. Similarly, health information is one of the most commonly searched topics on the Web and as a result content is being pumped in daily to attract readers: some sites provide reliable and useful information, others provide sketchy or limited information or are designed to push a specific product or service.[2]

Many of us fall into the same trap that McCloud did: not thinking out our search strategy and popping on Google and looking at the first few sites listed. In fact, research shows that many people believe that just being listed in the top five hits of a Google search is a sign that a piece of information is credible.[3] We know enough to avoid the paid advertisements, but there is much more we could be doing to retrieve reliable information.

My search for health information was not a life or death issue. My goal was to justify my nightly glass or two of red wine by getting support from current health research. Unfortunately, like McCloud the bank robber, I decided to start with a simple Google search. But unlike McCloud, I have a degree in information science. I should know better. All I really wanted was an answer to a seemingly simple question:

Is red wine good for you?

The night was young. Down the rabbit hole I went.

BIASED INFORMATION SEARCHING

Like most people looking for complex information on the Web, I want information that confirms my current assumptions: that drinking red wine has positive health benefits. How I search for this information would, of course, influence my results. Psychologists refer to this as "motivated cognition," which includes:

- *Biased information searching*: seeking out evidence that is congruent with existing beliefs.
- *Biased assimilation:* giving extra weight to information found that supports the searcher's goals.

Starting my search by asking questions that bias the outcome in favor of finding the answer I want puts me in good company. Even U.S. Supreme Court justices and their clerks search the Web and may be almost as likely to suffer from "biased information searching" as anyone else. This is a serious concern because justices are expected to rely on the facts submitted with legal briefs, and if they need additional information they should use objective researchers such as those at the Congressional Research Service. Because of "motivated cognition," justices may sometimes be seeking information in order to confirm certain biases they already possess, and this could interfere with their decisions. In a recent ten-year period justices have cited articles from local news sources like the *Sacramento Bee*, *Golf Magazine*, and even information from partisan think tank websites. In fact, half the information judges cite in their decisions now come from non-legal sources possibly because it is so easy to jump on Google and look something up. [4]

Starting out the research process with a biased agenda can skew the information uncovered. Unfortunately, many of our current assumptions are not predicated on reliable information. Psychologists have studied the tendency of people to seek out consonant information and avoid dissonant information for over sixty years. [5] My desire to prove red wine was good for me was especially fraught with the baggage I brought to the search table. My current beliefs hadn't exactly been formed by the scholarly research literature. I had recently watched the popular movie *The Kids Are All Right*. In one scene Annette Bening's character (Nic) starts drinking too much red wine. The following exchange takes place with her wife, played by Julianne Moore (Jules):

JULES: (sotto) *How about some green tea, honey . . .*
Nic slams her glass on the table. Explodes.
NIC: *You know what, Jules?! I like my wine! Okay? So f---ing sue me! And FYI, red wine has a chemical called resveratrol in it, which has been proven to significantly extend the human life span!*
JULES: *Yeah, if you drink a thousand bottles a day!*

It's too bad I didn't pick up on the "thousand bottles a day" comment and instead focused on the comment about extending the human life span. Motivated cognition strikes again: I heard what I wanted to hear.

Cass Sunstein, who writes about echo chambers on the Web, and Eli Pariser's concerns about a Filter Bubble suggest that a lot of what we view online is selected either by us, or for us, to reinforce our existing beliefs. [6] Echo chambers occur online when information or ideas are amplified, reinforced, and repeated in an enclosed system; for example, liberal news outlets simply repeat or echo news from similar sources with the same political slant. The Filter Bubble involves living in an information world that only reflects our own views: for example, only reading a personal Facebook feed or limiting ourselves to watching Fox News.

Most people tend to listen to people with whom they already agree, and the Web is set up in a way that reinforces our worldviews by showing us websites that we are apt to agree with and advertisements for items we are likely to purchase. By starting out the search process often in a biased manner, by asking the *wrong* questions, we frequently head down a road that has foregone conclusions. I started searching for *red wine, health, and resveratrol*, not *red wine, scam, and resveratrol*: Very, very different questions.

CONTEXT DEFICIT DISORDER

It wasn't just about what Annette Bening said in the film though, newspapers and blog writers kept reporting enthusiastically about the health effects of red wine, the Mediterranean diet, and something called "The French Paradox," which includes staying healthy by drinking wine like the French. The results of my simple Google search brought up the usual suspects: Wikipedia and the slew of sites like "WikiHow" and "Answers.com," that many people click on to answer their search queries.

While Google and Wikipedia can help with quick factual questions, there are disadvantages to relying solely on them for more complex or controversial questions. It is no coincidence that a Wikipedia entry typically comes up in the first few hits of a Google search. The symbiotic relationship between Google and Wikipedia is well known. Wikipedia gets almost 70 percent of its traffic from Google, and Google benefits by connecting people to an enormous amount of content and gains advertising dollars.[7] Now that Wikipedia has knocked out most of the competition, Google, Siri, and others rely heavily on Wikipedia. Google even inserts Wikipedia information into their own authoritative-looking "fact box" to answer queries, with the subtle implication that these are verified facts.

Knowing I am jumping into a hornet's nest, I glance at the Wikipedia article on resveratrol, the compound found in red wine that might have positive health effects. The 198 citations are a bit overwhelming. Some seem to have ties to industry, and when I look at the Wikipedia edit history I find that of the 2,022 edits made since the original entry, the second highest number of edits were made by a Wikipedia editor with the user name of the "Sceptical Chymist." There is a link directly to a Wikipedia article *on* this editor (not to be confused with an author by the same name who wrote a book in 1661). On this editor's Wikipedia page there is simply one line of "biographical" information:

Wikipedia, the online encyclopedia that is rapidly approaching a state of badly edited omniscience.[8]

I am not sure why this is what is listed on the editor's biography page, though I note a strong scent of cynicism. I suspect that the editor's agenda might be less than pure, and I am beginning to wonder why he or she cared enough to make fifty-nine edits to the entry on resveratrol. I wonder if he or she has since become burned out on the whole Wikipedia editing process. The "Sceptical Chymist" is not alone.

Many would like to believe that the content in Wikipedia is improving with its collaborative crowd-edited approach to assembling "all the world's knowledge." Unfortunately new research has shown that Wikipedia is now declining in quality and suffering from several intractable issues. The number of editors working on Wikipedia has declined dramatically by 39 percent in the last few years and new volunteers are discouraged from contributing and find their entries frequently deleted because they are not following proper editing rules and etiquette.[9]

The reduced numbers of editors are engaging in infighting and bureaucracy and are having trouble keeping on top of the ever-mounting pile of editing and repair work needed. Staying ahead of vandalism alone has become a tremendous undertaking. The editors also are a homogeneous lot, a problem in and of itself, made up of primarily male (some estimates are as high as 90 percent), with Western and "tech geek" biases.[10] Ultimately, though, Wikipedia's largest obstacle to providing reliable information is the anonymity of its authors. This makes it impossible to trace who is writing what, in order to understand their expertise or possible agenda. A recent report from MIT suggests that Wikipedia has gone from:

> The encyclopedia that anyone can edit to: The encyclopedia that anyone who understands the norms, socializes him or herself, dodges the impersonal wall of semi-automated rejection and still wants to voluntarily contribute his or her time and energy can edit.[11]

Wikipedia can still be useful and even wonderful for straightforward factual questions, if the stakes are not too high. It typically does a stellar job on popular music, culture, and online gaming entries to name a few. There have been many recent studies on the accuracy of health information on Wikipedia with most concluding there are significant concerns about accuracy.[12] At the same time, a number of people in the medical and other professions have noted that because so many people go to Wikipedia for information, partly because of its high ranking in a Google search, that if some of the editing challenges and anti-expert bias could be overcome and more health experts contributed that there may still be hope.[13]

For now, as a rule of thumb, Wikipedia (or any encyclopedia) should rarely be cited in formal research, and it should not be consulted for questions that involve any controversy, even if it's just for settling a bar bet.

Using Wikipedia to get a few citations to articles is a reasonable strategy, provided that the searcher quickly moves on to those citations. But there are usually better ways to track down the best studies on a topic or research question.

GOOGLE ADDICTION

While some people might find they can move past Wikipedia in their search process, moving past Google feels nearly impossible. But unfortunately Google is losing the war on finding reliable information, especially if the information is complex or nuanced. Google is unable, and perhaps in some cases unwilling, to stop the onslaught of search engine optimization (SEO) that controls which links make it to the top few screens of Google search results. [14] White hat (legal) and black hat (illegal) SEO has a powerful hold on what a Google search will turn up. While Google uses over fifty-seven signals to algorithmically rank websites to capture the most reliable ones, a whole sophisticated SEO industry has sprung up to assist companies in getting onto that top page of search results. [15] And, for every trick Google spots and creates a work-around for, five more hacks are developed to get onto that first Google results screen.

As most people know, Google and Wikipedia can accurately answer an amazing number of questions:

What was the name of the chicken restaurant in the TV show Breaking Bad?

Is a Komodo dragon a real lizard?

But they are not good at answering questions that are more complex:

What causes the high rate of divorce in the United States?

Is global warming a serious threat?

As companies grow increasingly sophisticated in gaming the system, Google searches become less useful for turning up reliable information. And, there is often a context deficit in the information we retrieve: we often cannot tell where it is coming from, who is generating it, and why.

Q&A FAIL

The Q&A sites such as WikiHow or Answers.com that often appear near the top of Google search results have serious reliability issues as well. Q&A crowdsourced collections are a motley crew with extremely variable quality, even on the better sites. They are often a "poor man's" Wikipedia, answering questions by the crowd without a sophisticated or effective editing or filtering process. Researchers worry that many Q&A sites suffer from their own popularity, with so many responses overwhelming the useful answers even with users voting on "best" answers.[16]

Quality tends to increase for sites that charge a fee and sites that provide names and credentials for people who post answers. Quality can be quite high for sites that rely on the wisdom of a crowd of experts, rather than the wisdom of anyone. But there is still a high degree of signal to noise and a lot of bad advice out there. If you want to know how to filet a fish or sew on a button, Answer.com or WikiHow are usually fine, but when it comes to legal or health concerns there are many good reasons *not* to use these sites. There is a reason why, if you Google "Yahoo Answers.com Fail" you get over 8 million hits.[17]

> Q: *What is masculine and feminine in French? What does this mean? Please explain I just started learning French.*
> A: *Armpit hair.*[18]

Fail blogs love to post answers from Q&A sites because many of them are humorous, crude spam or in some cases just unintentionally inept. Many Q&A sites use content farms. They analyze what people are searching for and then hire a stable of thousands of freelancers to churn out mediocre but targeted content for a few cents an answer. By pushing out lots of new content Q&A sites can get a high page ranking in a Google search and attract readers to advertisements. Other Q&A sites have more of a social purpose with the quality of the answer often being less important than the social interaction.[19]

When I ask Quora, one of the Q&A sites with a better reputation for tapping into experts and linking to better quality answers, I get enthusiastic responses reporting that red wine and resveratrol are great for me. Responses are posted from a vineyard owner and a communications manager from the Australian Wine Research Institute. When I look up the institute I see that their main purpose in life is to: "work exclusively for the benefit of the Australian wine industry."[20] This makes their information a tad suspicious at best. I suppose they could be the same people writing Wikipedia entries; at least with Quora I know who is answering my questions.

There may come a time when general Q&A sites are able to filter out the garbage and become more reliable, but that time has not yet come. For some smaller crowds, such as the crowds of computer programmers sharing answers and advice on Stackoverflow.com, Q&A sites work well and have a high degree of reliability. Crowdsourced wisdom connected to hobbies, skills, expertise, or work can sometimes provide a great source for information, depending on the degree to which it can be divorced from commercial interests or zealots.

For casual questions where the need for a reliable answer is low, popping on to a Q&A site is comparable to sticking your head in a noisy bar and yelling out your question. You might get some weird responses, but you also might pick up a morsel or two of useful information. Sometimes though it might resemble getting advice from the neighbor that lives downstairs, has no visible means of employment, but has a ready opinion on almost any topic. Whether I drank a glass of red wine or not every night was certainly not a high-stakes question, but I really wanted to know whether the research was real, or just some commercial bunk.

PANDA VS. CONTENT FARMS

Getting back to my Google search, in between the Wikipedia article and the Answers.com advice, I find a website on the first page of search results called "Refinery29": "Could Red Wine Save Your Life?"[21]

Refinery29 is not the most promising site name, but the title of the article seems encouraging. The article is peppy and full of positive information:

- *Light to moderate alcohol consumption reduces risk of death from a heart attack by 30 to 50 percent.*
- *The beneficial ingredients may counter the effects of fatty foods, perhaps delaying or decreasing their absorption into the body.*
- *Recent studies have shown that alcohol—and red wine in particular—may potentially decrease the risk of colon cancer and prostate cancer if consumed in moderation.*

The writing style gives me pause though. Perhaps it is a little too peppy? The article ends with: "So we should eat, drink, and be merry? Done, done, and dunzo!" But not really "dunzo" when I need scientific research to justify my habit. I had already spotted trouble when I saw that Refinery29 was a "dot com," not a "dot org." In fact Refinery29, according to its "About Us" is:

> the largest independent fashion and style website in the United States . . . a
> lifestyle platform that delivers nonstop inspiration to live a more stylish and

creative life . . . connects over 10 million visitors every month . . . giving them all the tips, tricks, and tools they need to live a more beautiful life.

As much as I am all for lifestyle platforms and living a more beautiful life, my antennae are up, and I know that this lifestyle platform has gotten into the top search results in Google for one of several possible reasons, none of them good. Posting new content and having massive amounts of content boost the page ranking a website can get in Google. Refinery29, though carefully disguised, was yet another content farm full of freelance writers with their perky articles displayed next to carefully customized advertisements.

Content farms are the bane of the Web, and at times they threaten to topple Google with their armies of low-paid "astroturfing" freelance writers and video creators who crank out enormous piles of poor-quality content. Though Google has tried hard to quash the junk that gets churned out by content farms, it has been an ongoing battle. Demand Media, one of the biggest content farms, was worth more than the *New York Times* in 2011, due to its ability to generate lots of cheap "how to" content. Demand Media developed a system to algorithmically assign and publish articles based on user data gathered from Google and social media searches.

In late 2013, Demand Media fell on its face due to the development of Panda, a new search algorithm developed by Google.[22] Panda works to ferret out lower quality articles, specifically "farm" sites, but it still cannot stop the more carefully disguised junk like Refinery29. Content farms are running for cover and regrouping with some actually improving their content and others pursuing more sophisticated ways to outmaneuver Google. The battle between Google and the adaptive and evolving world of content farms will not be won any time soon, and the loser will continue to be those who rely on the first few Google hits rather than devise more strategic searches and more strategic selection of sources.

Google has experimented with different ways of pulling up higher quality in-depth resources, especially when it is clear the searcher does not want a short answer. For example, if the searcher is requesting information about stem cell research, Google will tweak its algorithm to focus on somewhat more in-depth articles and sites that have strong track records for reliability and at least some depth such as *National Geographic, Science*, and *Discovery,* though Google did not do this for my resveratrol inquiries. Google sometimes pulls in a few results from Google Scholar, their database of citations to scholarly journal articles, when the search question seems to warrant it. Unfortunately the SEO marketing consultants often stay one step ahead of the game, advising people wanting to increase Web traffic to write longer articles, use citations to other articles in their writing, and perform other adjustments to appear on the top page of search results. Too bad it doesn't make sense to just spend the time writing high-quality articles.

While Google results can sometimes be "good enough," they have yet to find a way to effectively compete with the scholarly databases that contain carefully vetted articles and other published resources and filter out all the riffraff like About.com and WikiHow. While scholarly databases are not good at answering questions like: "How do I flush out my hot water heater?" they are good at providing carefully filtered reliable scholarly articles in all subject disciplines.

THE PARALLEL INFORMATION UNIVERSE

David Carr, the longtime media columnist for the *New York Times*, said: "What I don't look at is the web. The web has kind of gone away for me."[23] He meant that when he gets online he does not hop on Google to find information. Carr would go directly to the sources he thought would have the information he wanted, or he would get his information pushed to him through Twitter feeds and other strategies so that he could filter his information to sources he felt were useful and reliable. Because he was a famous journalist, he also probably got on the phone a lot to talk directly to experts.

Recently, at a conference I attended, the speaker was bemoaning how hard it was to devise good filters in Google so that searches would pull up the most reliable information and not include all the junk developed by marketers. The speaker said: "If only there were a place where we could search without having to plow through all this junk!" I sat in the back row mumbling quietly but intensely to myself "There *is*, there *is*!" For anyone connected to an academic, research, or public library there is a whole array of subscription databases that provide access to all the high quality vetted information while not including "unpublished" infotisements such as About.com or Refinery29. Even hopping on the free Google Scholar will weed out most of the marketing information.

The Invisible Web or Deep Web is defined in various ways, but includes all those sources that are hidden within academic databases, behind pay walls, or are buried several layers down on a website out of the reach of search engines. For many of us, the Invisible Web can be anything that does not hit our Facebook or Twitter feed, or is not in the top page of a Google search, because we do not see it. Oscar Wilde once said: "The pure and simple truth is rarely pure and never simple." This was certainly true of the articles I was finding on red wine and health. Every new piece of research seemed to generate a flurry of blog posts about red wine being the next penicillin, and most of the articles I had found up until now were pretty useless in terms of presenting any kind of scientifically valid information or citing any hardcore research.

Over 80 percent of people in the United States who search the Web have searched for health information, and of those 60 percent report that they have used the information found online to make a decision about their own health or the way they cared for someone else. [24] Because of the popularity of health searches there are a lot of health "information" sites that have been created in the last few years. Just type in the words "sore throat" or "cholesterol" and the Web is buzzing with sites like "medicinenet.com" and "health.com."

The famous movie critic Roger Ebert admitted to searching the Web when he was diagnosed with thyroid cancer. Googling for information, he ran across articles on neutron radiation and became convinced that this would lead to his recovery. Just prior to his death he blamed himself for succumbing to an appealing idea he found online:

> *I believe my infatuation with neutron radiation led directly to the failure of all three of my facial surgeries, the loss of my jaw, loss of the ability to eat, drink and speak, and the surgical damage to my right shoulder and back as my poor body was plundered for still more reconstructive transplants. . . . Today I look like an exhibit in the Texas Chainsaw Museum.* [25]

While there is a tremendous amount of health information available online it is often difficult to access reliable information. A group of researchers recently found that using a search engine such as Google or Yahoo with simple search terms was not effective: about 75 percent of the content retrieved on the first page of search results was not relevant to the searcher's needs. [26] Lucky for all of us that there are thousands of librarians out there developing guides that point to some of the more reliable free as well as fee-based sites. In fact, if you search any broad topic area—say Bolivia or Veterinary Medicine or Economics—and pair it with the word "LibGuides," chances are good a librarian has created a selective list of reliable sources for that area of study. There are over 400,000 LibGuides online that are regularly updated and link to valuable information within many disciplines and subdisciplines.

LibGuides are typically designed for use by a particular group of students connected to an academic institution, so often they connect users with customized expensive search engines that focus on the research literature in a particular discipline that are only accessible to students who are enrolled at a particular institution. But in many cases LibGuides will also point users to reliable resources that are available free online or are available via local public libraries. For example, here is a search at Libguides.com for cancer. (This search pulls up about fifty guides, most of them have a specific focus: nursing, history, type, biology, etc. Just the first two are shown below.)

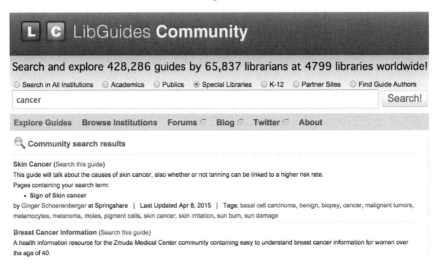

LibGuides provide thousands of specialized guides of curated online resources on specific topics.

In the case of health sites, there are hundreds of good LibGuides for general as well as specific sites, and the Medical Library Association (MLA) also has a highly selective guide that points to the best Web resources for health.[27] While it feels like an extra step, clicking on the sources listed in the MLA guide will pay off. Not surprisingly, sites like PubMed and Mayo Clinic make the cut, but other sites that might seem credible, like WebMD and ShareCare do not.

On first glance Mayo Clinic and WebMD seem similar. Both have physicians writing articles and both accept advertisements on their sites. Mayo Clinic, however, is run as the information arm of the world-famous Mayo Clinic, whereas WebMD is owned and run by the pharmaceutical industry.[28] While it is subtle, there is often a push on WebMD toward buying prescriptions to solve a health issue, whereas Mayo tends to provide more objective treatment options.[29]

While WebMD has disclosed that it partners with pharmaceutical companies such as Lilly, the line drawn between advertising and information is blurry. For example, on WebMD a general information page on depression links to a "Depression Quiz" that takes the reader to a screening page funded by Lilly, the manufacturer of the antidepressant Cymbalta. The Cymbalta-sponsored pages include a page titled "Learning to Treat Depression" with a strong push toward asking your doctor about Cymbalta.[30]

The blurring lines between information and advertisement are common on the Web, and early pharmaceutical company innovators include Roche, the makers of a flu medicine called Tamiflu. When the movie *Happy Feet* came out in 2006, just at the start of flu season, Roche partnered with Disney and developed a Happy Feet flu website where children could play fun penguin games while learning "flu facts." Though the site was pushed out as an "education" site, the fun penguin pages were closely paired with unbranded banners pushing parents and kids toward finding out more about a pill that could be taken to treat the flu. It was an extremely successful campaign and sales of Tamiflu skyrocketed the year the website was introduced. [31]

Advergames have now become a common way to sell many products, but for the pharmaceutical industry the direct to consumer advertising is finally starting to raise some eyebrows. The Federal Drug Administration pulled down Pfizer's Viva Cruiser game, which involved players guiding a motorcycle rider down a desert road picking up gifts for a date including roses, candles, gift boxes, and little blue Viagra pills to the tune of a "Viva Viagra" theme song. It was not the tacky game quality that caused the advergame to be pulled down, but the failure to disclose risk information about the drug.

Avoiding all the content farms and advergames, I hop on Mayo and search for resveratrol. The Mayo article states, over the course of a dozen paragraphs, that:

> *Red wine's potential heart-healthy benefits look promising. Those who drink moderate amounts of alcohol, including red wine, seem to have a lower risk of heart disease.* [32]

But they also say that many of the studies have been on animals, and that the jury is still out. I also notice that it was published in early 2011 and the most recent studies referenced in the article are more than four years old. This wasn't enough information, and it wasn't current enough. It was time to move deeper.

DIGGING DEEPER: DR. DAS AND HIS WEB OF DECEPTION

According to Web of Science (WOS), [33] one of several comprehensive databases linking to scholarly research, over 2,000 scientific articles have been published in scholarly journals on resveratrol and red wine. Google Scholar lists over 24,000, but Google Scholar casts a much wider net than WOS, and what they define as "scholarly" is broadly defined. If you have access to a library and are doing a lot of research it is worth using WOS, which has a lot of fancy bells and whistles, but Google Scholar or PubMed would also suffice, and both are free and PubMed focuses solely on medical journal articles.

The 2,000 articles I find on WOS feel a little overwhelming, but I remain optimistic and continue on my quest. WOS indicates that the first article on resveratrol and wine was written in 1993. The number of articles published since then has dramatically climbed, going from 1 a year in 1993 to over 180 a year in 2012. Clearly scientific interest in resveratrol is gaining ground.

Unlike a magazine article or blog post, a scholarly article is one that is written by a professor or credentialed researcher: An expert. It is published in a scholarly journal that uses blind peer review to filter out poorly done research.[34] A typical peer review process might look like this:

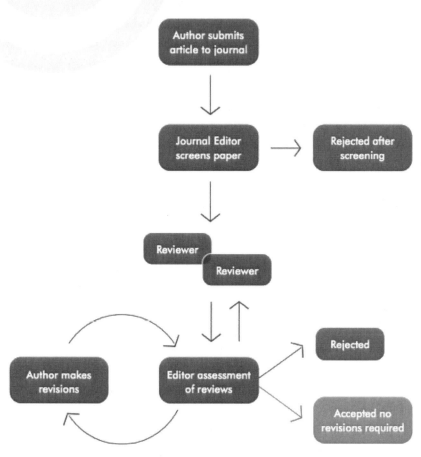

A typical peer review process.[35]

Just because an article appears in a scholarly journal does not mean the information is *true*, but it often means that this carefully vetted information represents the current state of research at the time it was written. Often the reputation of the journal can be a stronger indicator of credibility than even the author's credentials. Some journals are very selective and turn away almost 90 percent of the research articles submitted to them.[36] While publication in a prestigious journal does not guarantee accuracy, it may be as close as we can get. This review and vetting process is the antithesis of the Refinery29 article referenced above, which was neither trustworthy nor written by an expert.

Scholarship is a beautiful and awkward dance. Sir Isaac Newton called the research process "standing on the shoulders of Giants." When a group of researchers decides to conduct a study they work within what is called the "invisible college." This collaborative process connects researchers who share similar interests in order to build off of each other's results. Good research never occurs in a vacuum and always links back to the groundwork that has already been completed. Another way to judge good research is to see whether subsequent scholars have linked back and cited specific studies that they respect and are using as a basis for their own studies.

But, before we get all starry-eyed discussing scholarship, it is important to note that though science is a collaborative effort it is also fraught with large egos, competition for research awards, fame, and the push to discover something new. In the case of the red wine and resveratrol fountain of youth claims I decide to use extra caution in my search for proof, given the loaded nature of the type of research and the high stakes involved.

There are many ways to parse the 2,000 articles on resveratrol. Unlike its free counterpart Google Scholar, WOS has a bucketful of filtering bells and whistles so I filter the articles and review them by:

- Most recent two years (343)
- Comprehensive review articles (39)
- Elimination of keywords on areas outside my interest (varied)

I skim through the recent articles that look promising and read over a few review articles to get a sense of the current state of the field. Then I apply a filter that organizes the 2,000 articles by author to look at the major players currently involved. Through all these machinations I waded knee deep into the literature and found myself surrounded by Dr. Dipak Das. Das had published the *most* research on resveratrol according to WOS: eighty-nine articles. This is typically a good sign that the research is worth reviewing, indicating some expertise in the field. Das has a Ph.D. and was a professor and Director of the Cardiovascular Research Center at the University of Connecticut School of Medicine. He not only published in many scholarly journals, but at least some of the journals he published in were well respected according to their Journal Impact Factor, a calculation related to citation counts.[37] There are many ways to measure journal prestige, but if you ask any professor in a particular field they can immediately rattle off the names of the most prestigious journals in their discipline. According to my sources, Das had done pretty well for himself.

Many of Das' findings indicate that resveratrol has a positive association with health and heart health in particular. Just before his death, Das produced research indicating that resveratrol pills might be a replacement for the daily aspirin many people take to decrease the risk of heart attacks. As I did some further investigation of Dr. Das I was dismayed to find him listed as a "media contact" on a website that sells a resveratrol supplement called Longevinex. Citing his own studies, Dr. Das is quoted on the website encouraging people to buy Longevinex in order to provide "pre-conditioning" for their heart to protect it from the effects of a heart attack and mentioning that resveratrol's preconditioning effect is "the best yet devised method of cardioprotection."[38]

Das' articles are widely cited by other researchers in the field, despite recent attempts by these same researchers to distance themselves from him. It turns out that Das was fired in 2012 based on a tip the University of Connecticut received about research irregularities. A three-year investigation of Das' work turned up 145 counts of fabrication and falsification of data.[39] Dr. David Sinclair, a famous resveratrol researcher at Harvard, said he had never heard of Das, though it appears that Sinclair has published articles that cite Das and has served on scientific committees with Das.[40] Sinclair later admitted that he had misspoken about his connection to Das' work. In recent news reports most researchers said his fabricated work would not detract from the overall encouraging research being conducted related to resveratrol.[41] All this is to say that in the tightly wound field of bottling a fountain of youth, transparency is hard to come by.

RESEARCH SUCCESS: COMING UP EMPTY-HANDED?

Undeterred, I decided to investigate the scientific literature on resveratrol that had *not* been conducted by Dr. Das and his team. Sinclair, a Harvard biologist, has been extremely active in resveratrol research. In addition to being present in my favorite scholarly database, WOS, Sinclair is an active participant on the media circuit. He toasted glasses of red wine with Barbara Walters while discussing his work with resveratrol and mice, talked with Morley Safer on *60 Minutes*, appeared on *Nightline,* and made a TEDx talk in Sydney called "A Cure for Aging."

Sinclair may have been following in the footsteps of Dr. Serge Renaud a decade or two earlier. Renaud, a scientist from Bordeaux University in France, was credited with coining the term "French Paradox" in the early 1990s. When interviewed on the news show *60 Minutes* in 1991, Renaud proposed a theory that moderate consumption of red wine was a risk-reducing factor for heart disease for the French, and that wine may have significant positive health benefits that would be worth further study. In the year following the broadcast, sales of red wine increased 44 percent over previous years.[42]

Unlike Renaud, Sinclair was doing actual research and not just *proposing* a theory. His team found that there was evidence that resveratrol lengthened the life-span of yeast and later research showed positive effects for mice, worms, fruit flies, and fish. Many people extrapolated from these studies that if resveratrol was good for little critters, it was probably good for people. Sales of red wine again jumped, and Dr. Sinclair and his friends formed a biotechnology company to develop a drug that would mimic resveratrol. In 2008 GlaxoSmithKline bought Sinclair's company Sirtris for $720 million and Sinclair moved into the role of consultant. Around that same time many scientists began to question whether Sinclair's findings were significant. It was also about this time that the University of Connecticut started their three-year investigation of Dr. Das.

Researchers, such as Dr. David Gems at University College London, have unsuccessfully tried to replicate some of Sinclair's research findings. Gems' research found that resveratrol in fact did not appear to play a role in anti-aging.[43] While some scientists were skeptical of Sinclair's findings, other scientists that serve on the science advisory board of Sirtris seem more optimistic about his results.[44] The plot has thickened over the years as Sinclair plows ahead in his work to develop a pill that will "cure aging."[45] Sinclair has just put out new research that refutes what his critics have reported, but as of this writing there has not been corroboration of Sinclair's research, though some experts are encouraged by his recent results.[46]

Sinclair's statements announcing his recent findings give me pause:

I've spent the last ten years figuring this out. . . . It almost brings me to tears to think how hard it's been. There were so many people that didn't believe in this, that I'm really grateful to the scientists who did stick with us and believe it was right.

We like to think of scientific research as an unbiased process of testing, replication, and open-ended inquiry; where research interests are pursued based on objective measures rather than simply pursuing agendas that will be funded and prove that initial hypotheses were correct. But, according to meta-researcher Dr. John Ioannidis, who is one of the world's foremost experts on the credibility of medical research and one of my personal heroes:

Even when the evidence shows that a particular research idea is wrong, if you have thousands of scientists who have invested their careers in it, they'll continue to publish papers on it. . . . It's like an epidemic, in the sense that they're infected with these wrong ideas, and they're spreading it to other researchers through journals.[47]

Ioannidis has discovered that the errors being committed in medical research were widespread. Errors and bias were introduced at every step of the process from what questions researchers posed, to how studies were conducted, to which patients were selected to study, to which measurements were taken, and to how the data was analyzed and published. The big picture was that researchers went into their work wanting certain results, and not surprisingly they were getting these results. There is strong pressure on researchers to find the results that are going to get funded and published, the exciting results that present positive and marketable results, especially in health research.

A related issue is that much of what we read in the news are the results of observational studies where vast amounts of data are sifted and a hypothesis is formed such as "red wine may be good for health." Journalists sometimes translate this into: "red wine *is* good for health!" when in fact no smaller randomized trials have been done to isolate a specific variable such as resveratrol. Prasad and other researchers reviewed almost 300 scientific papers and half these articles gave some kind of medical advice based on their observational studies, yet only 14 percent of these articles called for randomized trials to be conducted in order to validate their hypotheses. [48]

For the resveratrol studies it was perhaps more telling to find out that GlaxoSmithKline has started to step away from this research and has shuttered its offices in Cambridge, Massachusetts, where the resveratrol research was being conducted. They found Sinclair's ideas on genetics and aging useful and are continuing to pursue some of these same avenues Sinclair was exploring, but not connected to resveratrol.

All this is *not* to say that we should go back to our Wikipedia and Google searches and abandon scientific research! While Ioannidis has found that an obsession with winning funding has weakened the reliability of medical research, not all medical research is faulty. Partly to blame is our lack of understanding of what scientists should be doing, and this has caused some of the confusion and media frenzy. Many of the problems with the way scientific research is conducted today could be solved, according to Ioannidis, if all of us stopped expecting scientists to be *right*. Being wrong in science is expected and necessary, and studies that do not work out need to be reported on and funded as much as the rare breakthrough study.

Unfortunately, until career rewards are disconnected from producing "successful" and marketable results, science will continue to sometimes turn up flawed research and the media will sometimes push it out to the public as the latest "truth." Science needs to shift into the mode of being a "low-yield" endeavor, and until funding can be separated from the drive for sexy and marketable results, science is unlikely to change.

So where did that leave me in my quest to justify my wine-drinking habit? Like any good researcher I had strayed from my original research question by following the research trail where it took me: from red wine to resveratrol to resveratrol supplements containing huge doses of synthetic resveratrol. I had even run across a probiotic yogurt touting its resveratrol content!

> Yovivo! Yogurt with Resveratrol, the antioxidant found in red wine that's linked to heart health benefits! [49]

I have to say I am disappointed by all the interviews with Sinclair and the members of the media that continually emphasize the red wine connection—Dr. Sinclair and Barbara Walters toasting each other with red wine, an image of a large glass of red wine at the top of a *New York Times* article about resveratrol, the early articles showing Dr. Das sitting at a table with large glasses of red wine. The irony is that none of this is directly related to red wine at all. The amount of red wine needed to achieve some possible resveratrol health effect would surpass 100 glasses a day! Often the researchers would explain this during their interviews, but no one would then remove the images of red wine, or the little jokes about drinking, from these videos or articles.

As I wind down my research adventure, while a bit anticlimactic, I feel I have achieved some success. I have done the hardest thing there is to do in research: come up empty-handed. It is much harder to prove a negative than a positive, especially with so much noise out there about the potential for red wine and resveratrol. If more scientists and funders were willing to report negative findings, the state of science research would be vastly improved. But like Annette Bening's film character Nic, I will continue to have my nightly glass of red wine, hoping that the much larger quantities of resveratrol that showed positive effects in rodents might yield some minor positive benefit. But unlike Dr. Sinclair, I won't be tossing down resveratrol supplements any time soon. [50]

BREAKING IT DOWN: THE SIX STRATEGIES

When searching for health information, or any information, it is crucial to consider the following strategies:

1. Start at the Source

Let's go back to Sarah McCloud, the bank robber who is now serving time. Rather than strategically formulating her research question, instead she searched for:

What happens to someone when they rob a bank?

And rather than doing real research she likely popped onto the first few hits that Google returned. Here is what Wikipedia says:

> *While it is likely but not certain that the first time someone robs a bank they will not be caught, it is highly likely that if they continue they will be caught [citation needed].*[51]

Not good advice at all: in fact most people who rob banks are apprehended, even the first time.[52] The handful of hits on Google that follow the Wikipedia hit do not answer the question well either. They are off topic: newsy articles about what to do if you are working at a bank being robbed and video footage of two people robbing a bank.

If instead McCloud had thought first about searching for a *source* rather than a piece of information, she may have had better results. If she poked around a little on the topic of bank robbery generally, she would discover that it is a federal crime and that the FBI, the police, and criminologists all study bank robbery. She could have used this information to devise a more strategic search query to get at the right kind of source:

Google: *FBI rate of apprehension first-time bank robbers*

By using words like "FBI" and "apprehension" she would retrieve or see mention of a source called the FBI *Uniform Crime Reports* that reports on numbers and clearance rates for crimes and she could easily look up recent figures and avoid jail time. She also could have gone to Google Scholar or a library database that covers either criminology or vetted newspapers and zeroed in on the information she needed that would not turn up at the top of a Google search. For example:

Google: *Criminal Justice Databases*

This leads to both library-owned and free criminal justice databases such as the National Criminal Justice Reference Service. A quick free search on the NCJRS for "bank robbery" leads to a U.S. Department of Justice summary report listing clearance rates.

Starting by searching for a source rather than a piece of information can be challenging. It is a different way of thinking about searching. Rather than let Google control the process, a few extra words can help zero in on a reliable source and avoid getting pulled in by appealing but unreliable information. We often develop, over time, favorite sites for the weather, sports, and so on and either put these on a search dashboard, have them in our list of favorite apps, or use keywords to combine our trusted site name with a Google search. For example, for everyday health questions there are credible sites such as the Mayo Clinic. Go ahead and search Google, but just use a slightly more calculated search strategy:

Google: *Mayo knee pain*

For simple health questions Mayo can be enough. For more complex issues you may want to search PubMed for medical journal articles or you can track down a good "meta" site, such as the American Diabetes Association website, but review it carefully and make sure it is a ".org" or a ".gov" and not a ".com" that may be pushing a particular product. The Medical Library Association has a list of reliable health sites for many common diseases and illnesses, and MedlinePlus Health Topics website is free and constantly updated with extremely reliable information.[53] Go to these places first instead of Google.

2. Pay Attention to the "Psychology of Search"

There are many components to how we approach a search: The questions we ask, the keywords we use, and the information we find and then select. All these components impact the reliability of the information we ultimately use. Often we rely on "heuristics" or shortcuts that can be helpful and save time, but some shortcuts can skew the reliability of our results. I was guilty of "motivated cognition" when I started my red wine search: I was looking for information that meshed with what I already believed (biased information searching) and I wanted to give more weight to information that supported my goals (biased assimilation).

Sometimes this process takes time. I started out with biased searches about health and resveratrol (Is red wine good for you?), because I was motivated to justify my red wine habit. Later I started digging deeper to find out what the scholarly research was reporting. I then dug even deeper to see if different scholars were agreeing with the research that was receiving the most publicity: they weren't.

3. Expert, Amateur, or Crowd?

Most people seek health information from an expert, especially if they have a serious health problem. For day-to-day quick remedies for health issues 50 percent of people consult a friend or family member, but if the issue turns serious they typically consult a doctor.[54]

On the other hand, for getting emotional support and practical coping advice, the crowd—whether fellow sufferers online or family or friends—can be useful for some people, in addition to consulting an expert.[55] But be careful about getting actual treatment advice from the crowd. And experts, like all people, can have flaws. In some cases it pays to fully investigate expert advice and perhaps bring in the wisdom of a crowd of experts by getting a second or third opinion, or by accessing the medical journal literature on PubMed.

There are many places where crowdsourced information shows significant potential in healthcare—such as tracking the spread of the flu—but at this point in time crowdsourced treatment advice is risky.

4. Context, Motivation, and Bias

The old journalism adage "if your mother says she loves you: *Check it out,* is only partially a joke. It helps to remember that every piece of information, no matter how good the source, needs to be checked out. Kick the tires and take it for a test spin. Does it seem too good to be true? Context is an important component of figuring out the motivation of a particular author or site. Sometimes context is challenging to glean as information on the Web can be disintermediated: separated from its original author or source. If you can't tell who wrote it or who is sponsoring it, determining motivation and bias can be difficult but not impossible.

Ask the following questions when you read a piece of information online:

- What is the author (or site's) point of view?
- Is the article trying to influence your opinion?
- Is this a commercial site? Is the purpose of the site to promote or sell any products?
- Does the document come from a server sponsored by an organization with a specific agenda (political or commercial)?
- If the information refers to controversial issues, does the author acknowledge such a controversy or only present one side of the story?

All information has some inherent bias: Authors construct information for a reason or a particular motivation. Motivations need to be factored into the equation. Sites like Refinery29 are like cheerleaders: *Rah rah rah! Drink red wine and read our advertising!* They are not reporting on carefully vetted health advice, they are merely rebroadcasting content that will attract readers in order to lure them to advertisements.

5. Comparison and Corroboration

Comparing the information you find with other sources takes time and perseverance. The more important the need for accurate information the more crucial it is to find other sources that confirm what you have already found. If you are working with scholarly research, search Google Scholar or WOS to see if a particular article you are investigating has been cited by other researchers after it was released. If the article is from a website or an online magazine, try to verify the information with a stronger source. As you compare several articles or websites that cover the same topic, investigate which ones go into more depth, which ones verify sources, which ones acknowledge controversy about a topic or provide a balanced analysis. If you start with a heavily vetted search, such as MedlinePlus Health Topics, less verification is needed as this source is heavily vetted and continually updated.

Corroboration is slightly different from comparing sources. To corroborate information, identify a few specific facts found in a piece of information and look for other sources that either confirm or refute the specific facts. As you gather information see if much of what you find is supporting or refuting your original information, and verify whether each piece of information is coming from a credible source. Gradually you will be able to determine which way the research is currently leaning. Sometimes this means you have to adjust your own initial assumptions about whether a piece of information is credible.

6. Go Deep, or Not

With health information going deep often makes sense. Take the extra time to sort out the full story; do not just rely on the first article you find online. On the other hand, if you are just looking the best home remedy to treat a sore throat, Googling Mayo plus sore throat or even asking a friend could be sufficient.

NOTES

1. jatrahan, "New Bank Robbery Stats Show Lure of The Loot. But at What Cost?" *Dallas Morning News*, April 17, 2009, http://crimeblog.dallasnews.com/2009/04/new-bank-robbery-stats-show-lu.html/.

2. Susannah Fox, "Health Topics Report," Pew Internet and American Life Project, February 2011, http://www.pewinternet.org/Reports/2011/HealthTopics/Summary-of-Findings.aspx.

3. Eszter Hargittai, Lindsay Fullerton, Ericka Menchen-Trevino, and Kristin Yates Thomas, "Trust Online: Young Adults' Evaluation of Web Content," *International Journal of Communication* 4, no. 27 (April 2010), http://ijoc.org/index.php/ijoc/article/view/636.

4. Allison Orr Larsen, "Confronting Supreme Court Fact Finding," Faculty Publications Paper 1284, 2012, http://scholarship.law.wm.edu/facpubs/1284.

5. S.M. Smith, L.R. Fabrigar, and M.E. Norris, "Reflecting on Six Decades of Selective Exposure Research: Progress, Challenges, and Opportunities," *Social and Personality Psychology Compass* 2 (2008).

6. Cass R. Sunstein, *Republic.com 2.0* (Princeton: Princeton University Press, 2007); Eli Pariser, *The Filter Bubble* (New York: Penguin, 2011).

7. Matthew Ingram, "Google and Wikipedia: Separated at Birth?" Gigaom Research, February 18, 2010, http://gigaom.com/2010/02/18/google-and-wikipedia-separated-at-birth.

8. See http://en.wikipedia.org/wiki/User:The_Sceptical_Chymist.

9. Tom Simonite, "The Decline of Wikipedia," *MIT Technology Review,* October 22, 2013, http://www.technologyreview.com/featuredstory/520446/the-decline-of-wikipedia.

10. Ibid.

11. Aaron Halfaker, R. Stuart Gieger, Jonathan Morgan, and John Riedl, "The Rise and Decline of an Open Collaboration System: How Wikipedia's Reaction to Sudden Popularity Is Causing Its Decline," *American Behavioral Scientist* 57, no. 5 (2013).

12. For example, see Jennifer Phillips, Connie Lam, and Lisa Palmisano, "Analysis of the Accuracy and Readability of Herbal Supplement Information on Wikipedia," *Journal of the American Pharmacists Association* 54, no. 4 (2014), doi: 10.1331/JAPhA.2014.13181; Samy Azer, "Evaluation of Gastroenterology and Hepatology Articles on Wikipedia: Are They Suitable as Learning Resources for Medical Students?" *European Journal of Gastroenterology & Hepatology* 26, no. 2 (2013); Peter G. Volsky, Cristina Baldassari, Sirisha Mushti, and Craig S. Derkay, "Quality of Internet Information in Pediatric Otolaryngology: A Comparison of Three Most Referenced Websites," *International Journal of Pediatric Otorhinolaryngology* 76, no. 9 (September 2012), doi: 10.1016/j.ijporl.2012.05.026; Andreas Leithner, Wener Maurer-Ertl, Mathias Glehr, Joerg Friesenbichler, Katharina Leithner, and Reinhard Winhager, "Wikipedia and Osteosarcoma: A Trustworthy Patients' Information?" *Journal of the American Medical Informatics Association* 17, no 4 (July/August 2010), doi: 10.1136/jamia.2010.004507.

13. Several recent comprehensive literature reviews of Wikipedia have been conducted that focus on a variety of factors, including comprehensiveness, quality, and currency. Specifically in terms of reliability the findings have been mixed. See M. Mesgari, C. Okoli, M. Mehdi, F. Å. Nielsen, and A. Lanamäki, "'The Sum of all Human Knowledge': A Systematic Review of Scholarly Research on the Content of Wikipedia," *Journal of the Association for Information Science and Technology* 66 (2015), doi: 10.1002/asi.23172. Another researcher, a philosopher, concluded that "interacting with Wikipedia involves assessing where it is likely to be reliable and where not." See P.D. Magnus, "On Trusting Wikipedia," *Episteme* 6(1),(2009), doi: 10.3366/E1742360008000555.

14. Search Engine Optimization (SEO) refers to the methods used to boost the ranking of a website in results returned by a search engine, in an effort to maximize user traffic to the site. Some SEO is just good business sense, while other methods used are ethically and sometimes legally suspect.

15. Pariser, *The Filter Bubble.*

16. Gang Wang, Gill Konark, Haitao Zheng, and Ben Zhao, "Wisdom in the Social Crowd: An Analysis of Quora," in proceedings of the International World Wide Web Conference Committee (IW3C2), 2013, http://www.cs.ucsb.edu/~gangw/quora-www13.pdf.

17. Ibid.

18. See https://answers.yahoo.com/question/index?qid=20120801163909AAqmHRr.

19. Erik Choi and Chirag Shah, "User Motivation for Asking a Question in Online Q&A Services," *Journal of Association for Information Science & Technology* (in press); C. Shah, Vanessa Kitzie, and Erik Choi, "Modalities, Motivations, and Materials—Investigating Traditional and Social Online Q&A Services," *Journal of Information Science* 40, no. 5 (2014).

20. See http://www.awri.com.au/about_the_awri/business-model.

21. See http://www.refinery29.com/red-wine.

22. Felix Gillette, "Digital Drought Wrecks the Great American Content Farm," *Business-Week,* October 17, 2013, http://www.businessweek.com/articles/2013-10-17/digital-drought-wrecks-the-great-american-content-farm.

23. Jesse Hicks, "The Verge Interview: David Carr on Curation, Crowdsourcing, and the Future of Journalism," April 3, 2012, http://www.theverge.com/2012/4/3/2912487/david-carr-interview-dnp.

24. Susannah Fox, "Health Topics Report," Pew Internet and American Life Project, February 2011, http://www.pewinternet.org/Reports/2011/HealthTopics/Summary-of-Findings.aspx.

25. Maureen Dowd, "The Roger Ebert Show," *New York Times,* September 23, 2011, http://www.nytimes.com/2011/09/25/books/review/life-itself-a-memoir-by-roger-ebert-book-review.html?pagewanted=all.

26. G.K. Berland, M.N. Elliott, L.S. Morales, J.I. Algazy, R.L. Kravitz, M.S. Broder, D.E. Kanouse, J.A. Muñoz, J.A. Puyol, M. Lara, K.E. Watkins, H. Yang, and E.A. McGlynn,

"Health Information on the Internet: Accessibility, Quality, and Readability in English and Spanish," *Journal of the American Medical Association* 285, no. 2 (2001).

27. See http://www.mlanet.org/resources/userguide.html.

28. Virginia Heffernan, "A Prescription for Fear," *New York Times,* February 6, 2011, http://www.nytimes.com/2011/02/06/magazine/06FOB-Medium-t.html?_r=0.

29. Ibid.; Curtis Brainard, "Dr. Search Engine: NYT Prompts Needed Discussion about the Relative Merits of Health Website," *Columbia Journalism Review,* February 17, 2011, http://www.cjr.org/the_observatory/dr_search_engine.php?page=all.

30. Jim Edwards, "WebMD's Depressions Test Has Only One Sponsored Answer: You're at Risk," CBS News, February 22, 2010, http://www.cbsnews.com/8301-505123_162-42844266/webmds-depression-test-has-only-one-sponsored-answer-youre-at-risk.

31. M. Mackert, B. Love, and A.E. Holton, "Journalism as Health Education: Media Coverage of a Nonbranded Pharma Web Site," *Telemedicine and E-Health,* March 17, 2011.

32. See http://www.mayoclinic.com/health/red-wine/HB00089.

33. Web of Science is one of two "comprehensive" databases to the scholarly literature that is available in some academic libraries. Scopus has similar coverage and search features.

34. Double-blind peer review involves the reviewers of a paper and the author of a paper to remain anonymous to insure objectivity. Blind peer review involves just the author remaining anonymous to the reviewers.

35. "Voice of Young Science. Peer Review: The Nuts and Bolts," A Guide for Early Career Researchers, Standing up for Science 3 Report, http://www.senseaboutscience.org/data/files/resources/99/Peer-review_Thenuts-and-bolts.pdf. Reproduced under Creative Commons License.

36. Journal acceptance rates can usually be found on the journal website homepage under "information for authors." For a complete guide to understanding acceptance rates and selectivity, see http://guides.lib.umich.edu/content.php?pid=98218&sid=814212.

37. Thomas Reuters Journal Impact Factor provides a gross approximation of a journal's impact on research by calculating citation counts for articles published in a journal. A journal impact factor is only one measure of prestige, and it can sometimes be manipulated by authors citing their own work or by playing politics and heavily citing specific peers to increase their research reputation.

38. See http://www.longevinex.com/ and http://multivu.prnewswire.com/mnr/longevinex/42390.

39. Chris DeFrancesco, "Scientific Journals Notified Following Research Misconduct Investigation," *UConn Today,* January 11, 2012, http://today.uconn.edu/blog/2012/01/scientific-journals-notified-following-research-misconduct-investigation/.

40. Adam Marcus, "So How Peripheral Was Dipak Das' Resveratrol Work, Really?" *Retraction Watch,* January 11, 2012, http://retractionwatch.wordpress.com/2012/01/12/so-how-peripheral-was-dipak-das-resveratrol-work-really/.

41. Tom Bartlett, "Red Wine and Lies," *Chronicle of Higher Education* Blog Post, January 16, 2012, http://chronicle.com/blogs/percolator/red-wine-and-lies/28345.

42. M. Franz, "Merlot's Bad Press," *Washington Post,* May 4, 2005, http://www.washingtonpost.com/wp-dyn/content/article/2005/05/03/AR2005050300419.html.

43. Bartlett, "Red Wine and Lies"; Linda Patridge, David Gems, et al., "Absence of Effects of Sir2 Overexpression on Lifespan in C. elegans and Drosophila," *Nature* 477 (September 22, 2011), doi: 10.1038/nature10296.

44. Carolyn Johnson, "Study Supports Anti-Aging Effects of Red Wine Ingredient Resveratrol," Boston.com Blog, March 7, 2013, http://www.boston.com/news/science/blogs/science-in-mind/2013/03/07/study-supports-anti-aging-effects-red-wine-ingredient-resveratrol/jUzPDw0d2yj7HHUo5kMuDK/blog.html.

45. David Sinclair, "A Cure for Ageing?" TEDxSydney, http://www.youtube.com/watch?v=vCCdmGKtxPA.

46. I. Johnson, "Study Supports Anti-Aging Effects."

47. David Freedman, "Lies, Damned Lies, and Medical Science," *Atlantic,* October 4, 2010, http://www.theatlantic.com/magazine/archive/2010/11/lies-damned-lies-and-medical-science/308269/.

48. Vinay Prasad, Joel Jorgenson, John P.A. Ioannidis, and Adam Cifu, "Observational Studies Often Make Clinical Practice Recommendations: An Empirical Evaluation of Authors' Attitudes," *Journal of Clinical Epidemiology* 66, no. 4 (April 2013), doi: 10.1016/j.jclinepi.2012.11.005.

49. See http://www.indiegogo.com/projects/yovivo-probiotic-yogurt-advancing-access-to-better-health-for-all.

50. Charlie Rose interview with David Sinclair, "Red Wine and Its Effects on Mice: David Sinclair, Harvard Medical School," November 2 2006, http://www.charlierose.com/history.html.

51. See http://en.wikipedia.org/wiki/Bank_robbery.

52. Federal Bureau of Investigations, "Robbery," *Uniform Crime Reports,* 2010, http://www.fbi.gov/about-us/cjis/ucr/crime-in-the-u.s/2010/crime-in-the-u.s.-2010/violent-crime/robberymain.

53. See https://www.mlanet.org/resources/medspeak/topten.html; and http://www.nlm.nih.gov/medlineplus/healthtopics.html.

54. Susannah Fox, "Medicine 2.0: Peer-to-Peer Healthcare," Pew Research Internet Project Report, September 18, 2011, http://www.pewinternet.org/2011/09/18/medicine-2-0-peer-to-peer-healthcare/; "Health Fact Sheet," Pew Research Internet Project, http://www.pewinternet.org/fact-sheets/health-fact-sheet/.

55. Mowafa Househ, Elizabeth Borycki, and Andre Kushniruk, "Empowering Patients Through Social Media: The Benefits and Challenges," *Health Informatics Journal* 20, no. 1 (2014), doi: 10.1177/1460458213476969.

Chapter Two

Five Stars! Four Girls and Free Brunch

Finding Reliable Restaurant Reviews

Criticism . . . doesn't necessarily mean heaping scorn. It means making fine distinctions. It means talking about ideas, aesthetics and morality as if these things matter (and they do). It's at base an act of love.

—Dwight Garner (2012)

Yeah, well, you know, that's just, like, your opinion, man.

—*The Big Lebowski* (1998)

My husband Tom thinks he can spot fake restaurant reviews. I disagree. I send him a link to some TripAdvisor reviews of Oscar's, an upmarket restaurant located on a fishing trawler along the quay in Brixham, England. Because Oscar's is new it has only eight reviews. Seven reviews rate the restaurant "excellent" and one review says it is "terrible." Here are excerpts from the positive reviews.

-The big surprise here was what Colette and her staff do in the kitchen, something bordering on sorcery.
-The most amazing meal my family and I have ever had.
-Trying to book a table can be a nightmare. Getting a table midweek for two . . . is a major achievement.
-I am fortunate enough to live in Catalyuna, home to some of the best restaurants in the world. I have dined at both elBulli and El Celler de Can Roca. Is Oscar's as good? No not quite - but as has been mentioned already, there is an unbelievable quality about it.

27

Researchers are now investigating fake online reviews to develop software to filter out the fakes. Tom feels confident he can spot fake reviews because he knows that people writing fake reviews tend to do the following:

- **Use over-the-top raves.** Fake reviews tend to be excessive and emotional with lots of superlatives and phrases such as "the best ever" or "the number one barbeque ribs place in Texas!!"[1]
- **Use a large number of personal pronouns.** People who are lying and want to convince people that something happened tend to use phrases such as "I ordered the chicken and it was delicious," rather than "The chicken was delicious."[2]
- **Overuse certain words and avoid others.** Words in restaurant reviews such as *options, seat, helpful, overall, serve,* and *amount* show up much more frequently in fake reviews.[3]

But people often overestimate their ability to spot fake reviews. Researchers at Cornell have found that people can only spot fake reviews with about 50 percent accuracy. People tend to fall into two camps: they either accept way too much at face value, or are overly skeptical and reject many reviews that are in fact true. So, which of the reviews about Oscar's were fake? I'll get to that soon.

Fake reviews are only the tip of the iceberg when it comes to selecting reliable recommendations for restaurants or for any service or product. There are also choices to be made about quality: do you simply need a "thumbs up" type of review or are you looking for a more nuanced description? While this chapter focuses on restaurant reviews, it also touches on issues relevant to book, movie, product, and theater reviews. Are there easy ways to zero in on a reliable restaurant review? Yes, if you keep in mind the following:

1. Start at the Source

While finding a good restaurant is a low-stakes game compared to finding health information, there are times when we want to make sure we get a trustworthy recommendation for a great restaurant. This chapter investigates how to choose among crowdsourced sites like Google Reviews or Yelp, amateur food bloggers, and professional reviewers. Google is a great search engine for some types of information, especially for pointing to factual information like the weather or a store location. But in order to find a reliable review it is often better to go after a specific source. Sometimes we can use specialized search engines to help us locate what we want. For example, Yelp is not thought of as a search engine, but in fact it is a very good niche search engine for providing quick information about restaurants. It is not, surprisingly, a good place for reviews!

2. Pay Attention to the "Psychology of Search"

Like the other chapters in this book, we investigate the psychology of search—the motivations, biases, and behaviors that operate behind our searching choices. This chapter investigates source amnesia: the tendency to remember information but forget the source of the information. This can happen even when we view information from an extremely unreliable source.

3. Expert, Amateur, or Crowd?

Expertise is a tricky business when it comes to restaurant, film, book, or theater reviews. Many argue that an amateur review is fine, especially with food. What's the big deal? But what we think is an amateur may be a shill, and what we think is some crowd wisdom might be skewed or so overly positive it is not helpful. On the other hand, there are limitations to solo professional critics who may have lost touch with the average diner's experience or are influenced by the resume of a famous chef. The good news is that a middle way is emerging: a tuned-in reliable critic that is also connected to, and interacting with, the crowd.

4. Context, Motivation, and Bias

Online reviews frequently suffer from a context deficit: It is difficult to tell who posted a review and why. Not only is the source of a piece of information sometimes missing, at times it is masked or distorted. For restaurant reviews it is usually better to head for sites that have posted a code of ethics and use editors or have some mechanism for ensuring the integrity of the reviews they post.

5. Comparison and Corroboration

When looking at restaurant reviews, the biggest challenge is fake reviews. While some crowdsourced sites are combating this practice, they have not won the battle. Maintain a healthy skepticism. Fast and simple corroboration techniques are all that are needed to double-check on a restaurant review.

6. Go Deep, or Not

This is a personal decision with restaurant reviews. If you just want a pizza at a restaurant that does not have a serious health code violation, search Yelp for "pizza" plus the name of the city you are in to get a restaurant name and then:

Google*: restaurant safety scores and Name of City*
Or:
Google: *restaurant health code violations and Name of City*[4]

The results are not for the fainthearted! But if you want more than just a clean bill of health, there is a pleasure and richness of experience that comes from reading a knowledgeable amateur blogger or a professional restaurant critic. This can heighten your restaurant adventure. For example, you might learn about José Andrés, who experiments with molecular gastronomy and strains mojitos over cotton candy at Los Angeles's SLS Hotel, or the "roof to table" movement involving rooftop gardens above restaurants that is taking locally sourced food to a whole new level.

THE CHALLENGE: 1 OUT OF 4,000

My husband and I are celebrating a milestone wedding anniversary next month by flying out to San Francisco. He has agreed to find a hotel and get the plane tickets. I have been charged with finding the perfect place for dinner. Not a big deal right? San Francisco is only, arguably, the culinary capital of the world.[5] With roughly 4,000 restaurants to choose from, how hard can it be?

The first task is to figure out if I can simply use a site like Yelp restaurant reviews to make my selection. Following the crowd when it comes to choosing a good restaurant seems like an effective strategy. But is it?

FOLLOWING THE CROWD

If you suddenly became a Pentecostal minister in West Virginia, where they still practice snake handling to prove their faith in God, you would want to bring in an expert who had experience handling cottonmouths, copperheads, and rattlesnakes. A herpetologist could advise you on how to avoid being bitten. Scientists have been puzzled by how rare it is for these pastors or their congregants to be bitten in this century-old practice. Recently, herpetologists looked more closely at the snakes being used in these churches and found that the snakes were often dehydrated, underweight, and sick from being underfed and closely confined in cages. These practices make the snakes much less likely to strike, and the venom they produce if they do strike is much weaker than that of a healthy snake. Consulting with an expert can sometimes save your life.

But food reviewing does not seem to require expertise. We all eat, and as the saying goes, "everyone is a critic." Consulting crowdsourced amateur reviewers could work, and the downside is not death, but simply a mediocre meal. In practice, the crowd *does* follow the crowd. Searchers greatly prefer crowdsourced restaurant review sites with as many as 42 percent of searchers using Yelp, Zagat, or TripAdvisor-type sites, while only 14 percent use professional reviewers.[6] But it might be a chicken and egg situation. Whenever anyone searches for restaurant reviews on Google, the top sites are typically Google Reviews, Yelp, TripAdvisor, and other heavy hitters. So do users *choose* to head straight for sites like Yelp, or do they head for sites like Yelp because these sites come up first in the search? Professional reviewers like the food critics for the *New York Times* or *San Francisco Chronicle* rarely come up in Google top search results.

Getting "real reviews from real people," as Yelp claims to do, combined with averaging these reviews should lead to a safe bet in choosing a restaurant. Is the wisdom of the Yelp crowd enough? I decide to dig a little deeper. Americans have had a long-held distrust of professionals telling them where to eat a meal.[7] There has been broad appeal for user-generated reviews dating back almost one hundred years, to a time when the middle class first started venturing out regularly to restaurants.

ADVENTURES IN GOOD EATING: A BRIEF HISTORY

Duncan Hines used to say that more people died of restaurant food poisoning than hit-and-run accidents.[8] Hines was a traveling salesman who began writing restaurant reviews in the 1930s to help travelers find safe places to eat. He was a far cry from a professional food critic, and his reviews were often just a few sentences long. He wrote as much about the experience as the food when recommending restaurants to other travelers.

> **San Francisco. The Oyster Loaf. 30 Kearny St . ACond.**
> *There is a tradition that in the early days of San Francisco the imbibing males who made the rounds on the cocktail route never failed to bring home an Oyster Loaf as a "peace offering." The present Oyster Loaf Restaurant is an old established dining place which has been rebuilt and newly reopened. As the name implies, seafoods are featured dishes although charcoal broiled steaks and chops are also on their menu. A la carte.*[9]

Today Hines is considered one of the inventors of anonymous crowd-sourced restaurant reviews. His guide, *Adventures in Good Eating,* incorporated the reviews of other travelers, and the reviewers remained anonymous. His guidebooks garnered enormous trust and reader loyalty at a time when people were wary of restaurant food and "greasy spoons," before the advent of chain restaurants. As Hines' fame grew he remained dedicated to his readers. He never accepted a free meal or advertising, and he required restaurants to be modern and to agree to open their kitchens for customer inspection if they wanted to be included in his guide. But like other reviewers that followed Hines, he struggled with maintaining this integrity. In a 1946 guide he states in the forward:

Warning to Places Listed.
It is a distinct disappointment to me to learn that a surprising number of people have gone to listed places and received free meals and lodging because they have claimed to be relatives of mine traveling through the country to check on places, or that they were responsible for the place being included in my book. Please remember I have authorized no one to make such demands and they should be refused.

Because his name was associated with high standards in the food business, Hines agreed to having his name on boxes of cake mix that are still found in grocery stores today.

In the 1970s going out to eat became increasingly popular and other restaurant guides emerged, such as one written by staff from *Forbes* magazine. In 1982, Tim and Nina Zagat entered the restaurant review scene. At a dinner party their guests were complaining that the small handful of professional restaurant critics in New York were often unreliable. After the party, the Zagats began informally surveying their friends about favorite restaurants. This led to the compilation of 200 amateur critic reviews and ratings of 100 top New York restaurants. The Zagats felt that the shared opinions of many consumers were more accurate than the opinions of one or two critics. The first Zagat guide for New York sold 7,500 copies and the Zagats later expanded their guides to more than seventy cities and 250,000 reviewers. [10]

Like the Hines guides, Zagat was known for reliability and carefully edited crowdsourced reviews. Influenced by the Michelin Guides in France, their focus was on their rating system so that restaurant goers could see separate aggregated scores for food, décor, service, and cost. Hines and the Zagats knew that maintaining the quality of their reviews tied directly to their success.

Unfortunately, the Zagats kept their online guide partially behind a paywall while continuing to sell print guides. Because of the paywall their Google ranking was lower than free review sites, and despite their quality reviews they lost audience share. Recognizing the quality and quantity of Zagat reviews, Google purchased Zagat in 2011 and combined it with their fledging local review site. They wanted the Zagat reputation and thousands of data points in order to compete with Yelp. As Zagat has merged with Google Reviews, it has lost its unique features and quality and become more like Yelp, its chief rival.

THE POWER OF YELP

Following in the footsteps of Zagat, Yelp was started in 2004 as a site for sharing recommendations on local services. Unlike Zagat, Yelp was free and quickly grew in popularity, making use of new social media tools and gaining a top spot in Google search results. In 2014 Yelp received over 120 million unique visitors a month. Yelpers have written more than 53 million reviews of restaurants and other services.[11] Many reviewers take great pleasure in contributing reviews viewing it is a community service, a hobby, a record of their eating adventures, and a social opportunity.

Yelp exerts a powerful influence over many businesses because of their popular reviews. A Harvard study found that when the average star rating on Yelp goes up by one star, the revenue of that restaurant goes up by 5 to 9 percent. A related study by two economists correlated evening reservation rates with their ratings on the Yelp website. An upgrade from 3.5 to 4 stars resulted in a 19 percent increase in the sellout rate for 7:00 p.m. reservations.[12] The average star rating is what people attend to while the text of reviews plays a secondary role.[13]

Yelp and similar review sites such as TripAdvisor and UrbanSpoon have sent "nervous ripples through the restaurant world."[14] Roughly 93 percent of people in the United States use the Internet to buy or research a purchase and about 25 percent do this on a daily basis.[15] Many a chef or restaurateur stays up late into the night worrying about, and sometimes responding to, negative reviewers. But are popular sites like Yelp the best place to get a true sense of the quality of a restaurant? Are crowdsourced restaurant reviews credible?

WISE CROWD?

Yelp may be powerful, but it is also considered the bane of professional restaurant critics, passionate foodies, and independent restaurant bloggers. Yelp's many detractors have led to popular sites such as *F@#$ You Yelpers* on Tumblr, a site that curates the most offensive Yelp reviews and posts them for their entertainment value. A rude waiter or long wait often has an overly influential impact on many a Yelp amateur reviewer who may only visit a restaurant one time:

> *Seriously the service is* [sic] *here is soooooo weird. They try to be extra nice to you, but somehow ends up being fake. I dont know, the whole experience was super off and I don't mean off in a quirky cute way, I mean off in a, I wanna hurry up and eat what I ordered and get the hell out of this place way. Honestly, the service of the waistaff and the management seemed cultish for some reason.*
> *NEVER EVER GOING BACK TO THIS HELL HOLE!*

1-star review of Chilbo Myunok by Stacey R.[16]

Other Yelpers do not even feel obligated to try the food, but this does not keep them from sharing their review and star rating.

> *Well, Ive never even eaten here. so why, you ask, do I even bother to rate this place? Because I did walk in here, sit down, and read the menu. Then I looked at my friends and said, Theres no way I can eat this. It was all grease and fat and a whole buncha yuck jumbled together. NO WAY. Im just not into that kind of eating or food combinations.. so NOT appealing to me. So we left. Yet, it's a local institution of sorts. Oh well.*
> 1-star review of Roscoe's House of Chicken and Waffles in Hollywood by Claudia B.[17]

For my own restaurant search I am hoping what is helpful in using Yelp is the "wisdom of the crowd" effect derived from aggregating Yelp reviews. Many people report using this strategy and pay attention to the averaged rating while finding individual reviews not that helpful. I am thinking that by averaging hundreds of reviews the Yelp score is probably an accurate measure of restaurant quality, but I am skeptical. Averaging a lot of data is good, but not if much of the content is of poor quality. I decide to give it a try and see what happens. I type the following into Google:

Google: *Yelp San Francisco*

Up comes the Yelp site for San Francisco and the words "Best Restaurants in San Francisco." I can choose by neighborhood, price, and type of restaurant, so I choose Italian and then see a large image of Sotto Mare, the top-ranked "best" Italian restaurant in the city. Because such a huge percentage of restaurants in Yelp end up with high rating scores, it is pretty hard to choose between hundreds of restaurants that all received 4.5- or 5-star aggregated reviews. To determine the "best" restaurants, engineers on Yelp's data-mining team use "a technique based on the Wilson Score to compile their list by pulling in both the star rating and the number of reviews to get at popular highly rated restaurants."[18]

Most social media sites on the Web try to leverage the "wisdom of the crowd" to create useful information and there have been many success stories. For example, the Weather Underground (WU) is a good example of a wise crowd. The WU takes data from the National Weather Service and combines it with 20,000 amateur-run personal weather stations around the world. These stations provide real-time weather reports for specific, and sometimes hard to get to, locations where rapid weather changes can occur. The WU has developed an algorithm that performs a "sanity check" and then removes a station that is reporting incorrect data. The "sanity check" cross-references data from one local station to data from a nearby station. Over time they have had to drop about 50 percent of their reporters, often because their stations were not set up properly.[19]

Amateur weather geeks differ from YELP reviewers in several ways. The weather is factual, quantifiable, and not subjective. Weather geeks are committed to accuracy and do not have a stake in, for example, boosting the ratings of a friend or trampling a competitor. They invest over a hundred dollars to set up a station and provide real-time weather data independent of any data being provided by other stations.

Crowdsourcing at the WU succeeds because it meets the criteria for a successful crowdsourced system. The "wisdom of the crowds" is an effect first investigated by Frances Galton in 1907 when he found that a crowd was better than any individual at guessing the weight of an ox at a country fair. More recently popularized by James Surowiecki, the theory states that when making quantitative decisions about uncertain outcomes, averaging the estimate of a crowd is usually a better predictor than the estimate of any one individual, even if that individual is an expert.[20] Often misinterpreted by social media platform developers, Surowiecki was clear that crowdsourcing depended on individuals not knowing, and therefore not being influenced by, other people's contributions and that it typically worked well with quantifiable objective information. These factors make applying the "wisdom of the crowd" effect to sites like Yelp, TripAdvisor, or UrbanSpoon, a bit of a stretch.

AVERAGING APPLES, ORANGES, AND TROLLS

Another concern with sites like Yelp is that reviews often do not focus on the food. Yelp is notorious for mean-spirited posts that are obsessed with minor affronts that then plummet a review score. A recent study from Purdue University found that user-generated reviews devote a far greater percentage of their word count to service and price than do semi-professional and professional restaurant reviews.[21]

> *The sushi here is amazing! It literally melts in your mouth. BUT little did I know, this place charges 18% gratuity no matter how big your party is. That really really really disappointed me and definitely hurt their rating.*
> 2-star review of Sugarfish by David N.

> *wtf, try to go to Langers on the day after Thanksgiving, and it is CLOSED! For four days!!!*
> 1-star review of Langer's Delicatessen Restaurant by Carla B.

Angry reviews directed at service are frequently one-star reviews that impact the averaged rating, even though the reviewer is not rating the food. Though some Yelpers identify themselves, most use a pseudonym. Being able to post anonymously on social media sites can bring out the worst in some users. Trolls are users that post comments on social media sites that are specifically designed to stir up trouble. Combined, these aggrieved reviewers and trolls provide unreliable data points that throw off aggregated star ratings. Certainly the star rating on a restaurant with hundreds of reviews provides a better predictor than a restaurant with only a few reviews, but many people pay little attention to how many reviews a restaurant receives and focus on the aggregated star rating. [22]

Researchers have been investigating whether by weighting reviews Yelp could achieve greater reliability. [23] Unfortunately, Yelp has decided not to weight reviews and so it rates a review that is three years old the same as one that is three days old, and the ranting of a reviewer that had to wait in line for fifteen minutes is rated the same as a more balanced reviewer. The bottom line is that Yelp ratings can usually call attention to a really terrible restaurant, but they are not much help in my tracking down a great restaurant in San Francisco.

THE WISDOM OF HERDS AND SELECTION BIAS

A further problem with tapping into the crowdsourced ratings on Yelp is that the site suffers from what many crowdsourced sites experience: herding behavior and selection bias. When Galton's fairgoers guessed the weight of the ox, none of them heard any of the other guesses because that would have influenced their guess. Independence is essential for a "wisdom of the crowds" effect to work. Instead of wisdom on sites like Yelp, a herd mentality tends to overinflate online ratings.

Here is how the ratings look for Sotto Mare, the "best" from Yelp:

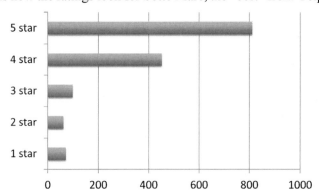

Ratings for Sotto Mare, the "best" from Yelp.

This positive data skew is common for online review sites.[24] A study published in *Science* found that researchers could easily sway people into overinflating their enthusiasm by giving an "up" vote to user comments about news stories online.[25] The study showed that a "wisdom of the crowds" effect only works if each person brings their own independent observations. When everyone is able to see everyone else's opinions there is a tremendous bias effect. The bias occurs typically in the overly positive direction. Working with large numbers of "reviews" (up and down votes), the researchers demonstrated that by intervening early and voting a news story up right after it was posted, there was a massive snowball effect on that comment and it was then much more likely to receive an overall high rating by the crowd.

The power of social influence to impact choices made by others is not a new phenomenon, but social media greatly magnifies this effect. In the 1950s research demonstrated this effect in numerous studies. In one experiment people were asked to choose which of three lines was the same length as another line. If people planted in the room by the researchers made an obviously wrong choice, many study participants also went along with this wrong choice. An economist at Harvard found similar results of positive herding behavior when he tracked how Yelp restaurant reviews evolve over time.[26]

This herding behavior does not occur when the aggregated crowd data is factual and unbiased. A data point for books such as the "Amazon Best Sellers Rank" is meaningful. It is objectively measuring how many copies of the book Amazon has sold. An Amazon rank of 10,000 suggests a frequently purchased book, compared to one with a rank of 400,000. But the reviewer star system in Amazon is, like Yelp, subjective and prone to gaming behavior whether by publicists, social media experts, or trolls.

Selection bias is another problem that occurs with consumer rating sites for restaurants, movies, books, or other goods. With selection bias, amateur reviewers tend to *choose* restaurants or other items that they expect to like, and then, not surprisingly, they rate them positively. Professional critics go to many more places, and editors often control where they go, so this effect is minimized.

Researchers studying theatergoers found a strong selection bias occurring, with amateurs giving out many more 5-star reviews and tending to be more extreme in their ratings and comments. Trying to get at the sensibility of one reviewer is difficult, because many amateurs only provide a handful of reviews. But for those who provide more of a track record, it is possible to gauge such items as how quick they are to hand out 5 stars. Interestingly, in one study focused on theater reviews, amateurs who rated many shows started to resemble the more nuanced rating distributions of professional reviewers. These amateurs gave out fewer 5-star ratings as they built up their experience and were able to compare each show to those they had already rated.[27] They were gaining expertise. The research on amateur theater re-viewers concluded that it was possible to use these to spot a dud, but for making a choice between several shows that are all highly rated it makes sense to read a published professional review.

THE INTERNET WATER ARMY IS WINNING

Depending on crowdsourcing for restaurant reviews is also a problem be-cause of fake reviews. Thousands of paid reviewers with fake email and Facebook accounts post fake reviews every day.[28] In China they are called the Internet Water Army because they can quickly and effectively "flood" the Internet with comments, information, reviews, and gossip. Recently a stealth team of researchers went undercover posing as members of the Water Army to discern how to spot fake postings. As they analyzed fake postings they developed a software system that could weed out similar types of fake re-views. Unfortunately, as soon as the first version of the software goes on sale the Water Army will figure out a way to modify their posts to avoid detec-tion.[29] It is a zero-sum game.

Spotting fake reviews or "likes" is like playing Whac-a-Mole. Every time a mechanism is developed for filtering fake reviews, a work-around is creat-ed. Mechanical Turk, an Amazon site advertising for "human intelligence workers" used to heavily recruit for crowdturfers to post fake comments and reviews. They have now cracked down on these types of ads, reducing their numbers from 41 to 12 percent.[30] As Amazon reduced their ads for crowd-turfers, other sites such as Fiverr.com and Freelancer.com were quick to fill the gap. Almost one-third of Freelancer.com jobs relate to crowdturfing.[31] On Fiverr, workers offer to write fake reviews or assist with optimizing Google search results for $5.00.

> *I will write a glowing review for your restaurant for $5. Are you a restaurant,*
> *bar, or café owner? I would love the opportunity to help you increase your*
> *customer base by writing a positively glowing review for you! All reviews that*
> *I complete will be well thought out, thorough, and realistic. I will write up to*
> *200 words catered to your unique needs.*
> Post on Fiverr.com by alisharenee05

Yelp has also developed a "sanity check" that algorithmically weeds out many fake reviews, though their success is unclear. Software developed by Cornell claims to be able to detect fake online reviews with about 90 percent accuracy, but other researchers contend that for every algorithm developed and thought to be game-proof, clever people will find ways to beat the system.[32]

Between 10 and 30 percent of online reviews are fake.[33] Researchers predict an increase in litigation from the Federal Trade Commission against hiring people to post fake reviews.[34] Recently nineteen companies in New York were fined more than $300,000 for hiring crowdturfers. Unpacking the data, two Harvard professors found that the most active offenders in the restaurant business were restaurant owners seeking to offset negative reviews or posting fake negative reviews about their competitors.[35] During an investigation into allegations that millions of TripAdvisor reviews might be fake, TripAdvisor changed their slogan from: "Reviews You Can Trust" to "Reviews from Our Community."[36]

FUNNY, COOL, AND USEFUL?

One way that Yelp, Amazon, and others try to combat the issue of fake reviews and the growing clutter of trolls is by calling attention to, and rewarding, their most prolific reviewers. Yelp reviewers who write many reviews and are rated by fellow Yelpers as "funny, cool, or useful" are given the title Elite Yelpers. Elite Yelpers are invited to exclusive parties with vendors who provide free food, drinks, and other goods in exchange for reviews.

David Ferrell, a reporter for the *Orange County Register*, writes about Suki Beasla, an Elite Yelper who attends monthly Yelp parties. Suki has written more than 950 reviews for Yelp and has over 1,000 "friends" on Yelp. She provides free marketing in the form of "reviews" in exchange for perks such as food and going to Yelp social events. While Suki claims to be impartial, of the fifty-two reviews she has written for Yelp-sponsored restaurant events, fifty-one of them received perfect 5-star ratings.[37]

Reviewers who accept free food or other items in exchange for positive reviews cannot remain objective. Receiving freebies occurs commonly in the age of social media marketing. In the product review industry, researchers have been investigating Amazon's prolific "Vine" reviewers. Vine members receive enormous amounts of free goods in exchange for reviews, but claim that they provide unbiased reviews. New York University professors Michael Erb and Anindya Ghose disagree. They found that Vine members were likely to review things much more positively than people who pay for the items.[38]

TAME YOUR YELP ENGINE

My first choice for finding a restaurant in San Francisco is a failure. Yelp proves to be unreliable for locating a great restaurant, and possibly even harmful. But Sotto Mare sticks in my mind and I still think of it as the best Italian restaurant in San Francisco, as I lose sight of the fact that it came from an unreliable set of reviews. This is a common occurrence with online searching or even searching for information in print. It is called "source amnesia." Frequently an information searcher remembers the information retrieved and treats that information as "true," having forgotten the source of the information and that it came from an unreliable place. [39]

Though not reliable for reviews, Yelp can be used effectively in several other ways. Yelp is good at calling attention to extremely bad restaurants. If you look up a restaurant and it has a very low star count—steer clear. Yelp is also particularly great at being the "Google" of restaurants. While many foodies disparage Yelp as a review site, they use it frequently to search for information *about* restaurants.

> Want to find out what bakeries in Philadelphia make sticky buns?
> Google: *Yelp Philadelphia*
> Yelp search box: *sticky buns*

Want to know what restaurants have a gluten-free menu or are child friendly? Yelp has that data as well. Yelp can be helpful as a crowdsourced site for locating factual information, even if that information is just a location or whether a restaurant is expensive, or cheap, or serves eggplant. But Yelp's take on Sotto Mare? Pretty limited:

> *The food was decent, actually, but the service was so terrible I would never go back. After we placed our order, we were asked to move tables even though the place was nearly empty. We were obviously annoyed, so they offered to comp our wine but then forgot to take it off the bill. Our waiter was overly chatty and rude as well.*
> 1-star review from Lauren H.

IT'S NOT ROCKET SCIENCE

I decide to give up on all of the crowdsourced review sites and go to the other extreme: a professional critic. I look up my restaurant pick with the high Yelp score on the main online newspaper site for San Francisco to see if their professional critic has reviewed it.

> Google: *San Francisco newspaper*

This gives me the name of the top newspaper in San Francisco, the *San Francisco Chronicle*. Google excels at this kind of search. I could also do the same search in Wikipedia and get a list of a few dozen news sites if I want to look at some of the alternative weeklies or other dailies in San Francisco. I decide to stick with the biggest news site. I combine it with my restaurant choice:

Google: *San Francisco Chronicle Sotto Mare*

Good news! Michael Bauer, who has spent almost thirty years reviewing for the *Chronicle,* has written a lengthy review. But before I look at his review, maybe it would help to understand just what defines a professional critic. When it comes to food and restaurant criticism, what qualifies someone like Bauer as an expert?

The popular expression "It's not rocket science!" comes up all too often when laypeople feel they can step in and do the work of a professional. But in some cases professionals provide a degree of expertise that is justified. We accept this in fields such as brain surgery, but we are less likely to value expertise in areas where we might have some experience, like photography, or . . . eating. But sometimes amateurs overstep their boundaries resulting in potentially dire consequences. When Christina Hale went foraging in her backyard for mushrooms to make soup she had no idea that the poisonous Death Cap mushroom looks similar to the edible Caesar. Without the expertise of a mycologist, Christina was dead within four days from complete organ failure caused by the twenty toxins found in Death Caps. [40] Calling on an expert when mushroom hunting makes sense. Only a handful of people in the United States die each year from poisonous mushrooms, but dozens more become extremely ill and about half of these cases are the result of overconfident amateurs selecting the wrong mushrooms. [41]

Like mycologists, the talents of wine experts are frequently underestimated. Many people dismiss what they view as snooty oenophiles using words like buttery, tight, or crisp to describe particular wines. In fact, research investigating the skills of wine experts indicates a high degree of agreement among oeniphiles in their analysis, descriptions, and selections of top wines. Restaurant critics, even more than mycologists or oenophiles, have jobs that many feel could be done by anyone with a mouth. As a result we have thousands of bloggers and Yelpers jumping into the fray. But professional restaurant critics, whether working for a blog or a newspaper, can possess expert knowledge that adds richness, veracity, depth, ethical standards, and cultural context to their reviews in an arena where most of us barely scratch the surface.

A QUESTION OF DEGREE AND DEGREE?

To be an expert is to have expert knowledge. Sounds simple, but scholars like Carl Bereiter have spent a lifetime becoming experts on how individuals develop expert knowledge. Bereiter and other researchers have sliced up expert knowledge into five pieces. The more straightforward parts are the expertise that comes from skill development called *procedural knowledge* and the *formal knowledge* that we gain from education and reading. The other three types of expert knowledge are harder to pin down: *informal, impressionistic*, and *self-regulated*.

Informal knowledge is the expert's specialized and finely honed form of common sense that is fed by a deep well of skill and education.[42] Closely related to informal knowledge is *impressionistic knowledge*. Some people label it intuition or instinct because it seems to come from gut feelings, but these are highly informed gut feelings. I observe impressionistic knowledge being used by my husband, a social worker, when he responds to emergency cases and needs to make a quick judgment about whether someone might be a danger to himself or others. He uses the knowledge gained from formal learning and practice, but it is that hard-to-articulate instinctual response that often helps him make the final judgment call.

Impressionistic knowledge develops after years of experience. Bereiter says it is "what we are left with after we have forgotten all the explicit content of great literary or artistic work."[43] We use words like connoisseurship or professionalism when we discuss this kind of knowledge. The wine amateur provides an example of someone who has "impressions" about the taste of a wine, but lacks the impressionistic knowledge of the oeniphile. In studies focusing on amateur wine tasters there was little agreement in ratings or words used to describe wine not only *between* amateur reviewers, but the same amateur tasting from the same bottle at different times does not report the same impressions.[44]

The last type of expert knowledge is *self-regulatory knowledge*, meaning knowledge about oneself that is needed in order to function effectively in a particular domain.[45] It is not about *how* to be, for example, a wine expert. It is about how to manage yourself, with all your strengths and weaknesses, within that field. As professionals solve challenges that come up, an ongoing feedback loop occurs that can strengthen that expertise over time. While many people have the capacity to develop all these kinds of expert knowledge, the difference between an amateur and an expert is in how well integrated and regulated their knowledge has become.

CRITICISM AND ITS HUMBLE COUSIN, REVIEWING

Professional restaurant critics possess the skills and formal knowledge of their field. They typically have a strong educational background in journalism and a deep knowledge of food, the restaurant business, and cultural criticism. They often work for old media such as newspapers and magazines online and in print, though more are crossing over to new media publications and blogging.

Restaurant criticism is a relatively new field that was largely invented in the 1950s by Craig Claiborne, the food and restaurant critic for the *New York Times* for almost thirty years. Claiborne developed a code of ethics that is still followed by many professionals today. It specified that:

- The review would be written and signed by one individual.
- The restaurant would be visited a minimum of three times and a small group would go so that many of the dishes on the menu could be sampled.
- Some dishes would be eaten more than once to check for consistency.
- The publication would pay for the meals and the reviewer would never accept free food or other gifts.
- The reviewer would visit the restaurant anonymously and not give any indication that the restaurant was being reviewed. [46]

Professionals who become famous struggle to remain anonymous. Some reviewers, such as Robert Sietsema, go to great lengths to stay undercover in the age of Google and Facebook, while others have given up after being "outed." Ruth Reichl described the disappointment of being "outed" after her fourth visit to one restaurant:

> *When I was discovered, the change was startling. Everything improved: the seating, the service, the size of the portions. We had already reached dessert, but our little plate of petit fours was whisked away to be replaced by a larger, more ostentatious one.* [47]

Professional critics write *criticism* rather than *reviews*. A review is brief and to the point: here is where I went, here is what I ate, and it was good or not so good. Yelpers and many amateur bloggers write reviews. Unfortunately our language does not help make a distinction between criticism and reviews, because much of what we would define as formal criticism is referred to by using the word "review."

There are also food bloggers who write marketing pieces that resemble reviews, but they are written in exchange for free food and lack objectivity. The Boston Brunchers are a group of young adults who attend free food events at restaurants and agree to honestly "review" the restaurant. Their reviews are overwhelmingly positive:

> *On June 2nd, the Vine Brook Tavern was awesome enough to host a group of food-loving, blog-writing ladies from the area: the Boston Brunchers. And guess what? I was one of those ladies! Refreshing cocktails, delicious food, and a serenade by one of the waitstaff made for a really amazing experience. I apologize in advance for the cell phone photos—I was clearly underprepared, but I think they get the point across!* [48]

Food industry specialist Joyce Goldstein has said that unlike simple reviews, criticism "implies having a scale of knowledge and having a range of
things that serve as a basis for comparison. It involves a certain level of
intelligence, a frame of reference, a big picture, and some depth behind the
words."[49] Andrew Keen, in his book *The Cult of the Amateur*, bemoans the
onslaught of amateur commentators who are "delivering . . . superficial observations of the world around us rather than deep analysis, shrill opinion
rather than considered judgment."

Writing about books, the critic Richard Schickel complained of the decline of professional reviews and the rise of amateur review bloggers. While
many celebrate blogging as a democratic response to the stranglehold that a
few elite reviewers have maintained over movies, books, restaurants, and
theater, Schikel feels there is a place for a few dependable voices that maintain ethical standards. He states that:

> *criticism and its humble cousin, reviewing—is not a democratic activity. It is,*
> *or should be, an elite enterprise, ideally undertaken by individuals who bring*
> *something to the party beyond their hasty, instinctive opinions of a book (or*
> *any other cultural object). It is work that requires disciplined taste, historical*
> *and theoretical knowledge and a fairly deep sense of the author's (or filmmak-*
> *er's or painter's) entire body of work, among other qualities.*[50]

The difference between the Boston Bruncher who wrote about her "awe-
some" experience while providing photos in lieu of description is strikingly
different from the writings of a professional food writer who conveys a much
deeper portrait of a restaurant by bringing in finer points about the food, the
setting, the clientele, the chef, and other cultural details about the experience.

Restaurant critics have maintained Claiborne's ethical standards while
deepening the field and branching out beyond their coverage of high-end
restaurants. The famous critic Ruth Reichl brought in techniques used in
literary and theater criticism, and the equally famous Gael Greene provided
an informal writing style as well as detailed descriptions of the food and
context.[51] Robert Sietsema, writing for many years for the *Village Voice* in
New York, went foraging outside of the mainstream restaurant world to
investigate hundreds of small ethnic restaurants in the outer boroughs with
the aim of better representing the typical restaurant diner on a tight budget.

Many feel that Claiborne lifted the restaurant review out of the territory of
marketing and made it into a public service, a profession defined by ethics
and expert knowledge. I can see the appeal of relying on a professional such
as Michael Bauer at the Chronicle. I search:

Google: *Michael Bauer San Francisco Chronicle Biography*

Bauer is the executive food and wine editor and restaurant critic and is in charge of the largest food and wine staff of any newspaper in the United States. Bauer's review is lukewarm on Sotto Mare, despite Yelp's claim that it is the best Italian restaurant in San Francisco. He uses words like "cramped," "cluttered," "no dessert," and "uneven pastas." Bauer states that he will not review a restaurant if it is not good, so it is confusing that Sotto Mare received a good rating but then received a negative review. Bauer's critics say he gives 80 percent of the restaurants he reviews a high rating of 2 or 2.5 stars on his personal rating scale (Sotto Mare got a 2), so his rating system may be no more useful than Yelp's.

Like any profession, critics can be uneven in their talent. For cities that have held on to their professional reviewers, there may be only a handful to choose from, and of course for smaller cities there may be only one or two. If you find a professional who matches your sensibilities then you are set. Your search is over. However, for me, Bauer seems a little stuffy and traditional. I do not find his reviews useful and feel reluctant to use him as my only source. My search continues.

BOOTS ON THE GROUND

In the 1960s the founders of the *Village Voice* decided to start an alternative newspaper in New York to "demolish the notion that one needs to be a professional to accomplish something in a field as purportedly technical as journalism." Early rock critics that wrote for the *Voice* felt that to write about a cultural movement it was essential to be a part of it. This flew in the face of the traditional journalists of the day who failed to recognize pop culture as being worthy of news coverage.

While the journalists at the *Voice* were often not professionally trained, they did have extensive experience with popular music, film, and art, and they had boots on the ground—they were heavily involved in the youth countercultural uprising and the music that accompanied it. The writers of the *Voice* helped invent a new form of journalism where the boundaries defining what was acceptable writing for publication shifted. Writing became more informal, and writing in the first person using the common vernacular and even using epithets became acceptable in print publications.

Devon Powers, the author of the book *Writing the Record: The Village Voice and the Birth of Rock Criticism*, writes that the anti-professional ethic of the time was not the same as the widely held notion today that everyone can be a critic. The writers who contributed to the *Voice* may not have had formal training, but many had expertise in music, recognized their potential power, and carefully devised an objective structure that would separate them from turning in to advertising machines.[52]

Amateur bloggers are revolutionizing the way reviews are done for restaurants, art, music, and books. They are disrupting the industry and influencing the work of professional critics. Time will tell whether this disruption has been positive. Currently in the restaurant review business the number of paid professional critics is in decline while 20,000 amateur food and restaurant bloggers have flooded the market. These bloggers range from barely comprehensible to incredibly articulate, and their ethics are all over the map.

Restaurant and food bloggers have diverse motives that drive their writing. One pioneer food blogger, Julie Powell, kept a blog of her experiences taking 365 days to try every recipe in Julia Child's *The Art of French Cooking*. The Julie/Julia blog became a best-selling book and a hit Hollywood movie with Powell being played by the actress Amy Adams. Not every food or restaurant blogger is looking for a Julie/Julia moment, but many are. Other bloggers have appeared on the scene after leaving, or being forced out of, their traditional media perches and are joining the exciting ranks of the new food writers. There are also other types of casual bloggers that simply want to share advice and create grastronomic memories for themselves. Restaurant blogging for this last group is simply a hobby—an outlet for creative expression. They do not view themselves as journalists or professionals.[53]

WILL WORK FOR FOOD

One casualty of the new blogging climate is that ethical considerations are falling by the wayside. The new bloggers have shredded the old-school rules: many do not remain anonymous, some accept free food or avoid standing in line, and most do not wait for a restaurant to settle in before popping in to review them. The restaurant industry has adapted quickly by hosting review parties and is finding great marketing synergy in wining and dining the more popular amateur bloggers in exchange for positive "reviews."

Some bloggers adhere to newly devised ethics codes that are a much looser version of the Association of Food Journalists Food Critics Guidelines. Most newbies feel it is fine to accept free food, as long as the blogger acknowledges the gift. The Federal Trade Commission agrees, calling on bloggers to follow journalistic standards of integrity and transparency and to disclose gifts or face fines. The problem is that some bloggers identify not as journalists, but simply as diarists recounting their personal experiences.

And then there are some bloggers who throw all ethical considerations to the wind. Philadelphia blogger Sarah Lockard emailed area restaurants offering them an opportunity to host her family dinner on Christmas Eve in exchange for coverage on her website, Facebook posts, and Instagram photos. She ended her email to the restaurant owners with: "Be THE top restaurant we recommend this Christmas Eve to our HUGE audience!!!!"[54]

Bloggers are not alone in failing to adhere to journalistic standards of independence, verification, and accountability. Professional journalist Josh Ozersky wrote a glowing review for *TIME* magazine about the food that top New York chefs provided at his wedding reception.[55] Unfortunately he failed to declare that all the food was provided for free. As the critic Robert Sietsema pointed out in an open letter to Orzesky, the problem was not that Ozersky wrote the piece, but that he failed to disclose that the food he reviewed had been provided for free. In 1974 Pauline Kael said, speaking about film though the same could be applied to restaurants: "Criticism is all that stands between the public and advertising."[56]

Some observers see a battle being waged between innovative but sometimes naive bloggers versus expert, but sometimes stodgy, professionals.[57] But as the dust settles we may be able to have our cake and eat it too. There seems to be more of a blurring of the lines between the professional and the amateur, rather than a showdown.[58] Amateur bloggers are pushing more traditional critics to get back on their game, or to devise a new game, while some professionals are crossing over to write for more innovative sites. Meanwhile, some successful amateur bloggers are getting their Julie/Julia moment and becoming the newly anointed voices of professional criticism.

FINDING YOUR SOUL MATE

It dawns on me that finding a great restaurant critic is like finding your soul mate: impossible, but something to shoot for. The search is *on* for someone with strong ethical standards, but also for someone who matches my sensibilities when it comes to eating out.

There are two choices at this point: either I need to look at the other local news sources in San Francisco and see if I like their reviewers better than Bauer, or I need to do what is called *primary research*. If I was in a smaller city and did not like the restaurant critic I would be heading straight to primary research, but because San Francisco is large, there are more than a dozen other vetted restaurant reviewers and I quickly find a few that I like by searching:

Google: *San Francisco Restaurant Reviews*

Here is the trick: I have to breeze past all the Yelps, TripAdvisors, and Google reviews that come up first in my search results. It is worth the extra few minutes and I find Anna Roth, who writes for *SF Weekly*. She is creative and interesting and reviews everything from noodle shops to fancy multi-course haute cuisine. I could easily settle on one of her reviews. There are several other choices, including a *New York Times* article by Pete Wells, a talented critic who has covered San Francisco for his column "Critic on the Road."

So why not stop now? Curiosity. I know this is insane but I cannot stop. Are there exciting amateur bloggers out there that I have missed? My husband thinks I am possessed. He is more than willing to go with Anna Roth or Pete Wells. I embark on primary research by formally interviewing by phone a bunch of food writers in the San Francisco area to find out their favorite reviewers, amateur or professional. I also verify their choices with lists of writers who have won awards such as the James Beard Foundation Awards and the Association of Food Journalists Awards. Facebook and Twitter, for people heavily connected to social media, are good places to do quick primary research as well.

From my research I come up with a list of ten, all of whom fall under the category of professional, but many no longer work for traditional news outlets. I plug in each of their names combined with Sotto Mare and receive useful results. *None have bothered to review Sotto Mare!* This is telling. The choice of whether or not to review a restaurant often speaks as loudly as the review itself. By not reviewing Sotto Mare the critics have "spoken." This serves to corroborate my findings with Bauer's negative review and further reinforce my disappointment in the Yelp rating of top Italian restaurant in the city.

After skimming the ten choices, I settle on Jonathan Kauffman, who has written for several San Francisco publications in the past decade. In the review below, Kauffman approaches noodles the way I approach research—with passion and thoroughness. Here is a sample from his piece called "The Great Noodle Quest" from *San Francisco Magazine*:

> *Given this overwhelming abundance of noodles to choose from—both high and low—how did the 21 finalists emerge? The hunt started with spelunking trips into memories of past meals, from a rabokki expedition in Seoul to a search for knife-cut noodles in Shanxi train stations—not to mention notes from my 12 years of working as a restaurant critic. I spent hours sifting through local food blogs and Chowhound posts—tipping the hat, of course, to Melanie Wong [an amateur noodle expert] and Yimster, two of my stalwart guides. I also milked information from food writers, friends, and my dentist's assistants, who are always sending me off with the names of Filipino restaurants to try. Even Yelp was an amazing source of leads—once I learned to scan for phrases like "Even my mother approved" or "All you haters are ordering completely wrong." . . . All this research was followed, of course, by weeks of eating.*

In Kaufman can be seen all that is good in the new world of food criticism. Everyone from Yelpers to food bloggers keep the professional critic on his toes. What was once a solo voice shouting at the masses has become more of a dialogue between a professional and his fellow eaters. We have entered a world in which an expert does not have to be just a lone wolf dictating his or her tastes onto the community. There is the benefit of expertise combined with a feedback loop bubbling up from the crowd. This is similar to research on art criticism, which has shown that expertise is still thriving in the art world because it instills trust based on experience, training, and institutional linkages. The traditional experts have not been replaced by the crowd, but "new voices have been added to the chorus," that help to inform professional criticism.[59] The challenge for new restaurant reviewers will be to find a good revenue model and high placement in search engine results.

So, Sotto Mare is out, and I have fallen in love with my new soul mate: Johnathan Kaufman. He and his colleague, John Birdsall, have just written "The Masters of Masa," for *San Francisco Magazine* after spending two months(!) researching the Mexican restaurant scene in San Francisco.[60] They recommend the twenty-two best Mexican restaurants and describe them. I will sit back, relax, and read this online tome and choose the one that seems best for an anniversary dinner. Mission accomplished.

BACK TO OSCAR'S ...

So by now perhaps you have forgotten all about Oscars and the positive reviews that were posted at the beginning of this chapter. Despite my warning that most people possess a 50-50 chance of spotting a fake review, you may be a competitive person and have popped back to the first page of this chapter and are ready to cast your votes.

Well, my apologies, because it was a bit of a trick question. Not only are all the reviews fake, but Oscar's is fake as well. There is no restaurant called Oscar's! This did not prevent dozens of people who read these reviews on TripAdvisor from showing up looking for Oscar's in Brixham, England. When readers went to the address listed on the review site all they found was an alleyway full of trash cans next to the quay. The TripAdvisor posting and reviews were made up by a disgruntled businessman who was unhappy because a close friend's hotel had received a lot of negative postings on TripAdvisor. He suspected the reviews were from a rival hotel. With more than sixty pieces of content created every minute on TripAdvisor, it is not a shock that Oscar's remained on the site for much too long. It has now been removed.[61]

TIME SINK OPTIONAL

Finding a restaurant review does not have to be a time sink, unless you want it to be. Information-obsessed people like me feel rewarded by going the extra mile and digging deep. Comprehensive research works the same way whether it is scholarly or just for everyday-life information: the more you pick away at it the more you start seeing the same names, the same sites, the same articles and you know you have come full circle. In San Francisco the same dozen sites and same dozen food journalists' and bloggers' names come up again and again. In academia this research process is called the systematic or comprehensive literature review, but it works just as well for finding good restaurant reviewers.

The lesson to be learned in finding restaurant reviews is that the crowd-sourced sites are not reliable enough yet, and it is too easy to get swayed when you start seeing 5-star reviews even though the five stars are pretty meaningless. Locating a reliable amateur blogger is difficult. In her book *Food and Social Media: Tweet What You Eat*, Signe Rosseau laments that maybe amid the thousands of restaurant bloggers the best we can hope for is something that will help us evaluate who is worth listening to when we are trying to choose a restaurant.[62] If only! So far this has not happened. For now it makes sense to focus on an online publication such as a local newspaper or online magazine that has built up a reputation over time of providing a home for high quality ethical reviewers, whether they are columnists or bloggers. In other words, to start at the source.

NOTES

1. J. Hancock, M. Ott, Y. Choi, and C. Cardie, "Finding Deceptive Opinion Spam by Any Stretch of the Imagination," in proceedings of the 49th Annual Meeting of the Association for Computational Linguistics, 2011, http://aclweb.org/anthology//P/P11/P11-1032.pdf.

2. Ibid.

3. Arjun Mukherjee, Bing Liu, and Natalie Glance, "Spotting Fake Reviewer Groups in Consumer Reviewers," in proceedings of the 21st International World Wide Web Conference, Lyon, France, April 16–20, 2012. http://www.cs.uic.edu/~liub/piblications/WWW-2012-group-spam-camera-final.pdf

4. Some cities, such as San Francisco, have made health code scores available via Yelp.

5. Charlotte Drukman, "San Francisco: Culinary Capital," *Wall Street Journal,* December 5, 2013, http://online.wsj.com/articles/SB10001424052702303610504577418871114965262.

6. Molly Aronica, "More People Read User Reviews Than Restaurant Critics," *Daily Meal,* August 23, 2011, http://www.thedailymeal.com/where-do-you-get-your-restaurant-recommendations.

7. Robert Sietsema, "Everyone Eats . . . But That Doesn't Make You a Restaurant Critic," *Columbia Journalism Review* 48, no. 5 (February 2, 2010), http://www.cjr.org/feature/everyone_eats.php?page=all.

8. Bill Daley, "The Man, Not the Cake Mix," *Chicago Tribune,* March 20, 2013, http://articles.chicagotribune.com/2013-03-20/features/sc-food-0315-giants-hines-20130320_1_cake-mix-restaurant-food-poisoning-guidebook.

9. Duncan Hines, *Adventures in Good Eating* (Bowling Green, KY: Adventures in Good Eating, 1946).

10. See http://www.zagat.com/about-us.

11. "Ten Things You Should Know About Yelp," www.yelp.com/About.

12. Michael Anderson and Jeremy Magruder, "Learning from the Crowd: Regression Discontinuity Estimates of the Effects of an Online Review Database," *Economic Journal* (September 2012), doi: 10.1111/j.1468-0297.2012.02512.x.

13. Michael Luca, "Reviews, Reputation, and Revenue: The Case of Yelp.com," Harvard Business School Working Paper 12-016, http://www.hbs.edu/faculty/Publication%20Files/12-016_0464f20e-35b2-492e-a328-fb14a325f718.pdf.

14. Ike DeLorenzo, "Everyone's a Critic," *Boston Globe,* June 2, 2010.

15. A.J. Flanagin, M.J. Metzger, R. Pure, and A. Markov, "User-Generated Ratings and the Evaluation of Credibility and Product Quality in Ecommerce Transactions," in proceedings of the 44th Hawaii International Conference on System Sciences, 2011.

16. "F@#$ You Yelpers," http://fuckyouyelper.tumblr.com.

17. See: http://www.yelp.com/user_details_review_search?userid=p4UcEYTLJyh96o1 R8wrJaQ&q=roscoe%27s

18. Hannah C., "Yelp Data Reveals Top 100 Places to Eat: Bookmark These Babies Now!" Yelp Official Blog, February 26, 2014, http://officialblog.yelp.com/2014/02/yelp-data-reveals-top-100-places-to-eat-bookmark-these-babies-now.html.

19. Daniel Slotnik, "Users Help a Weather Site Hone Its Forecasts," *New York Times,* March 20, 2011, http://www.nytimes.com/2011/03/21/technology/21weather.html.

20. James Surowiecki, *The Wisdom of Crowds* (New York: Anchor, 2005).

21. Anish Parikh, "User Generated Restaurant Reviews: Examining Influence and Motivations for Usage," Ph.D. diss., Purdue University, 2013.

22. Flanagin et al., "User-Generated Ratings."

23. Luca, "Reviews, Reputation, and Revenue."

24. Dalvi Nilesh, Kumar Ravi, and Bo Pang, "Para 'Normal' Activity: On the Distribution of Average Ratings," in proceedings of the Seventh International AAAI Conference on Weblogs and Social Media, July 8–11, 2013, https://www.aaai.org/ocs/index.php/ICWSM/ICWSM13/paper/view/6117.

25. Carolyn Y. Johnson, "Study Finds That Herd Mentality Can Overinflate Online Ratings," *Boston Globe,* August 9, 2013.

26. Luca, "Reviews, Reputation, and Revenue."

27. Matthew B. Welsh, "Expertise and the Wisdom of Crowds: Whose Judgments to Trust and When," in Building Bridges Across Cognitive Sciences Around the World: Proceedings of the 34th Annual Meeting of the Cognitive Science Society, Sapporo, Japan, August 1–4, 2012, ed. N. Miyake, D. Peeble, R. P. Cooper, http://digital.library.adelaide.edu.au/dspace/bitstream/2440/74412/1/hdl_74412.pdf.

28. Adrienne Jeffries, "Facebook's Fake-Name Fight Grows as Users Skirt the Rules," The Verge, September 17, 2012, http://www.theverge.com/2012/9/17/3322436/facebook-fake-name-pseudonym-middle-name.

29. Cheng Chen, Kui Wu, Venkatesh Srinivasan, and Xudong Zhang, "Battling the Internet Water Army: Detection of Hidden Paid Posters," ArXiv.org, November 18, 2011, http://arxiv.org/pdf/1111.4297v1.pdf.

30. Gang Wang, Christo Wilson, Xiaohan Zhao, Yibo Zhu, Manish Mohanlal, Haitao Zheng, and Ben Y. Zhao, "Serf and Turf: Crowdturfing for Fun and Profit," in WWW Conference Proceedings, 2012, doi: 10.1145/2187836.2187928.

31. M. Motoyama, D. Mccoy, K. Levchenko, S. Savage, and G.M. Voelker, "Dirty Jobs: The Role of Freelance Labor in Web Service Abuse," August 8, 2011, https://www.usenix.org/legacy/event/sec11/tech/full_papers/Motoyama.pdf.

32. Jaron Lanier, *Who Owns the Future?* (New York: Simon and Schuster, 2013).

33. Mukherjee et al., "Spotting Fake Reviewer Groups in Consumer Reviewers"; Luca, "Reviews, Reputation, and Revenue"; "The Consequences of Fake Fans, 'Likes' and Reviews on Social Networks," *Gartner Report,* 2012, http://www.gartner.com/newsroom/id/2161315.

34. Michael Learmonth, "As Fake Reviews Rise, Yelp, Others Crack Down on Fraudsters," AdAge, October 30, 2012, http://adage.com/article/digital/fake-reviews-rise-yelp-crack-fraudsters/237486/.

35. Michael Luca and Georgios Zervas, "Fake It Till You Make It: Reputation, Competition, and Yelp Review Fraud," Harvard Business School NOM Unit Working Paper No. 14-006, http://papers.ssrn.com/sol3/papers.cfm?abstract_id=2293164.

36. Marnie Hunter, "TripAdvisor Scolded by UK Ad Regulator for 'Trust' Claims," CNN Travel, February 1, 2012, http://www.cnn.com/2012/02/01/travel/tripadvisor-advertising-uk/.

37. David Ferrell, "Elite Yelp Reviewers Live Like Stars," *Orange County Register,* November 8, 2013, http://www.ocregister.com/articles/lifestyle-535271-writing-live.html.

38. Lisa Chow, "Top Reviewers on Amazon Get Tons of Free Stuff," NPR Planet Money Blog, October 29, 2013, http://www.npr.org/blogs/money/2013/10/29/241372607/top-reviewers-on-amazon-get-tons-of-free-stuff.

39. D.L. Schacter, J.L. Harbluk, and D.R. McLachlen, "Retrieval Without Recollection: An Experimental Analysis of Source Amnesia," *Journal of Verbal Learning and Verbal Behaviour* 23, no. 5 (1984).

40. Hailey Dixon, "Mother Dies After Eating Poisonous Mushrooms from Garden," *Telegraph,* May 9, 2013, http://www.telegraph.co.uk/health/healthnews/10046676/Mother-dies-after-eating-poisonous-mushrooms-from-her-garden.html.

41. Michael Beug, "Toxicology: Reflections on Mushroom Poisoning in North America," *Fungi Magazine* 1, no. 2 (2008). http://www.fungimag.com/summer-08-articles/12_Beug_Final.pdf.

42. Carl Bereiter and Marlene Scardamalia, *Surpassing Ourselves: Expert Knowledge and How It Comes About* (Chicago: Open Court Publishing, 1993).

43. Carl Bereiter, *Education and Mind in the Knowledge Age* (Hillsdale, NJ: Lawrence Erlbaum, 2002).

44. Ibid.

45. Ibid.

46. Rien Fertel, "Past and Repast: Craig Claiborne," Oxford American, October 12, 2012. http://www.oxfordamerican.org/articles/2012/oct/12/past-repast-craig-claiborne/.

47. Robert Sietsema, "Everyone Eats . . . But That Doesn't Make You a Restaurant Critic," *Columbia Journalism Review* 48, no. 5, February 2, 2010, http://www.cjr.org/feature/everyone_eats.php?page=all.

48. Mary Mallard, "The Vine Brook Tavern with Boston Brunchers," Where Is My Sandwich Blog, June 11, 2013, http://whereismysandwich.me/2013/06/11/the-vine-brook-tavern-with-boston-brunchers/.

49. Andrew Dornenburg and Karen Page, *Dining Out: Secrets from America's Leading Critics, Chefs, and Restaurateurs* (New York: John Wiley and Sons, 1998).

50. Richard Schickel, "Not Everybody's a Critic," *Los Angeles Times,* May 20, 2007, http://articles.latimes.com/2007/may/20/opinion/op-schickel20.

51. Sietsema, "Everyone Eats."

52. Devon Powers, *Writing the Record: The Village Voice and the Birth of Rock Criticism* (Amherst: University of Massachusetts Press, 2013).

53. Isabelle De Solier, "Why Foodies Are the New Food Critics," *InDaily, Adelaide Independent News*, December 2, 2013, http://indaily.com.au/food-and-wine/2013/12/02/why-foodies-are-the-new-food-critics/.

54. Raphael Brion, "Philly Blog Publisher Asks Restaurants for a Free Dinner," EATER.com Blog, December 11, 2013, http://eater.com/archives/2013/12/11/sarah-lockard-email-philadelphia-blogger-restaurants-dinner.php.

55. Robert Sietsema, "An Open Letter to Josh Ozersky," *Village Voice,* June 23, 2010, http://blogs.villagevoice.com/forkintheroad/2010/06/an_open_letter.php.

56. Armond White, "Do Movie Critics Matter?" First Things, April 2010, http://www.firstthings.com/article/2010/04/do-movie-critics-matter.

57. Singe Rosseau, *Food and Social Media: Tweet What You Eat* (Lanham, MD: Rowman & Littlefield, 2012). See also De Solier, "Why Foodies Are the New Food Critics."

58. Joseph Turow, "The Experts vs. the Amateurs: A Tug of War Over the Future of Media," Knowledge@Wharton, March 19, 2008, http://knowledge.wharton.upenn.edu/article/the-experts-vs-the-amateurs-a-tug-of-war-over-the-future-of-media/.

59. P. Arora and F. Vermeylen, "The End of the Art Connoisseur? Experts and Knowledge Production in the Visual Arts in the Digital Age," *Information Communication and Society* (2012), doi:10.1080/1369118X.2012.687392.

60. John Birdsall and Jonathan Koufmann, "Our Big, Hot (Sometimes Fancy, Sometimes Not) Mexican Moment," *San Francisco Magazine*, January 24, 2014, http://

www.modernluxury.com/san-francisco/story/our-big-hot-sometimes-fancy-sometimes-not-mexican-moment.

61. Hugh Merwin, "Oscar's Restaurant," Grub Street, July 2013, http://www.grubstreet.com/2013/07/oscars-brixham-trip-advisor.html.

62. Rosseau, *Food and Social Media.*

Chapter Three

The Wisdom of a Crowd of Experts

Finding Reliable Scholarly Research

No truths—not even mathematical truths—can be considered secure for all time. But over time and with the openness afforded by the Internet, we have a greater likelihood of establishing truths than during any previous era of human history.

—Howard Gardner, *Truth, Beauty, and Goodness Reframed* (2012)

Ray Tomlinson, a sixty-two-year-old from Warren, Michigan, just wanted to get home quickly: driving from Arizona to Michigan was a long trip. When his girlfriend sitting in the passenger seat turned out to be not sleeping but dead from a drug overdose, he knew what to do. Whipping out his smart phone he searched for the laws in Arizona on how soon you were required to contact the police if someone dies. Warren police Sergeant Stephen Mills, who later arrested Ray, related:

> "He then does an Internet search via his phone . . . He says he finds on the Internet that he has 48 hours to take her to a medical examiner."[1]

The police Sergeant then explains that the information on the Internet was incorrect.

What did Ray do wrong? Where do I begin . . .

By starting and ending with a Google search and not thinking through his search strategy, Ray probably violated all six of the following strategies for finding reliable information online.

1. Start at the Source

Ray likely popped into one of the first items that came up in his Google or Siri search rather than "starting at the source." He should have at least gone to an official law website and started his search there. He could have started with a Google search if he was thinking about searching for a *source* rather than a piece of information:

> Google: *Arizona Statutes "report a death"* [2]

He also could have relied on librarians who have created guides, called "LibGuides," for every topic imaginable. These guides link to free and proprietary resources online. If you have access to a library these guides link directly to library-owned sources, but they also point the way to the best free resources, such as Findlaw, a great source for finding legal information.

> Google: *Libguides Free Legal Resources Web*

Legal searches are tricky. They are a unique kind of scholarly research. Often the best way to find official laws or regulations is to take a back-door approach. The search above will lead you to some unofficial legal sites that provide easy access and will identify the law by name and number. That gives you the information you need to then locate the official law. Once you have the statute number, in this case Title 36:344, you can go straight to the Arizona statutes.

> Google: *Arizona Statutes*

Then simply look up the Title number to make sure that this law is still accurate, up to date, and in force—that it is still "good law."

2. Pay Attention to the "Psychology of Search"

Ray was suffering from a strong case of *motivated cognition*. He really wanted to drive quickly from Arizona to Michigan and not be bogged down with reporting the death of his girlfriend. He searched and found what he wanted to find. That did not make it true. In addition, *confirmation bias*— giving greater credence to information that agrees with Ray's personal perceptions—and *false certainty*—not even recognizing the possibility of uncertainty—were also at play here. This is human nature, many of us automatically start searching online for what we *want* to be true.

3. Expert, Amateur, Crowd?

In the case of law the searcher needs to consult official documents or an expert. It is not a good idea to rely on WikiHow or About.com for legal advice.

4. Context, Motivation, and Bias

If you are on an official legal website—such as the Arizona Revised Statutes that are on a .gov site—then you are all set. Ray was not on an official site.

5. Comparison and Corroboration

Ray only looked at one site, an unofficial site. For a legal question, if you are verifying that something is not a potential felony, you may want to consult a few sources or even call a lawyer. In Ray's case he was committing a misdemeanor and the police went pretty easy on him, though he did get into the national news. Perhaps that was punishment enough for poor judgment *and* poor search skills.

6. Go Deep, or Not

Relying on the first page of search results in a Google Search is the opposite of going deep. For a legal question like Ray's, expect to spend more than two minutes wading through the law. A surprising number of people believe that coming up in the first five search results in Google is a sign that a piece of information is trustworthy. [3]

Often when we search for something online we think we are shooting for a "yes" or "no" or one-sentence answer:

Who won the World Cup in 2014?

But many questions do not have simple answers, even when it seems like they should:

Does bologna contain lard?

Research questions are frequently more nuanced and complex. In the social sciences, such as psychology or anthropology, there is typically no right answer, but some answers are better than others and represent current knowledge in the field. In his book *Thinking, Fast and Slow*, Daniel Kahneman writes about our tendency toward fast thinking and experiencing false certainty. [4] We default to fast thinking and draw instant conclusions based on whatever information comes up first in a search. Instead, we should dig a little deeper, check out the source of the information, and understand that the answer might be more nuanced. Some bologna may contain lard and some may not.

GOING DEEP

When a new client approached me about helping her with a research question she had already gone way past our Arizona driver Ray in doing her home-work, but she had turned up conflicting results and was confused about how to proceed. Maya is the CEO of a tech start-up that is about to design a new office space. They just received an infusion of venture capital and are plan-ning the usual type of start-up space: an open-plan shared workspace with primary colors, connected couches, shared desks, ping pong tables, and Ra-zor scooters. Many start-ups mimic the open-plan office layout found at successful workplaces such as Google. Maya read in the business section of the *New York Times* an article by an experienced journalist:

> *They've [Google] looked at the data to see how people are collaborating. Physical space is the biggest lever to encourage collaboration. And the data are clear that the biggest driver of performance in complex industries like software is serendipitous interaction.*[5]

But Maya has also just read the following opinion piece in the *New York Times* written by a respected author:

> *Studies show that open-plan offices make workers hostile, insecure and dis-tracted. They're also more likely to suffer from high blood pressure, stress, the flu and exhaustion. And people whose work is interrupted make 50 percent more mistakes and take twice as long to finish it.*[6]

Journalists are famous for using phrases like "studies show," but unfortu-nately, many newspapers do not provide citations to these "studies" that "show." Maya asks me to do a comprehensive literature review. She wants a summary of all the research to date on this topic so that she can make an informed decision. In essence, she wants me to go deep, but also go fast.

Go Deep is my middle name.

GO DEEP, BUT FIRST POKE AROUND

Spenser, the fictional detective in Robert Parker's novels, typically starts his search for the bad guys by doing a little poking around. Like doing research, Spenser wants to get a sense of where things currently sit:

Hell, I don't know [what I'm doing]*, Mr. Esteva. I don't know what's going on so I wander around and ask questions and annoy people and finally somebody says something or does something then I wander around and ask questions about that and annoy people and so on. Better than sitting up in a tree with a spyglass.*[7]

A comprehensive literature review involves methodically finding any relevant research that has been done on a topic, but there are also elements of serendipity. It helps to start by poking around to see what is out there, to come up with a list of keywords to search for, to carefully define and refine the topic, and to see who the expert players are that are working in a particular area and find out the current buzz.

You cannot do a comprehensive literature review on any topic. If a client came to me and asked me to do a comprehensive review of the research on ADHD I would say: "Give me a ten-year contract or forget it!" Really, what I would say is:

"What about ADHD? ADHD and medication? ADHD and young children?"

Interestingly, you can discover the most common searches that people do for ADHD by typing ADHD into Google. Google has an "autocomplete" feature called "Google Suggestions" that lists a handful of the most common searches that have been done recently related to ADHD. If you search:

Google: *ADHD*
The suggestions are:
ADHD test
ADHD in adults
ADHD medications

Bing and Yahoo have a similar mechanism for calling up frequently searched terms. The practice can be surprisingly powerful and controversial. A skydiving company was upset when searchers entered their company name in Google and the first suggested autocomplete word was accident. There had been a recent accident at the company, but they did not want to have that be immediately associated with their name in a Google search. Some companies hire *mechanical Turks* to do thousands of searches on a company name combined with positive words in order to push down negative words that come up next to their company name in autocomplete.[8]

What is great about Google autocomplete is that it will reflect recent searching trends, it is not just a sum total of searches. If President Obama were to suddenly confess he has ADHD, that item would likely come up in autocomplete when searching ADHD. In short, autocomplete can suggest the most recent popular ways people have tried to break down a topic, and this can be helpful in pointing to the recent thinking about a topic.

I riff on a number of different keywords for the concept of open offices and find that "open-plan office" seems to be the most common term. Then I search simply:

> Google: *open-plan office*

If I type a space after office, I get suggestions like "vs. cubicle" or "office etiquette." If I add a space before my search I get "advantages of" and "working in."

Though not always useful, autocomplete can sometimes provide a quick pointer to what key issues relate to a topic. For example:

> Google: Dalmatians SPACE
> Retrieves:
> 101 Dalmatians
> 102 Dalmatians
> Are Dalmatians mean?
> Are Dalmatians deaf?

Interestingly, Dalmatians are more likely to be deaf than any other dog breed, and they can also be overly aggressive, and sometimes this is related to hearing issues.

Starting a literature search on anything is a process of finding out how big that something is. What is included? What is left out? I search:

> Google: *open-plan office* (490,000 results)
> Google: *"open-plan office" design* (206,000 results)

Using quotes to get the exact phrase and adding another keyword limits and focuses my results. Many of the articles that come up first are free articles that are plugging a particular furniture company. Several of the top items retrieved are articles in *Forbes* and *Businessweek* that are interviews with office design companies pushing their products while discussing "the research." But no one actually cites a scientific research article. While I used to think of *Forbes* as a reliable business magazine, I was surprised at the quality and amount of content I was seeing. By generating oodles of fresh content *Forbes* was guaranteeing a top landing place in search results, and by having content that was connected directly to advertising—native advertising— Forbes was ensuring a high revenue stream. In 2013 Joe McCambley, an advertising expert, interviewed by David Carr, the former media critic for the *New York Times,* said:

What I love about Forbes *is that they have the guts to take risks, to experiment, but I think some of it is dangerous. When you go to Forbes, you expect sound business advice and news, information that has been fact-checked and vetted. But what you get instead is a mix of staff content, contributor content and sponsored content. It's hard to know where you are.* [9]

I decide to better define my question to avoid the sponsored content and get at something deeper. What my client is really interested in is office design in relation to productivity. I add this filter to my search:

Google: *"open-plan office" productivity* (38,000 results).

It may seem silly to gauge hit counts because for now I am only going to view the first few pages of results, but adding in specific words such as productivity to narrow my results can limit the type of information I retrieve. I can also use words like "research" or "study" and so on. I again breeze past the puff pieces and notice a *Scientific American* article listed in my results. Though it is not research per se, *Scientific American* is better at citing sources and presenting unbiased journalism than some of the lighter business oriented publications that are more focused on selling advertising.

The *Scientific American* article gives me a nice introduction to the history of open-plan offices. I also pick up a few articles from the *New York Times* and the *New Yorker*. Both publications are famous for fact checking their stories, especially the *New Yorker*. They are the gold standard of fact checking, spending weeks and in some cases months corroborating every fact mentioned in a story. [10]

I pull together enough background information to get the big picture: designers and architects invented open-plan offices to improve office life. These designers felt that by bringing down walls and bringing people together office life would become more democratic and less hierarchical. Modern architects such as Frank Lloyd Wright designed spacious and flexible open plans that would "liberate" office workers, but employers often saw open offices as an opportunity to save space and money. They plunked office workers into rows of desks squished together. These are sometimes called "bullpens" and they predate cubicles and open-plan offices. In the 1950s a German design group suggested breaking up the uniform rows of desks in a bullpen into smaller groupings based on work assignments.

In 1964, following in the footsteps of the German designers, Bob Probst, an artist and sculptor, joined forces with the furniture company Herman Miller to create the "action office." [11] Their goal was to provide more flexibility for the worker: desks at standing and sitting height, larger surfaces, and modular components that could be re-configured when needed. Unfortunately, many employers again saw cost savings and control advantages and selected the parts of the modular plan that would allow them to squeeze as many workers as possible into the same space. Probst was horrified by what had been done with his idea of modular flexible space. The bullpen later morphed into the cubicle by inserting dividers when people had trouble working due to distractions, noise, and lack of privacy.

Today 68 percent of all offices have an open floor plan, with or without partitions, and the number is increasing.[12] At the same time, people seem to fall into two camps on whether the open-plan office increases or decreases productivity:

> *This open style of work, insists Mr. Rouady, an employee of Netscape Communications, is best done in an open setting—where workers are separated only by low partitions instead of being walled off behind closed doors in individual offices. "The programming code we write has to work together seamlessly so we should work together seamlessly as well," he said.*[13]

The computer company Intel, like Netscape referenced above, has been pro-cubicle and open-plan since just after its founding in 1968. On the other side of the fence, Microsoft's corporate offices follow the vision of Bill Gates and Paul Allen, who are crystal clear that software programmers work best alone with individual offices and few distractions:

> *"Every time we revisit the issue of having open-plan offices, it is roundly rejected," said Nick MacPhee, the general manager of real estate and facilities. "The reaction borders between horror and hysteria."*[14]

Recently Microsoft has gravitated toward a combination of private office space and open plan. One extremist in the debate has been Michael Bloomberg. When he served as mayor of New York from 2002 to 2013 he went retro and put almost everyone in city hall into one large bullpen with Bloomberg's desk front and center. Bloomberg adopted the plan from his days working on the Wall Street trading floor and also designed his corporate offices this way. Incoming Mayor Bill de Blasio decided not to dismantle the bullpen due to expense, but he quietly took a private office on the floor below.

While some office design firms tout all kinds of new "research" advocating for open-plan offices, most of the web pages that come up in top Google searches rail against them:

- "The Open Office Trap." *(New Yorker)*[15]
- "Ending the Tyranny of the Open-Plan Office." *(Business Week)*[16]
- "Study: Open Offices are Making us all Sick." *(Wall Street Journal)*[17]
- "Open-Plan Offices Were Devised by Satan in the Deepest Caverns Of Hell." *(Guardian)*[18]

While the negative articles were in the majority, there were also a few on the other side of the fence:

"Open-Plan Offices: The New Trend in Workplace Design." *(Slate)* [19]

Many people would stop after reading five or six articles from recent and reputable newspapers and magazines touting the latest studies, and sometimes this can be enough. But for me this was just scratching the surface. I decided to wade deeply into the story behind the story, and the current quickly pulled me out, deep.

SATISFICING: EAT FISH!

Satisficing is an idea developed in 1956 to explain why people often pull together a limited amount of resources in order to find "good enough" information. [20] The theory predates the widespread use of the Internet by decades, and the behavior has probably gone on for centuries. It is not about being lazy. It is a practical coping technique because we are all bound by time limitations. Professor Metzger and others have shown that for important decisions we choose to spend more time searching for information, but for decisions we make daily and weekly at work or as consumers we tend to "satisfice" with a few quick searches. [21]

Often satisficing is combined with other strategies called "heuristics" to save us time. Confirmation bias, for example, is our tendency to view information as credible if it confirms our preexisting beliefs, and not credible if it counters our beliefs. [22] Combine this with the tendency people have to only look at the first five search results in Google and we get many people relying on a lot of unreliable information. Many of us also have a strong need for closure, and this also impacts our credibility assessments. Researchers have found that when people are experiencing a high degree of "need for closure" they are more likely to seize on the first piece of information they find because their primary goal is to get an answer quickly. [23]

In looking for information on office plans I could feel the urge to "satisfice," and also my confirmation bias was trying to gain control. I had worked as a research librarian for twenty years and in my last year there we transitioned overnight from having private offices to an open plan. I hated it. My initial foray onto Google was confirming all my deep-seated biases. Open plans were noisy, stressful, disruptive, and so on. I found myself wanting to minimize the handful of articles that were positive. While satisficing and the confirmation bias have been problems for many decades, this type of behavior is quickly magnified when searching online. Sometimes we even set ourselves up to confirm what we already believe by searching using terms that bias our findings from the start.

Newspaper and blog writers feed our need for satisficing. They grab one study and declare: *Eating Fish Is Good for Your Heart!* They do it because it works. Readers want a simple story with clear conclusions. They do not want to get bogged down with all the details: should the fish be farmed or wild? Tuna or salmon? Were the studies done with a randomized and large enough sample of subjects? We often just read the headlines anyway: Eat Fish!

PROOF BY REPEATED ASSERTION

It is always tempting to take a shortcut on the path to finding reliable information. I am committed to getting to the bottom of the research on open-plan offices, but if there is an easy way to get the full story quickly, that would be great. As I pop around looking at blogs and news articles a definite pattern was emerging. I keep seeing references to the same study and the same man. Apparently a researcher from Queensland University of Technology (QUT) in Brisbane, Australia, I'll call him "Dr. O.,"[24] had done an extensive review of the literature on open-plan offices. Dr. O. was quoted as saying:

> *In 90 percent of the research, the outcome of working in an open-plan office was seen as negative, with open-plan offices causing high levels of stress, conflict, high blood pressure, and a high staff turnover.*[25]

What is weird about the Dr. O. quote is that it is *everywhere*. In fact, almost every article I read as I pop around my search results has the Dr. O. quote of "90 percent." Dr. O. also offers heady sound bites about open-plan offices negatively impacting productivity and rails forcefully against this type of design by saying it caused so many problems there might be employee lawsuits down the road due to the stress the open-plan office might cause.[26]

Digging a little further, not surprisingly, I find that Dr. O.'s research is one of a handful of citations listed on Wikipedia under the subject of "open-plan offices." It is hard to know which came first: did Dr. O. do the study, get interviewed by a journalist, and then get cited in the Wikipedia article? Probably, and then all the other writers picked up the sound bite from either the first writer or from Wikipedia. Unfortunately, the link on Wikipedia does not go to the actual review study as promised, but instead links to yet another brief news article, this time from an Australian health site summarizing his research review.[27] In this summary, Dr. O. is quoted as saying:

> *The evidence we found was absolutely shocking!*

As I dig around more I find over 1,000 brief articles on the Web quoting Dr. O. saying how shocking his findings were, and just short of 1,000 of them cite the "90 percent" figure. I am stunned by the popularity of Dr. O.

Perhaps his review of the research is so extensive and his expertise so vast that this had made him *the* authority on open-plan offices.

Here is Dr. O. in Japanese railing against open-plan offices and referencing his study[28] (thank you Google translation!):

研究报告作者乌曼（**V▮▮▮ O▮▮▮▮**）指出，员工觉得压力大，血压升高，以及冲突多和流动率快，都与开放式的办公环境有关。 乌曼在这项发表于"亚太健康管理 ...

Here he is in Vietnamese, next to advertisements for cubicle partitions:[29]

Jul 4, 2014 - **V▮▮▮ O▮▮▮▮** một chuyên gia sức khoẻ cộng đồng của ĐH Công nghệ ứng dụng Queensland (Brisbane, Australia), cho...

And in Sweden, here is Dr. O., popping up like a "Where's Waldo?" in yet another article about open-plan offices making employees stressed and ill:[30]

Den **australiske forskaren V▮▮▮ O▮▮▮** har **funnit** att 90 procent av studierna om arbetsmiljön i öppna kontorslandskap talar emot en sådan ...

He is even featured in a brochure for an acoustic sound-masking company to help with the stress-inducing noise levels in open-plan offices, and he appears in a Google image search, a friendly smile on his face as he stands in front of a group of low-partitioned office desks.[31]

There is a phenomenon called "proof by repeated assertion" that occurs when a piece of information is repeated over and over again. This repetition reinforces the idea that because so many sources have reported it as true it therefore must be true. Combine this with the re-blogging and re-tweeting of the same story ad nauseam and you have a problem. When journalists and bloggers do not do their homework and then parrot each other, one piece of information becomes magnified a hundredfold. I wondered if the journalists who reported on the study had even *read* it. Many of them quoted Dr. O. in a way that implied they had each directly interviewed him, but it was the same quote in each story, suggesting that he was probably only interviewed once and then the story was parroted around what might be called "the shallow web."

With over 1,000 sources pointing to Dr. O. I think it possible that his study can answer all of my client Maya's questions, but my gut is telling me otherwise. There is something about his quotes in the articles online that seem off. It is rare for a researcher to say how "shocked" he is by the research or to make wild assertions about potential lawsuits. My guess is that the open-plan office issue is not as black and white as Dr. O. proclaims. It is time to track down the real research review and see if it holds water, and to do a little more digging into Dr. O.'s credentials.

Having just read Daniel Kahneman's book *Thinking, Fast and Slow*, I congratulate myself for not getting sucked into false certainty and not jumping to instant conclusions. Instead I recognize the possibility of uncertainty and know I need to investigate the quality of the information. Kahneman encourages us to think slow: "to doubt, hesitate, qualify."[32] He encourages skepticism. I am skeptical of Dr. O.'s study, but can 1,000 blogs and articles be engaged in fast thinking and false certainty? Even reputable publications like *Scientific American*? This seems hard to swallow.

WALKS LIKE A DUCK?

In the social sciences, like the sciences, there is primary research and then there are reviews summarizing and analyzing piles of primary research. Primary research consists of real experiments. To oversimplify: researchers take x number of subjects and expose them to some experimental condition and see what happens. The best research uses a randomized design for putting participants into control and test groups, they are double-blind, meaning participants and scientists do not know if a subject is in the experimental group or not, they use a large number of subjects, and the study results are repeatable by others. They are written up in scholarly journals and they follow a common format:

- Abstract
- Introduction
- Method
- Results
- Discussion
- Literature Cited

Most of these articles begin by touching on related research to demonstrate how this research builds on the work of previous studies. Those bumper stickers that read, "everything is connected" are not referring to the scholarly research process, but they could be. No one does useful research in a vacuum.

Below is a picture that demonstrates the interconnectedness of scholarly research. The image in the center is an article reporting on primary research. To the left are articles that the center article cites, the research that the center article is building on and thus obligated to cite. To the right are articles on research that took place after the center article had been published and cite it in their new research. This new research is furthering the conversation about a topic. It is easy to see that an article has followed proper etiquette if it contains a lot of citations on the left by citing previous research; it is also easy to see how influential an article and its research is by seeing how many researchers have cited the article after it was published, the pile on the right.

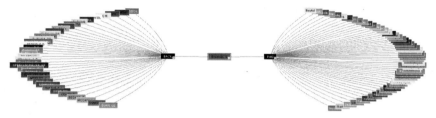

The Scholarly Research Process: Everything Is Connected. [33]

Reviews of the literature, on the other hand, take dozens and frequently hundreds of research articles and condense, summarize, and analyze the results. Sometimes they draw new conclusions based on their survey; sometimes they just provide a summary and analysis of the current state of the field.

Reviews of the literature vary in quality, sometimes cherry-picking studies to serve a particular researcher's agenda, but when they are done well they are comprehensive, systematically conducted, and cover a carefully defined area.[34] The authors will typically explain the procedures by which they conducted their review and they summarize and draw conclusions about the current state of an area of study. I know that if Dr. O's review holds up it will save me days of research and reading.

I track down Dr. O.'s review using Google Scholar, a fantastic and comprehensive search engine of published scholarship. Fortunately Dr. O.'s first and last names are unusual. If it had been a common name I would have thrown in subject keywords as well. Also, unlike many articles in Google Scholar, Dr. O.'s article was open access so the citation linked directly to a PDF. Had it been unavailable I would have been stuck paying for it or getting it via a library.

With the tremendous growth of information on the Web, evaluating information has been foisted onto the searcher. Publishers, libraries, and bookstores used to provide robust filters that excluded much of the commercial drivel that now populates the Web. The downside was that they also suppressed or curtailed innovative ideas that were not quite ready for prime time. There are many benefits to having access to greater amounts of information, but finding quality information has become more challenging as a result. While Google Scholar selects only scholarly information, it casts a large net and uses a broad definition of scholarship, but it provides access to much more reliable and scholarly information than a search on just Google, and it leaves out most of the marketing and advertisement pieces.

Just because an article appears on Google Scholar does not mean it is completely reliable research, though it is much more likely to be, and it is more likely to have been subject to some type of vetting and review process. My next step is to carefully evaluate Dr. O's article. Howard Rheingold and University of California Berkeley Libraries have both developed useful checklists and criteria for evaluating information (e.g., Currency, Reliability, Authority, Purpose).[35] At the same time, some experts, such as Marc Meola, warn searchers against leaning too heavily on checklists for evaluating information because checklists can encourage a mechanistic way of evaluating that is at odds with critical thinking.[36] Going down a checklist can become rote. Meola advocates using a contextual approach by shooting for peer- and editorially reviewed resources when possible, and using comparison and corroboration to verify information. Researchers from Hofstra University agree and state that the gold standard for evaluating research should be peer review, the credentials of the author, the reputation of the publisher, and the degree and quality of documentation provided.[37] I decide to use a combination of checklists and deeper contextual approaches.

Ultimately any evaluation strategy also needs to include a critical reading of the work using a healthy amount of skepticism while digging into the context of the research itself, where it came from, and what other research has been done in the field.[38] While I usually start with author credentials, I decide to dig into other evaluation criteria first:

1. Relevance?

This seems kind of obvious, right? It's about open-plan offices, so it must be relevant. Over 1,000 journalists and bloggers referenced it as pertaining to open-plan offices, but when I look at the title the focus is not what I expected:

> *Should Health Service Managers Embrace Open-plan Work Environments: A Review.*

Health service managers seem like a different type of worker than the software and marketing people that would be working in my client Maya's start-up. Health service managers face issues such as confidentiality that might impact whether they should be in an open-plan office. None of the online articles from the media had referenced the specific health service management focus. Perhaps Dr. O. reviewed the general research on open-plan offices to apply it to the needs of health service managers?

2. Context?

The discussion of context involves where the information is situated: is it on the web page of a corporation? Is it issued by an organization that has an agenda? Is it published by a scholarly body striving for objectivity?

Dr. O.'s information was wrapped in what appeared to be a scholarly journal titled *Asia Pacific Journal of Health Management.* Though the focus was on health management, not what I was looking for, the journal looked reputable. Scholarly journals contain articles written by researchers, professors, and graduate students. They are peer reviewed or refereed, which gives them a high level of credibility, because experts working in the same field review them.

To ensure that an article is in a scholarly journal, the quickest check is to search Ulrichsweb Global Serials Directory available online via most libraries. Pop the title of the journal in and a cute symbol of a referee shirt appears if the journal is peer reviewed. Dr. O.'s journal had the referee shirt—a good sign.

I decide to go one step further and figure out the Journal Impact Factor (JIF). This is an excessive move, but I am going deep. The JIF measures the frequency with which the average article in a journal has been cited year by year. It is a flawed measure, and is sometimes accused of being like a popularity contest, but I was not going for a high JIF, I just wanted to make sure the journal *had* a JIF score.

The JIF score can be found in the *Journal Citation Reports* within the proprietary database Web of Science (WOS)[39] that is found in many libraries. Strangely, Dr. O.'s journal is not included in WOS, a comprehensive database of scholarship. While WOS uses a more restrictive definition of scholarship than Google Scholar, almost all published English-language scholarly journals are found there. No go. Makes me think the *Asia Pacific Journal of Health Management* walks like a duck, talks like a duck, and is refereed like a duck, but maybe it is not a duck, or at least not according to WOS.

Searching Google to get to the publication website turns up a dead link. Information in the dead link provides me with a lead that the journal is a publication issued by the Australasian College of Health Service Management. While it is technically refereed, it is more like a newsletter that covers reviews of research and book reviews, which must be why WOS has snubbed it—no original primary research. I'm glad Google Scholar has a broader view of scholarship, because it provides a nice counterpart to WOS, and I never would have found the publication otherwise. Ultimately I conclude that though it is not a rigorous scholarly journal, the college that issues it has no specific agenda other than to share useful information with health service managers.

3. Length?

Often length does not seem important, but for a comprehensive literature review it should be long: A typical scholarly literature review is thirty or forty pages. Dr. O.'s review is only six pages.

4. Methodology?

For a literature review this is crucial. Dr. O. and company explained their search criteria: They had chosen appropriate journal databases to search, though they had included a preponderance of medical databases, including PubMed, Medline, and CINHAL (nursing). They listed the keywords used in searches and included negative words such as "office crowding," "office noise," and "office privacy," which could slant the search results. Not a deal breaker, but it would have been nice if they had searched for words like "collaboration" as well.

5. Timeliness?

Timeliness can mean different things. For some disciplines, like science, timeliness means the last year or two. A review of the literature from ten years ago for the treatment of colon cancer is useless. For my purposes I would accept something within the last few years. Dr. O.'s study was six years old, meaning the research reviewed would have been older than seven years, but more concerning was that Dr. O. indicated he had put no time limit on the research he reviewed. Many of the studies cited were old, from the 1970s and 1980s. While the expectation is that a deep review should cover older material, the older studies he referenced constituted half of the sixty studies cited.

In Dr. O.'s favor, they had used a snowballing strategy. This involves taking each article found and tracking down the articles cited at the back of that article. Unfortunately, they do not mention tracing forward to find out what articles were citing the articles they retrieved, so that they could get the most current research. This can be done with the click of a link on WOS or Google Scholar.

6. Balance?

In reading the review itself I find a balanced analysis of open-plan offices. The last page contains a chart listing seven advantages and ten disadvantages of the open office. This seems disconnected from the media reports that quote Dr. O. denouncing open-plan offices. I found no mention of the 90 percent figure so widely quoted online. The review itself makes no mention of that figure. Near the end of the review the authors write:

*Just because a workplace has an open-plan design, does not mean low em-
ployee productivity.* [40]

What had happened between publishing the literature review and Dr. O.'s
brush with the media? Had he gotten caught up in his "fifteen minutes of
fame" and let loose his feelings of hatred toward open-plan offices? Or had
the media misrepresented their interview with Dr. O.?

FINDING DR. O.

I decide that this "literature review" is not deep enough for my purposes. But
I am intrigued. Why had so many writers quoted Dr. O. and his study? Was it
just like a bad virus that spread around the Web? Was it a product of lazy
journalists? *Just who is this Dr. O.?*

According to the article, Dr. O. is listed as "Senior Project Officer," and
his coauthors are listed as "Executive Officer" and "Research Assistant,"
respectively. Dr. O. is listed as a "Dr." in the article, but there is no Ph.D.
following his name, instead he is listed as:

BDS, MHlthSC, CertMRC, DipMedDent, AFCHSE, CHE

I am not kidding: six degrees. I look up some of them and figure out that
DipMedDent may be some type of graduate degree in dentistry though it is
rare to see it listed as DipMedDent, even in Austalia. Not exactly the expertise needed for what falls under industrial and organizational psychology,
business management, or possibly architecture and design. The coauthors are
listed as "Mr." and "Ms." One has a physical education diploma and the
other has a nursing degree. Many of the media reports call Dr. O. "a researcher from Queensland." I had assumed he was on the faculty or was a researcher with a Ph.D.

I cannot locate his resume online and when I check Google Scholar for a
list of his other publications I found only a few on various medical subjects,
all published within a two-year period of the open-plan article. I decide to
email him and ask about the 90 percent figure: where did it come from given
that it did not show up in the research review? I look on the Queensland
website in the staff directory and do a search combining his name with
Queensland.

There is no Dr. O. listed there!

Any sane researcher would just move on at this point. It was time to see if
there was a better review article out there or create my own literature review.
But I am captivated. How had Dr. O. become *the* spokesperson against open-

plan offices? Was there some commercial payoff or personal agenda involved? I clear my schedule for the week to track down Dr. O., his study, and
everything I can find that relates to it.

I begin to feel like the central character in a detective movie with every
new piece of evidence dragging me in more deeply. My husband and children throw up their hands in defeat, slipping dinner under my study door . . .
again. My eyes are burning from too many hours on the computer, but what I
begin to uncover is too hard to resist—like pulling at a loose sweater thread
and watching the entire garment unravel.

THE ART AND SCIENCE OF FINDING PEOPLE

Finding information about people online is both an art and a science. If you
are trying to determine if a researcher is legitimate, a quick Google search
with their name and institution or logging on to the staff directory at their
university it typically enough. In most cases there will be a vita or resume,
publications list, courses taught, and information about research interests.
These people want to be found. If that fails, as it did with Dr. O., it begins to
raise a red flag.

Most of us, whether we admit it or not, have searched—maybe even a bit
obsessively—for someone on the Web. If their name is unique or unusual it
can be easy, but if they have a common name or are not active in social
media a more strategic approach is needed.

Once you have exhausted initial Google Searches—either because nothing is coming up or too much is coming up—searching for people can be
broken down into four types:

1. Social Media

Most people have a social media profile unless they are in a witness protection program. Facebook is the most widespread, but if it is a common name
and there is no known geographic location it can be challenging.

Graph search, on Facebook, lets you search for people by geographic
location, institutional affiliation, hobbies, college attended, and even whether
they "like" a certain restaurant. More people are turning on their privacy
settings, but they cannot prevent searchers from viewing their name and
profile image, if they have one. Sometimes you can glean just enough from a
Facebook page to then do an improved Google search.

As you pick up bits and pieces of information, combine them and plug
them into sites such as Twitter, LinkedIn, Google+, and Tumblr. You will
need accounts on these sites to do this. Try searching for their name in a
Google image search: If you find an image, then link back to its origin. [41] If
you find a photo they have posted on Instagram you can run it through a site

called The Beat. Developed by Rutgers students, it combines Instagram photos with a Google Street View of the photograph's location. Usually it will give you both the location of the photo and the time the photo was taken, helping you pinpoint the location of the person.

LinkedIn is becoming more useful for locating people and seeing where they work. If you are secretly tracking down an old flame or future romantic partner, *log out of your own account first,* before scanning their site. People who have enhanced subscriptions to LinkedIn can tell who has viewed their profile.

Twitter is also a place to find people if they want to be found, but unless the person identifies themselves in their "biography" it is not much use. Other social media sites are hit or miss. Remember that Google can search inside some social media sites but not others. There are niche vertical search engines that spring up and die out regularly, so to search Twitter, for example:

Google: *Search Engines Twitter*

Unfortunately, Dr. O. does not seem to be the social sort.

2. Contact Someone Directly

I know this sounds crazy, but sometimes the easiest approach is to email or call someone, or connect with someone who might know them. There are tricks to getting Google to pony up an email address or phone number. Try searching their name combined with @, or try their area code or workplace name if you have it. Several free (and many fee) white pages are available online. AnyWho.com and 411.com are useful. If you know the email of someone they work with, it can be easy to guess at the structure of your person's email: for example, Pedro_Martinez@Smithsonian.gov.

Cell phone numbers are difficult to find unless they are listed in some document out on the Web that can be accessed by Google. The "free" cell phone registries are rarely worth searching. They lead you on, but then try to charge for what is usually a landline number.

Unfortunately, I am not able to track down my Dr. O. The only information is that he has worked in some capacity at QUT, but was no longer there. I email the human resources department at QUT, but they cite privacy restrictions and are unable to respond.

I email Dr. O.'s coauthors listed in the QUT staff directory, but receive no response. I then email the coauthors that had worked with Dr. O. on his other published articles. Miraculously, one of them emails me back. She asks not to be quoted by name, but confirms that Dr. O. has "some sort of dental degree from India." This helps corroborate and confirm the *DipMedDent* degree listed next to his name in the article. She also reports that she thinks he might be "working for a small business in Queensland." This seems useful, but in poking around further with this information I find nothing.

3. People Search Sites

Finding information about people online is big business and big money: $31 billion a year and growing.[42] If you do a Google search for someone's name, you will quickly fall into the clutches of fee-based data brokers such as Spokeo, PeekYou, Zaba, Intellius, and Pipl. These sites scrape the Web and off-line sources for information and sell it for a subscription or fee. Much of this information is available online for free, but you have to do the leg work by popping into sex offender registries, court databases, social media sites, mortgage registries, and so on.

The compilers are savvy marketers. They will give you a teaser or will lead you on by promising that they have some hefty dirt on the person you are investigating:

Click here to find a criminal record for Leslie Stebbins!

Eventually this leads to a page asking for your credit card information. If you are short on time it can sometimes be worth paying, but many of these companies have gotten into trouble because their information is frequently inaccurate. They often make assumptions about data they have and link people to incorrect record information. This can have devastating consequences when someone's name gets linked to a felon who has the same name and lives in the same city.

The Federal Trade Commission (FTC) recently fined Spokeo $800,000 for selling personal information to employers and job recruiters. The collecting of personal information is not illegal, but the use of this information can violate the Fair Credit Reporting Act.[43] Spokeo was called on the carpet because they failed to verify how the information they were selling would be used and failed to ensure its accuracy. They were also fined for posting fake endorsements of their service on news sites.

A 2014 FTC report reveals how data brokers obtain and share information without consumer knowledge, and calls for new laws and greater transparency.[44] Data brokers collect information from on and off-line sources that include social media activity, purchases, warranty registrations, sweepstakes entries, voter registration lists, marriage and business licenses, birth records, magazine subscriptions, bankruptcies, criminal records, apartment leases, and mortgages. Using these services you can find out someone's race, religion, socioeconomic status, political affiliations, and more.

I am not willing to pony up the $39 fee for a data broker, and the initial information some of them gave me was what I had already gleaned on my own: that Dr. O. was quoted in many articles saying that 90 percent of the research on open-plan offices showed a negative impact on workers. Wow. Really.

4. The Exhaustive Search Engine Slog

To do an exhaustive Web search can sound a little insane, especially if you are dealing with a Jose Martinez or David Smith. But if you can add one more piece of information to your search, such as *Albuquerque* or *psychologist*, then it may be worth doing. Experiment with quotation marks to limit your search as well:

> Google: *"Jose Martinez" psychologist*
> But if Jose uses a middle name or initial you are out of luck. Do a second search with:
> Google: *Jose around(2) Martinez psychologist*

This will retrieve the word "Jose" with no more than two words in between it and "Martinez." If that still retrieves too many you could do *around(10)* next to the word psychologist as well to narrow the search.

For many of us it is a radical notion to move past the first page or two of Google search results. The reality is that there can be valuable information buried in search results. Some people even hire reputation companies who, if they cannot get negative information removed, will at least attempt to bury it by optimizing other newer pieces of information about the person.

For Dr. O. it means going through hundreds of pages of news articles and blogs about him and his comments about open-plan offices. But, buried way down at the end of the Google search results, hundreds of pages down, I find two vital pieces of information:

1. A link between Dr. O's name and a company name. The company is described as "Australia's first and leading online bullion store selling Swiss gold bars and silver bullion" founded in 2013. Dr. O. is listed as CEO in several-gold selling business directories.
2. A directory of gold sellers lists an address for Dr. O.'s company in New York!

I search the address online and cross check it with a reverse directory look-up and even "Google Earth" it to make sure the building exists. The address and suite number where Dr. O.'s company is allegedly located is connected to a lawyers' office that has the same suite number. I do research on the law office and find that they have received an "F" from the Better

Business Bureau and are not officially recognized as a legitimate business. Fraud reports and complaints were also listed against them. As I dig further in I discover that Dr. O.'s office mates are in the "business" of creating shelf corporations. Shelf corporations, similar to shell corporations, are companies that are created on paper, but do not really exist except to have an "address" in the form of a mailbox in an office building.

Things are looking dire. My plan to reach out to Dr. O. needs to be nixed. I had found my answer many days and many research hours earlier: Dr. O. had little expertise in fields related to office space and productivity and his review article was too narrow to be useful to me. There was nothing wrong with what Dr. O. had done. His article had been written for a university publication to inform health service managers. He probably gave a few interviews to local news outlets and that became magnified across the Web. My best guess is that he was a former staff member at QUT, a former dentist in India, and now appeared to be selling gold bullion. I have just blown off an entire week. Dr. O. may have struck gold. I have not.

GOING DEEP

I stand by the concept of starting research using the fine art of poking around to get the size and shape of a topic, but getting sucked into a black hole for a week is not recommended. Devise an exit strategy.

I still need a high-quality scholarly literature review—either to find one or to compile one myself—or some combination of the two. I need a literature review that is not too narrowly focused, was systematically conducted, and does not pull in an unrepresentative sample of studies to serve a particular agenda.[45]

Part of the problem has been that I was looking for a quick solution to a challenging research question. It is likely that there is no "yes or no" answer to the question about productivity and open-plan offices. It was a nuanced subject. When I got on Google I had been swept up into the "open-plan offices are Satan" type of thinking. Daniel Kahneham argues that we often revert to "substituting an easier question," as a way of avoiding doing the work to answer a more challenging question. Substituting an easier question is a type of fast thinking and needs to be countered by slow thinking: asking specific questions and evaluating arguments based on evidence rather than getting quickly swept up in the easy fix.[46] I decide to slow down and go deeper. I crack my knuckles, grit my teeth, and jump into the Deep Web.

The Deep Web is the best place to look for serious research, and I remain hopeful that I can find a good literature review, because I had not yet searched specifically for this when Dr. O.'s work fell into my lap. The Deep Web is not as mysterious as it sounds, but it is hard to pin down because it contains many types of resources that need to be found using different tools. The Deep Web is all the information on the Web that cannot be found by using a regular search engine such as Google or Bing. The vast bulk of the Deep Web includes scholarly articles and books that are behind paywalls or hidden within databases that traditional search engines cannot access. Pages buried several layers down in the site hierarchy are also part of the Deep Web, because search engines tend to skim mostly the top and second-layer pages, they do not go more than a few layers down unless a page has multiple links to it from other websites. [47]

The Deep Web also includes *some* government information (billions of pages), white papers, special archives, some blogs and wikis, many social media sites, corporate intranets that are behind firewalls, and, of course, pornography sites. Search engines also personalize search results and customize what they retrieve for each of us based on our past search interests, so parts of the Web might be more buried for some of us than for others. Some experts argue that because most people do not look through more than a few pages of search results, results that are buried on page 900 are also part of the Deep Web. [48] Often smaller sites that do not have a lot of links to them get buried, regardless of the quality of the information.

Content within the Deep Web is accessed through specialty, and sometimes proprietary, databases or vertical niche search tools. We use these all the time without thinking about it. If we are looking for a vacation house we might go to VRBO or Airbnb, if we want to buy a book we search Amazon, and if we want to buy new shoes we might go directly to Zappos or Nike. There is no single search engine for the Deep Web because it is not a single entity. In fact, many of us should be glad that some things on the Deep Web do not show up in our search results. Pornography sites, drug trade interactions, sexual predator solicitations, as well as the IRS Tax Code, thankfully, do not commonly surface in our search results.

COMMITTING TO THE WHOLE ENCHILADA

For my purposes, I wanted to access just the scholarly journal literature on the Deep Web from business and psychology journals. If you have connections to a library, you can choose a database that covers the discipline you think is most relevant to your subject. In my case I could search PsychInfo or Business Source Premier. The other option is to use Google Scholar, which indexes most scholarly journal articles and can be great for topics when you are using specific search terms such as "open-plan offices." Google Scholar is less good for a topic such as "diabetes" if what you want to focus on is just medical journals or just history journals.

Doing an extensive review of the research on a topic is a little like getting to know a potential partner really *really* well. It's a process that unwraps layer after layer of information. First you learn that, wow, they *too* like ping-pong and birding! Later you learn that they had a difficult childhood, are phobic about spiders, make a mean daiquiri, and have an abnormal fear of babies. In reviewing the scholarship on open-plan offices I couldn't just pick out the articles I liked. I had to take it all. You can't just accept the parts of your new partner that you like—you have to commit to the whole enchilada.

Every researcher who is doing their job conducts a mini literature review before starting their research. They need to know the current knowledge base of the little corner of the world that they are investigating. They need to tie their investigation to previous research so that they do not repeat the same mistakes. They need to build on the work of others in the field. Every few years a group of researchers will tackle a comprehensive review of the literature on a topic. This provides a service to researchers by analyzing all the scholarship on a topic so others can push on further, by "standing on the shoulders of giants."[49]

Most researchers work within an *invisible college*: a small group of researchers around the world that are investigating the same specific area. Typically they know each other or at least know *of* each other, see each other at conferences, and sit on boards and committees together. The invisible college also contains the scholars from previous generations. In a sense, scholarship is tapping into the wisdom of a crowd: The wisdom of a crowd of experts.

At the same time, it is important to acknowledge that researchers are not without an agenda. Everyone has an agenda. When researchers run a study, the way they interpret their findings can be influenced by their own ideas about a subject they are passionate about. That is why it is important to read the study carefully to identify the authors' conclusions and determine if the evidence they present directly supports their conclusions. The good news is that there is a correction mechanism in research. If someone publishes outlandish findings and runs too far afield, their work either will be ignored (i.e., never cited) by others in the field, or they will be dealt with directly when others try to repeat their studies and get different results.

Jacob Cohen, a psychologist at New York University, has pointed out that:

> *A successful piece of research doesn't conclusively settle an issue, it just makes some theoretical proposition to some degree more likely.* [50]

Office design and productivity research had started around 1910. It was a concrete body of knowledge and researchers working today in the field were all connected to previous research in this area. They could all point to important "Aha" moments that had occurred over the course of many decades of research. For example:

- A series of studies from 1924 to 1932 called the Hawthorne Experiments essentially shut down the subfield of office design and productivity research for more than two decades. There were numerous impacts from these experiments, including the idea of the famous "Hawthorne Effect" (workers behaving differently simply by virtue of knowing someone is studying their behavior). For office design researchers the important takeaway of these experiments had been that they could find no direct proof of a connection between the design of the work environment and worker productivity. So they stopped looking for many years.
- In the 1980s an influential study now referred to as the "Coding War Games" compared the work of more than 600 computer programmers at ninety-two companies. The study found an enormous gap in productivity between programmers working at some companies versus other companies. The programmers working at the highly productive companies performed better not because of higher pay or greater experience, but because they had more privacy, personal workspace, and freedom from interruption.[51] The takeaway here was not that everyone should always have their own private office, but that it was crucial to focus on people rather than processes and products, and for this large group of programmers, having fewer interruptions seemed to have a positive impact on their output.

Being the information extremist that I am, I return to Google Scholar and its fancier library-owned counterpart, WOS. I access Google Scholar, use my keywords and also try a few synonyms. I also click a small arrow to the right of my search terms and a drop down menu provides a few options. I limit by date and add the phrase "review of the literature." This is not foolproof. It will bring up false hits and also might eliminate good review articles that do not use that exact phrase. Generally it will get me most of the articles I want and I will pick up other important articles by snowballing through tracing citations of the articles I find.

Find articles		✕
with **all** of the words	productivity "review of the literature"	
with the **exact phrase**	open plan offices	
with **at least one** of the words		
without the words		
where my words occur	anywhere in the article ⇕	
Return articles **authored** by		
	e.g., *"PJ Hayes"* or *McCarthy*	
Return articles **published** in		
	e.g., *J Biol Chem* or *Nature*	
Return articles **dated** between	2011 — 2015	
	e.g., *1996*	

🔍

Google Scholar advanced search for a literature review on open-plan offices and productivity.

Doing an initial search on "open-plan offices" and "productivity" I retrieve over 2,000 articles, limiting by recent date and adding "review of the literature" narrows it down to seventy. I eliminate many of the seventy because they are narrowly focused or have given me a false hit—turning up articles on green design or office bullies. A few dozen look worth pursuing and I select one that seems perfect by Dr. Matthew Davis and two other researchers.[52]

I also go into WOS and run through similar searches. WOS has a number of advantages over Google Scholar because it defines scholarship more narrowly by using humans rather than spiders—bots that crawl websites and index them for search engines—to determine what sources are included. WOS also provides bells and whistles that allow me to analyze my search results. I can ask questions such as "What authors have published the most on this subject?" and "What journal articles have covered this topic the most frequently?" I can also limit my search specifically to literature reviews. On the other hand, Google Scholar is great for tracking down an obscure piece of scholarship, a needle in a haystack, or for extremely comprehensive searches. It is also free.

Combining Google Scholar and WOS I come up with a few dozen possibilities, with Dr. Davis again rising to the top of the pile. In a nutshell, here is why I like Dr. Davis so much:

1. Authority: Dr. Davis is on the faculty of Leeds University Business School and his resume on the Leeds site pops up quickly. He has a Ph.D. in Organizational Psychology, an MS in Occupational Psychology, and his specialty is, get this, workplace design! He has won dozens of honors, published dozens of related papers, and spoken at dozens of relevant conferences. His two coauthors have similar credentials.

2. Relevance: The article is spot on. In addition to giving background on research to date on open-plan offices, the review also serves to aid managers in making decisions about workplace design and reviews how open-plan offices are evolving to suit modern organizations. The end of the article focuses on managing the process of change that office design and optimization requires. A number of solid studies have pointed to the fact that it is the *process* of changing from one design to another that has a tremendous impact on morale and productivity, even more impact than the actual design of the office itself. Involving the employees in the process of designing an office is a crucial step in the process.

3. Context: His article is published in the *International Review of Industrial and Organizational Psychology*. Unlike Dr. O.'s journal, Dr. Davis's journal is included in WOS because it is considered "scholarly," it is also refereed, but it does not have a Journal Impact Factor because it is considered a serial book publication rather than a journal.

4. Length: The review article is forty pages and includes a review of 176 research studies.

5. Methodology: The authors have done a comprehensive job. They state that they are seeking "a fresh approach" to the study of workplaces and that the purpose of their review is to not only "collate and synthesize" all the research in this area, but also to review the ways open-plan offices are evolving, the implications of that, and how best to manage the process of design and identify how their field can contribute to decision making and current theory.

6. Timeliness: The article provides historical background, but then goes on to analyze recent research. The article itself was published three years ago.

7. Balance: Dr. Davis and his coauthors trace the history of research on office design and draw attention to the early research that showed improved team communications in open-plan designs. But as employers shifted to the open plan, many of them did so to reduce fixed overhead costs, and employees found themselves increasingly working elbow to elbow in closer and closer quarters. Later studies examined the density and proximity of workers, and how the openness of the design influenced worker effectiveness. Dr. Davis goes on to cover

the research on benefits of open-plan offices, the risks, individual and contextual factors that impact open-plan offices, research on balancing the tradeoffs between closed and open-plan offices, and the recent evolution of the open plan into more mixed-use spaces.

Dr. Davis's conclusions, though challenging to summarize in a few sentences, place the discussion within the context of research on organizational change management and office design. He finds that "pull-based user-owned change" in office design fares much better in terms of worker productivity than when "experts" come in and design a system and "push" it onto the workers. He then discusses ways to effectively involve workers in the design of the workspace. He also points to new trends in office design, including sustainable buildings, and the need for research in many of the new office configurations that are springing up that combine private and public space. He suggests that the focus has been on how the physical environment changes the way people work, but what researchers need to look at is the reverse: how can people craft their jobs to shape and change their environments to improve outcomes. Dr. Davis calls on organizations to be careful about assuming that they will save money by placing workers much closer together: in the short run possibly, but for knowledge workers this has been shown to result in significantly lower productivity, and Dr. Davis cites dozens of research articles that prove this.

PATIENCE AND PERSISTENCE

Because Dr. Davis's article was three years old, the last item on my list is to track the article forward in time. I embark on my own mini literature review of any articles that came out in the last three years by searching Google Scholar and WOS without the "review of the literature" limit in place, but limiting the date range. I also use a link in Google Scholar and WOS to check out who has cited Dr. Davis's article after it was published.

I find more than fifty new articles, but only a few stand out. One builds on Dr. Davis's ideas about building work environments that are more responsive to worker needs, another explains the current difficulty in actually measuring productivity in a meaningful way when examining the output of knowledge workers, and a third discusses younger workers liking the social aspects of open-plan offices better, but being less productive in them.

With Dr. Davis' article and the other three downloaded, I head to Maya's office to report back. While I am tempted to mention my adventures with Dr. O., I decide that it would only make me appear unprofessional. I had gone deep, and though the real depth had only taken two days of strategic research,

I could chalk my previous week's time sink up to experience gained and curiosity abated.

The differences between what I found searching the Deep Web and the shallow Google search results were dramatic. Why hadn't the bloggers and news sites that popped up in my initial Google searches—even *Scientific American*, FastCompany, and the *Times Higher Education Supplement*—picked up on Dr. Davis or another higher caliber article? Why had they instead pounced on Dr. O.? Low-hanging fruit? Anthropologist Alex Bentley has argued that the Web makes "academic research a popularity contest," because search engines prioritize information not based on scientific merit but instead on what will appeal to large audiences. [53] To increase readership, blogs and newspapers often overdramatize their stories: Open-plan office research is not nuanced and complex, it is "satanic." Accuracy often takes a back seat to entertainment. Just like high school, Dr. O. had won the popularity contest that Dr. Davis had not even entered. Dr. Davis was an academic interested in furthering research within his discipline, not getting "likes."

The famous educator Howard Gardner wrote:

> *Truth is about statements, propositions. The proliferation of information on the Internet makes it more difficult, initially, to determine truth. But with patience and persistence, we have a better chance than ever before to determine whether a proposition is true, false, or indeterminate.* [54]

With patience and persistence I had found Dr. Davis with the following strategies:

1. Start at the Source

After my initial poking around I centered in on Google Scholar and WOS as my two sources. Doing a dozen searches on each I was able to find a good literature review from three years ago and also trace it forward to bring my research up to date.

2. Pay Attention to the "Psychology of Search"

I had resisted the pitfalls of the psychology of search by not "satisficing," and by avoiding fast thinking. I had avoided false certainty by not settling for the first piece of information I found. I followed Kahneman's advice by thinking slow, "doubting, hesitating, and qualifying." [55]

3. Expert, Amateur, Crowd?

I had chosen the expertise of researchers, but I had chosen a "crowd" of researchers by selecting a comprehensive literature review providing me with all the nuances of the subject I was investigating.

4. Context, Motivation, and Bias

I had looked carefully at the context and motivation of the sources and authors I had dug up. By being skeptical of Dr. O. I had uncovered the shortcomings of his research in connection to my needs. Instead I had chosen a scholar who had conducted an extremely comprehensive review that was relevant to my needs.

5. Comparison and Corroboration

I had compared many studies, as had Dr. Davis, to come up with verification that the kinds of information I was passing on to my client reported on the current state of the field.

6. Go Deep, or Not

I had gone deep, and then some.

NOTES

1. "Man Drives Hundreds of Miles with Corpse Passenger," *Boston Globe,* June 5, 2014, http://www.bostonglobe.com/news/nation/2014/06/04/man-drives-miles-with-corpse-passenger/FiQvt8DrPyjDyQXkR5GokK/story.html.

2. Quotes can be placed around terms to indicate in Google to search for that specific phrase.

3. Ezster Hargittai, Lindsay Fullerton, Ericka Menchen-Trevino, and Kristin Yates Thomas. "Trust Online: Young Adults' Evaluation of Web Content," *International Journal of Communication* 4 (April 2010), http://ijoc.org/index.php/ijoc/article/view/636.

4. Daniel Kahneman, *Thinking, Fast and Slow* (New York: Farrar, Straus & Giroux, 2011).

5. James B. Stewart, "Looking for a Lesson in Google Perks," *New York Times,* March 15, 2013, http://www.nytimes.com/2013/03/16/business/at-google-a-place-to-work-and-play.html?_r=0.

6. Susan Cain, "The Rise of the New Group Think," *New York Times Sunday Review,* January 13, 2012, http://www.nytimes.com/2012/01/15/opinion/sunday/the-rise-of-the-new-groupthink.html?pagewanted=all.

7. Parker, Robert B. *Pale Kings and Princes.* New York: Random House (2009). Used with permission.

8. Danny Sullivan, " How Google Instant Autocomplete Suggestions Work," Search Engine Land Blog, April 6, 2011, http://searchengineland.com/how-google-instant-autocomplete-suggestions-work-62592.

9. Joe McCambley, quoted in David Carr, "Storytelling Ads May Be Journalism's New Peril," *New York Times,* September 15, 2013, http://www.nytimes.com/2013/09/16/business/media/storytelling-ads-may-be-journalisms-new-peril.html?pagewanted=all&_r=0.

10. Dan Duray, "Can't Handle The Truth? How a *New Yorker* Reporter and a Team of Fact-Checkers Took on the Church of Scientology," *New York Observer*, January 29, 2013, http://observer.com/2013/01/cant-handle-the-truth-how-a-new-yorker-reporter-and-a-team-of-fact-checkers-took-on-the-church-of-scientology/; John McPhee, "Checkpoints: Fact-Checkers Do It a Tick at a Time," *New Yorker*, February 9, 2009, http://www.newyorker.com/magazine/2009/02/09/checkpoints.

11. Don Goeman and Deanne Beckwith, "Design's Strategic Role at Herman Miller," *Design Management Review* 15, no. 2 (2004), doi: 10.1111/j.1948-7169.2004.tb00160.x.

12. Shari F. Epstein, "Space and Project Management Benchmarks," Report by the International Facility Management Association, 2010, http://wkpointe.com/pdf/Space%20and%20Project%20Management%20Report%2034.pdf.

13. Steve Lohr, "Rethinking Privacy vs. Teamwork in Today's Workplace," *New York Times*, August 11, 1997, http://www.nytimes.com/1997/08/11/business/rethinking-privacy-vs-teamwork-in-today-s-workplace.html.

14. Ibid.

15. Maria Konnikova, "The Open-Office Trap," *New Yorker*, January 7, 2014, http://www.newyorker.com/business/currency/the-open-office-trap.

16. Vanessa Wong, "Ending the Tyranny of the Open-Plan Office," *Bloomberg Business*, July 1, 2013, http://www.bloomberg.com/bw/articles/2013-07-01/ending-the-tyranny-of-the-open-plan-office.

17. Rachel Feintzeig, "Study: Open Offices Are Making Us All Sick," *Wall Street Journal*, February 25, 2014, http://blogs.wsj.com/atwork/2014/02/25/study-open-offices-are-making-us-all-sick.

18. Oliver Burkeman, "Open-Plan Offices Were Devised by Satan in the Deepest Caverns of Hell," *Guardian*, November 18, 2013, http://www.theguardian.com/news/2013/nov/18/open-plan-offices-bad-harvard-business-review.

19. Seth Stevenson, "Open-Plan Offices: The New Trend in Workplace Design," *Slate*, May 4, 2014, http://www.slate.com/articles/business/psychology_of_management/2014/05/open_plan_offices_the_new_trend_in_workplace_design.html.

20. H.A. Simon, "Rational Choice and the Structure of the Environment," *Psychological Review* 63, no. 2 (1955), doi:10.1037/h0042769.

21. Miriam J. Metzger, Andrew J. Flanagin, and Ryan B. Medders, "Social and Heuristic Approaches to Credibility Evaluation Online," *Journal of Communication* 60 (2010), doi: 10.1111/j.1460-2466.2010.01488.x; Judit Bar-Ilan, "Presentation Bias Is Significant in Determining User Preference for Search Results—A User Study," *Journal of the American Society for Information Science and Technology* 60 (2009): 135–49, doi: 10.1002/asi.20941; Lynn Silipigni Connaway, Timothy J. Dickey, and Marie L. Radford, "'If It Is too Inconvenient, I'm Not Going After It': Convenience as a Critical Factor in Information-Seeking Behaviors," *Library and Information Science Research* 33 (2011), doi:10.1016/j.lisr.2010.12.002.

22. Metzger et al., "Social and Heuristic Approaches."

23. A.J. Head and M.B. Eisenberg, "How College Students Seek Information in the Digital Age," Project Information Literacy Progress Report, Information School, University of Washington, 2009.

24. I am using the pseudonym "Dr. O." in this chapter to protect his privacy. He is a real person who, as far as I know, has not done anything illegal or unethical.

25. See, for example, Kevin Kruse, "Facebook Unveils New Campus: Will Workers Be Sick, Stressed, and Dissatisfied?" *Forbes*, August 25, 2012, http://www.forbes.com/sites/kevinkruse/2012/08/25/facebook-unveils-new-campus-will-workers-be-sick-stressed-and-dissatisfied/.

26. Terry Smyth, "Office Warfare," *Sydney Morning Herald*, April 30, 2009, http://www.smh.com.au/national/office-warfare-20090429-anfm.html.

27. Dr V—O—, "Why Your Office Could Be Making You Sick," *QUT News*. (Note: this is now a dead link, but the article existed and was viewed on July 15, 2014.)

28. See http://keywalker.afpbb.com/headline/search?q=%22Vinesh%20Oommen%22.

29. See http://dantri.com.vn/suc-khoe/ban-lam-viec-khong-vach-ngan-loi-bat-cap-hai-3032 15.htm.

30. Mattias Davidson, "Han Gör Tummen ner för Öppna Kontorslandskap," *Arbetar Skydd*, January 14, 2009, http://www.arbetarskydd.se/nyheter/halsa_ledarskap/halsa/article99507.ece.

31. See http://www.soundmask.com.au/pdf/intro_A4.pdf. See also Terry Smith, "Open-Plan Offices Sickening, Unproductive," *Brisbane Times*, April 30, 2009, http://www.brisbanetimes.com.au/national/openplan-offices-sickening-unproductive-20090430-anl0.html.

32. Kahneman, *Thinking, Fast and Slow*.

33. Reproduced under a license from Thomson Reuters. You may not copy or redistribute this material in whole or in part without the prior written consent of Thomson Reuters.

34. Pierre-Marc Daigneault. "The Blind Men and the Elephant: A Metaphor to Illuminate the Role of Researchers and Reviewers in Social Science," *Methodological Innovations Online* 8, no. 2, (2013), http://www.methodologicalinnovations.org.uk/wp-content/uploads/2013/12/Daigneault.pdf.

35. Howard Rheingold, "Crap Detection Mini-Course," video, February 20, 2013, http://rheingold.com/2013/crap-detection-mini-course/. See also "Evaluating Resources," http://guides.lib.berkeley.edu/evaluating-resources.

36. Marc Meola, "Chucking the Checklist: A Contextual Approach to Teaching Undergraduates Web-Site Evaluation," *Portal: Libraries and the Academy* 4, no. 3 (July 2004), doi: 10.1353/pla.2004.0055.

37. Alan Bailin and Ann Grafstein, "Evaluating Research: Beyond the Gold Standards," paper presented at the 13th Annual International Conference on Education, May 23–26, 2011, Athens, Greece. (Note: Bailin & Grafstein go beyond the gold standard, noting that we should also look at the financial interests of the researchers and sponsors, the dominant theoretical paradigms, and the potential political ideologies of the researchers and funders.)

38. For more on this, see Birger Hjorland, "Methods for Evaluating Information Sources: An Annotated Catalog," *Journal of Information Science*, April 18, 2012, doi: 10.1177/0165551512439178.

39. Scopus is a database that is similar to Web of Science. Large academic libraries typically purchase one or the other. In my examples I have used Web of Science.

40. Dr. V—O—, "Should Health Service Managers Embrace Open Plan Work Environment: A Review," *Journal of Health Management* 3, no. 2 (2008).

41. Google image search involves searching Google and then clicking on the word "image" that appears at the top of the screen right before the search results

42. Interactive Advertising Bureau, "Internet Ad Revenues Hit $31 Billion in 2011, Historic High up 22% over 2010 Record-Breaking Numbers," press release, April 18, 2012, http://www.iab.net/about_the_iab/recent_press_releases/press_release_archive/press_release/pr-041812.

43. Federal Trade Commission, "Spokeo to Pay $800,000 to Settle FTC Charges Company Allegedly Marketed Information to Employers and Recruiters in Violation of FCRA," press release, June 12, 2012, http://www.ftc.gov/news-events/press-releases/2012/06/spokeo-pay-800000-settle-ftc-charges-company-allegedly-marketed.

44. Federal Trade Commission, "Data Brokers: A Call for Transparency and Accountability," May 2014, http://www.ftc.gov/system/files/documents/reports/data-brokers-call-transparency-accountability-report-federal-trade-commission-may-2014/140527databrokerreport.pdf.

45. Mark Pettigrew and Helen Roberts, *Systematic Reviews in the Social Sciences: A Practical Guide* (Malden, MA: Blackwell, 2006).

46. Kahneman, *Thinking, Fast and Slow*.

47. Jane Devine and Francine Egger-Sider, *Going Beyond Google Again: Strategies for Using and Teaching the Invisible Web* (New York: Neal-Schuman, 2013).

48. Ibid.

49. This quote has been attributed to various scholars, including Isaac Newton.

50. Jacob Cohen, "Things I Have Learned (So Far)," *American Psychologist* 45 (December 1990).

51. Tim Lister and Tom DeMarco, "Programmer Performance and the Effects of the Workplace," in Proceedings of the 8th International Conference on Software Engineering, August 1985.

52. Matthew C. Davis, Desmond J. Leach, and Chris W. Clegg, "The Physical Environment of the Office: Contemporary and Emerging Issues," *International Review of Industrial and Organizational Psychology* 26 (2011).

53. Alex Bentley quoted in Rebeca Tuhus-Dubrow, "Group Think: The Turn to Online Research Is Narrowing the Range of Modern Scholarship, a New Study Suggests," *Boston Globe,* November 23, 2008.

54. Howard Gardner, "Reframing Truth, Beauty, and Goodness," *Education Week,* September 20, 2011, http://www.edweek.org/ew/articles/2011/09/21/04gardner_ep.h31.html?tkn=XMMFaK5jTQox%2FOEdDYf4lIWgs8fvbrX6l78B&print=1.

55. Kahneman, *Thinking, Fast and Slow.*

Chapter Four

Word of Mouse

Finding Reliable Travel Information Online

Quality, not just quantity, of information use should be considered when distinguishing between experts and novices.
— Rocio Garcia-Retamero and Dhami Mandeep (2009)

If you were a burglar, which of the following two properties would you break into?

Cue	Property A	Property B
Garden on the property	Tall hedges/bushes	Short hedges/bushes
Signs of care	Not well kept property	Not well kept property
Type	Apartment	House
Light on the property	On	On
Mailbox	Empty	Stuffed full of mail
Location	Corner of street	Middle of street
Access	Doors/windows on ground floor	Doors/Windows on second floor
Security on property	No alarm system	No alarm system

Choose a property to break into based on cues.[1]

If you guessed property A, you are correct. How did you decide? Would an expert be better at figuring out the likelihood that a particular house would be burgled? Who would that expert be?

Researchers have studied how people make decisions and whether experts make decisions differently and better than amateurs. In addition to studying burglars and police officers, researchers have studied economists, physicians, judges, chess players, and others.[2] Generally people use one of two types of strategies in making a decision such as the one above:

1. Novices tend to look at each "cue" in the list one by one, for example they might decide that tall hedges rather than short hedges would be more attractive to a burglar and give that cue a +1. Then they would add together the positive cues and choose the house with the most positive cues. This is called a "weighted additive linear model." Novices use this method because they do not have enough experience to choose the cues that are more salient and should be weighted more heavily.

2. Experts tend to focus on the cue that is the most important, if both properties are the same on that cue then they move to the second most important cue. As soon as they reach a cue that the two properties differ on, they have their choice. This is called "Take the Best." "Take the Best" is a heuristic—a strategy or shortcut—that usually results in a better and faster decision when the person weighing the cues has some degree of expertise.

But who is an expert in this case? Is it the police or the burglars? In a study involving 120 subjects, both burglars and police officers were found to use the expert strategy of "Take the Best," and the more experience they had the more they used this superior strategy. But these two groups differed in what cues they selected as most important and as a result differed in their prediction success. For burglars, an alarm system is pretty much a deal breaker, and they typically viewed that cue as the most important one. The police and novices, when asked to weight each cue in order of importance, tended to weight the "first floor access" as the most important. Because of this, police officer responses were no more successful than novices in choosing which residences were most likely to be burgled.[3]

So, are there different types of experts? Can some experts provide us with useful information from direct experience, and are some experts no better than novices in helping us make decisions? In the case of burglars, the researchers hypothesized that they were better at predicting which properties would be burgled because they had direct learning experience that gave them immediate feedback. This helped the burglars learn the best cues for selecting a property. Police officers learned indirectly through training and observation rather than getting immediate feedback about their observations.

For making good decisions, using heuristics such as weighted cues can help make better and quicker decisions, but only if you have some experience and feel you can weigh the different cues appropriately. If you do not have a lot of experience you may want to stick to the novice-favored linear additive model, and rely on an expert when the stakes are high. Underlining their key findings, the researchers point out that focusing on the quality of the information, not just the quantity, needs to be attended to when making a distinction between experts and novices.[4]

In the burglar study what was important was the quality of knowledge they had about alarms, just adding up cues was not going to cut it. I wish I had thought about all this more carefully when I started to plan my family vacation: *quality not just quantity.*

LEARNING FROM MEMPHREMAGOG

When searching for everyday-life information online, such as travel information, it is important to think about when an expert is needed and when using a crowd of amateurs might be better. What is a travel expert anyway? If someone has traveled a lot, does that make him or her an expert? Would an expert travel professional have some inside knowledge in the same way a burglar does? Or might they be more like police officers and differ little from the advice given by regular travelers? Maybe there are levels of travel information: for a weekend vacation a crowd of amateurs can help you select a hotel room, but if you are traveling to China maybe you need to consult an expert?

As I set off to search for travel information for a family vacation, I wondered if people traveling to the same area and rating hotels would provide me with reliable information. Would crowdsourced travel reviews resemble restaurant reviews or were they different? Would the challenge be which crowd, which travel website, to consult? Unfortunately, I have a spotty track record in planning vacations. Five years ago I planned a trip that turned into a nightmare: Family memories have been slow to fade. A friend had recommended going to Lake Memphremagog in Vermont; she had been there a decade ago. I had found a website advertising cottages and chose a cute one based on a handful of appealing images. It was long enough ago that this website did not have the user reviews or ratings that are now commonplace and can provide so much more information.

My research proved insufficient: the vacation was a disaster. The cottage was dark, dirty, and had thick sticky vinyl covers on the furniture. There were train tracks 500 yards away, and we woke several times during the night to the roaring and rattling as long freight trains barreled past our back door.

Worse still, the entire area had an unremitting eye-stinging smell of cow manure. After that experience my husband took over the reins for vacation planning for many years. It was a miracle I was being giving a turn again. I was determined not to blow it.

SIT OR SQUAT?

When our family goes on a trip we use our own unique bathroom rating system. It is an unspoken rule that whenever we stop for a meal, the first one to the bathroom reports back with a user rating on a scale of one to ten. Sometimes there is an abundance of highly granular information shared about décor, cleanliness, creativity, and color schemes; other times it is a somber concise report: "2" with a downward glance that indicates that waiting until our next stop for a bathroom break is advised.

Rating systems are a well-studied phenomenon, and there is widespread agreement that either a 5- or 7-point Likert scale provides the most reliable data. A scale like our family rating system of 1 to 10 is less helpful: it waters down the data with little understanding of the possible nuances between, for example, a "3" and a "4" or a "6" and a "7."

Many travel sites use a 5-star system, as do review sites for books, movies, and restaurants. They are simple and force people to choose only one of five numbers. For our family, the 10-point scale works fine. We know that when my teenage daughter gives a bathroom a "7" that it is high praise and probably the equivalent to a "9" rank by me. I'm known as an easy reviewer. With just the four of us it is simple to parse out what our ratings mean.

While my daughter and I have a very low inter-rater reliability score, for larger crowdsourced systems the higher the inter-rater reliability score, the more reliable the data. In medicine the Wong-Baker FACES scale is used to monitor pediatric patient pain. It has high inter-rater reliability. Dozens of studies have confirmed that it is an accurate measure of how much pain a patient is experiencing so that decisions can be made about treatment. The faces and text communicate just enough information so that each child can select the face that matches their level of pain.

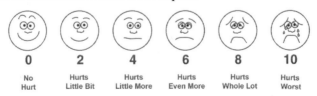

0	2	4	6	8	10
No Hurt	Hurts Little Bit	Hurts Little More	Hurts Even More	Hurts Whole Lot	Hurts Worst

©1983 Wong-Baker FACES® Foundation. Visit us at www.wongbakerFACES.org.
Used with permission. Originally published in Whaley & Wong's Nursing Care of Infants and Children. ©Elsevier Inc.

Wong-Baker Faces Pain Rating Scale. ©1983 Wong-Baker FACES® Foundation. [5]

Five-star rating systems on the Web vary widely in the degree to which they have inter-rater reliability, because what stars mean is often ambiguous and varies from site to site.[6] Three stars on Amazon are defined as just "good," whereas three stars on Yelp means "A-OK." Some sites make their ranking definitions easy to find, on other sites they are buried. Reviewers do not tend to read these definitions, and some reviewers tend to be overly kind or harsh. An email I received from an independent seller on Amazon asked me to review my purchase:

> *Please keep in mind that 4–5 are positive and 1–3 are negative feedbacks. If you feel the experience is negative PLEASE first respond to this email so we may resolve the problem ASAP.*[7]

One of the most reliable types of rating scales is called a nominal scale. These scales merely ask for a yes/no or good/bad response. To find clean bathrooms when traveling, the phone App SitOrSquat provides a nominal scale. Bathrooms that are good enough to sit down in are labeled green and bathrooms that you may want to avoid are labeled red. The ratings are averaged to provide travelers with information about the nearest clean public bathroom. It works like a charm. If only the rest of the travel information universe was broken down into a nominal scale, decision making would be so much easier.

DATA BLOAT AND WISE CROWDS

The wisdom-of-the-crowds is a well-studied phenomenon that demonstrates that aggregating the answers to a specific question from a large crowd of individuals often provides as good and in some cases a superior answer to the answer given by any one individual in the group.[8] The effect is dependent on answers being provided independently of knowing the answer given by any other individual, because the effect is easily undermined by social influence. Also, aggregated answers work best when they are responses to questions that have correct answers such as quantity estimates or factual knowledge.[9]

In Science, the "Wisdom of the Crowd" effect, referred to as Crowd Science, has been put to use in solving the problem of data bloat. Crowds of novices are successfully classifying hundreds of thousands of online images of galaxies, and providing data for cancer research; oceanography; gene mapping; and butterfly, bird, and bee counts. I knew that crowdsourced hotel review sites were different from the crowdsourced science projects: reviewers were likely to be influenced by seeing the ratings of other reviewers first,[10] and positive data skew is typical for these types of sites.[11] Selection bias was also likely, meaning amateur reviewers tend to *choose* hotels that they expect to like, and then not surprisingly, they rate them positively.[12]

While research on Amazon.com product reviews found that they tend to be overly positive, [13] I wondered if hotel reviews might focus on more objective issues such as whether the hotel was next to a noisy highway. I was hoping that these factual pieces of information would provide useful data even though the aggregated star ratings would not succeed in harnessing the true and unbiased "wisdom of the crowd" effect overall.

Writer Tom Slee points out that there are significant differences between review systems, and those differences impact the trustworthiness of particular sites. [14] On Netflix, users rate movies they have viewed and have a strong incentive to rate them accurately because Netflix takes their data and provides recommendations about what movies they may want to watch in the future. There is also *not* a commercial incentive for rating any movie high or low. Slee asserts that we can take Netflix ratings as a reasonable distribution of unbiased user ratings, such as the typical aggregation of Netflix user ratings below:

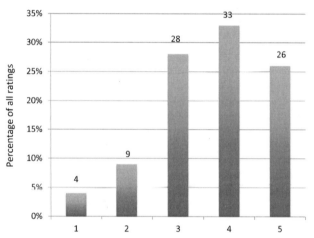

Typical aggregated Netflix movie-user ratings. [15]

While slanting to the positive—not surprising that users would tend to more often like a movie they chose to watch—there is still a significant number of low ratings. Slee compares this set of data to the data for BlaBla-Car, a European car-sharing company. There are more than one million registered users on BlaBlaCar, and their website provides user reviews of drivers and riders so that potential participants can check each other out before deciding to share a ride. Below is the distribution of ratings from 190,000 reviews on the BlaBlaCar site:

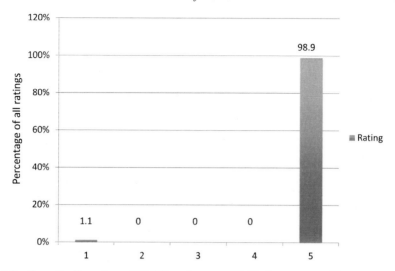

Distribution of ratings from 190,000 reviews on BlaBlaCar website. [16]

Clearly no useful information is to be found with more than 98 percent of the reviews positive. BlaBlaCar suffers from what many reputation review sites have to cope with: fear of retaliation. If I ride in your car and have a bad experience I may choose not to ride with you again, but if I give you a bad review you may retaliate by giving me a bad review as a passenger. On BlaBlaCar you can see who everyone is and see what they are saying about you. Often there is a tacit understanding that regardless of the experience people will give each other high marks so that they each can continue to participate in the service.

Would hotel review sites and travel information more closely resemble Netflix or BlaBlaCar? Or were they a different animal altogether? I knew many people who loved and relied on large review sites such as TripAdvisor, VRBO, and Airbnb, and I was hopeful sites like these would do the trick for me.

THE LANDSCAPE OF TRAVEL INFORMATION

The travel business has always depended heavily on Word of Mouth for generating a significant portion of its business and now Electronic Word of Mouth, also called "Word of Mouse," is a tool used by industry experts focusing on effective ways to commercialize consumer social media communications. Marketing research demonstrates that viral marketing—consisting of unpaid peer-to-peer communication through reviews, Facebook posts, Twitter feeds, and other tools—are invaluable for generating business. [17] Many Word of Mouth campaigns, online or off, are disguised as market research, providing free samples or discounts, participating in contests, or soliciting feedback and reviews. Some marketing campaigns are tied directly into user-review sites.

Word of Mouse dovetails with the idea discussed by many travel writers: that in looking for travel information it makes sense to find your "tribe," those who like the kinds of travel experiences you might like.[18] If your idea of fun is the *Queen Elizabeth II* you might want to check out CruiseReviews.com, if you want to backpack through Asia then Hostel.com is a good bet. More and more, participants in social media are congregating to their "lens of choice."[19] You don't want opinions from *everyone,* you want opinions from people who share your travel tastes.

Trouble was, I wasn't quite clear who "my people" were for this vacation. I had two teenage children (one who would prefer a five-star hotel, the other who would like to couchsurf in Cambodia), a husband who was more inclined toward traditional guidebooks and carefully vetted hotels, and me, the information addict, who wanted to corroborate each piece of information to plan the perfect vacation.

Poking around in the scholarly research that has been done on travel, I organize hotel information into four buckets:

1. Formal user-generated review sites: both massive and small.
2. More informal sharing-economy collaborative sites.
3. Traditional travel guidebooks with companion online sites.
4. Travel writers of all types from online newspapers, blogs, YouTube, and elsewhere.

I decide to sample from each type. Because there are so many choices in each category, I start with a brief detour to Alexa.com to determine the popularity of certain sites and which tribes are using them. Alexa.com provides demographics as well as the "bounce" rate: the percentage of people who view the home page and then leave (bounce) without viewing any more of the site. It also reports how many pages are viewed for the people who stay, and how many minutes the average user spends on the site.

For example, TripAdvisor has a global rank of a whopping 205, meaning it is number 205 of *all* the millions of sites people view on the Web. (For comparison, Google ranks number one, Facebook number two, and top pornography sites rank below 100.) On TripAdvisor, 41 percent of visitors bounce out after looking at the first page and spend an average of four minutes on the site. By contrast, GoatsOnTheRoad.com, a backpacking website, has a global rank of about 83,000, but its bounce rate is much lower at 25 percent, and the average time on site is thirteen minutes. Users of TripAdvisor spread out evenly across all educational levels, whereas everyone on Goats has at least some college and the majority of users have completed graduate school.

Alexa.com Data	TripAdvisor	Goats
Rank	205	83,000
Bounce Rate	41%	25%
Average Time on Site	4 minutes	13 minutes
Male/Female	High percentage female	Extremely high percentage female
Education Level	Evenly spread percentage from high school/college/graduate school	High percentage college, very high percentage graduate school

Alexa.com data on TripAdvisor and Goats on the Road.

Clearly different tribes were using TripAdvisor and Goats. I decided to start by going big.

ADVICE FROM 20 MILLION FELLOW TRAVELERS

I had wanted to go to Nova Scotia for years, but knew little about it. My parents had spent their honeymoon there in 1953 and spoke about its beauty, but also joked about their experience booking a cabin that turned out to be a shabby fishing camp with no plumbing or electricity. When they arrived late at night after their wedding, the owner handed them a flashlight and pointed to the outhouse that was down a trail through the woods that bordered the fishing camp. She also warned them of recent bear sightings and recommended making a lot of noise if they had to use the outhouse during the night. My parents' travel planning had consisted of a letter to the Chamber of Commerce in Nova Scotia and then selecting the cabin from a list of places with one-sentence descriptions in a travel brochure. What a different travel-planning process it would be for me! I could use Google, find a good crowd-sourced travel site, and rely on the advice of hundreds of travelers giving me information about their experiences. I popped on Google to see what it would choose as the best place to start my travel planning:

Google: *Nova Scotia Hotels*

Not surprisingly, Google indicates that *Google* is the top choice directly following the sponsored links that are labeled "Ads." In fact, the first search results for almost any place name combined with the word *hotel* brings up sponsored ads followed by the Google three-pack. The three hotels listed in the pack link to Google Reviews and booking information that in turn provides revenue to Google. Google recently purchased both Zagat and Frommer's and has fed review data from these and other entities into their collection to bulk up their reviews. [20] But I notice that the number of Google reviews dwarf in comparison to its rival TripAdvisor, which comes in at second or third place in many searches for hotel information.

TripAdvisor has several large competitors including Expedia, which disappeared from top search results on Google in 2014. Expedia lost 25 percent of its visibility on Google followed by a plunge in its stock price. Industry specialists speculate that Expedia was the victim of a negative search engine optimization (SEO) attack. [21] In a negative SEO attack a competitor builds up fake web pages with links pointing to, in this case Expedia, so that Google thinks Expedia is trying to game the system. As a result Google buries Expedia search results, decimating their business. Clever. The important takeaway for the searcher is if you depend on the first few hits of a Google search for information, what you are seeing is sites with the most sophisticated marketing strategies, but not necessarily those with the most reliable and high-quality information.

TripAdvisor is a dominant player, and because most people rely on the first few links in a Google search, its popularity continues to climb. TripAdvisor has more than 45 million reviews of more than 500,000 destinations. [22] Between 2010 and 2013, traffic on TripAdvisor increased from 20 million to 60 million monthly visitors with registered members rising from 15 million to 20 million. [23] They have also successfully distributed a software program to hotels that sends a "feedback survey" to guests with results automatically populating the TripAdvisor site.

TripAdvisor makes money by displaying prices from online travel agents alongside reviews and then charging agents for customer click throughs. This is called a "network effect." The more users post reviews, the more useful the site becomes to travelers, the more hotels and travel agents can make money and offer incentives, and that in turn increases traffic. In 2013 TripAdvisor had revenues of almost $950 million. [24]

Online review sites such as Amazon and TripAdvisor have transformed the way we purchase goods and services. They are wildly popular because we feel like we are getting the inside scoop from hundreds of people who have sampled the product, rather than having to rely on advertisers or journalists. Despite my suspicions about the trustworthiness of sites like TripAdvisor, I decide I will join the 20 million other members to determine whether they warrant their lofty reputation. I search the site for:

Search: *Nova Scotia hotels*

TripAdvisor is impressive. If nothing else, it is a niche search engine to almost all the hotels and other travel and lodging information in many parts of the world. Why get on Google when you can go directly to TripAdvisor?

Of the 192 hotels in Nova Scotia, the Antigonish Evergreen Inn comes up as the "Number 1 place to stay." It looks fantastic and everyone online is raving that it is "excellent" and "life changing."

Eighty-three images are posted on TripAdvisor for the inn, half from the inn and half from reviewers. Having photos is crucial to encouraging potential customers. Research shows that if you make a factual claim (e.g., "Large Rooms") and present it alongside a related photo, even if the photo does not actually establish proof of the claim people are more likely to believe it. Without photos, the same text is not nearly as persuasive. [25]

Photo manipulation is increasingly common, but is getting harder to spot with the naked eye. Dr. Hany Farid is a digital forensics expert at Dartmouth University who studies photo manipulation and provides a tool called "izit-tru.com." Upload a photograph onto this tool and it can determine if it has been altered. [26] Still in its infancy, the study of digital forensics is advancing and more automated procedures are being developed for running images through verification filters. At Oyster.com, now owned by TripAdvisor, they collect manipulated images from travel review sites and run them next to images that their professional review staff has taken showing what a particular hotel really looks like. It's eye-opening. [27]

Daniel Kahneman, in his book *Thinking Fast and Slow*, talks about the problem of thinking too quickly and assuming that "What You See Is All There Is." Fast thinking uses information at hand without asking whether other critical information might be missing. Trying my best to engage in slow thinking, I glance at the 409 reviews of the inn and they break down like this:

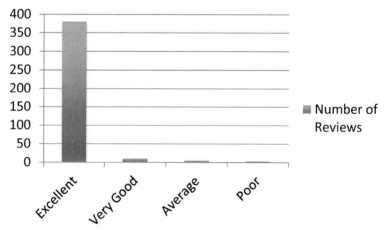

409 reviews of Antigonish Evergreen Inn on TripAdvisor.

Seems to resemble BlaBlaCar! Did *no one* have a bad experience at the Antigonish Evergreen Inn? I start looking over some of the other hotels in Nova Scotia and almost all have overwhelmingly positive reviews.

On TripAdvisor you can email members that have provided reviews, so I choose sixteen reviewers of the Evergreen Inn. I especially go after the more suspicious ones that have only written one review, for just this hotel, and I go after the prolific reviewers to gain their expertise. Of the sixteen I query, only three reviewers answer. Each of the three indicate that their reviews were completely fair and not coerced, but the third reviewer ends with:

> *I've been doing this out of my own interest. However, I've found some of my negative reviews deleted from TripAdvisor many times. I've complained to them. but haven't heard back.*

Perhaps this explains why the inn has no negative reviews? I wonder how long TripAdvisor can engage in this practice without some backlash, and perhaps the backlash is already happening, but being deleted? Cyndy K., a "Senior Contributor" on TripAdvisor did not have her negative review deleted, even though she was pretty angry at the reviewers who had posted positive reviews for a place that turned out to be a disaster:

> *I did extensive research for a hotel in San Francisco . . . much of that was based on tripadvisor reviews of hotels . . . and yeah, yeah, yeah . . . What did I expect for $100.00 in Union Square . . . you know what I expected? . . . I expected tripadvisor contributors to be honest and not lead me astray . . . how could anyone give this hotel an excellent, above average or even average rating . . . Who are you people?* [28]

Despite some blemishes I am, reluctantly, swayed by TripAdvisor. Research shows that consumers value and trust advice from other consumers much more than advice from travel "experts."[29] People are generally positive about online reviews: almost 80 percent of customers now trust online reviews as much as they trust a personal recommendation from a friend.[30] Given that it was a friend who had steered me to the fated Memphremagog trip, I was inclined to agree. Several hundred strangers rating something as positive seemed more powerful than one friend who had a good experience a decade ago.

Not surprisingly, researchers have also found a strong link between how credible a source is viewed and later purchases based on those sources.[31] For travel information specifically, research demonstrates that the more perceived credibility an online review site has the more likely a hotel room will be booked.[32] As long as a site like TripAdvisor can convince its users that their reviews are trustworthy, they can maintain their lucrative business. Unfortunately, both scholarship and news reports are starting to bubble up questioning the reliability of TripAdvisor reviews. Howard Orlarsch, writing to "The Ethicist" advice columnist in the *New York Times Magazine* in 2014, explains:

I recently spent several days at a relatively expensive hotel. The place was deplorable and unsanitary, with an unresponsive front desk. I gave it a poor write-up on TripAdvisor.com, the travel website, titling my review "An Over-priced Dung Heap." [33]

Howard goes on to explain that the very next day the owner of the hotel contacted him and offered to refund almost half the cost of his stay if he would retract the review. He says he accepted the offer and deleted his post. He asks "The Ethicist": who was the most unethical? Howard (for accepting the bribe), the owner (for offering the bribe), or TripAdvisor (which enables these untrustworthy reviews).

The advice columnist tells Howard that he *and* the hotel are unethical, but that TripAdvisor is in the clear because they state on their site that people should not engage in deceptive practices. In Europe they are taking a more aggressive approach to review fraud. When a group of hotels alleged that there were more than 27,000 legally defamatory reviews on TripAdvisor, the UK Advertising Standards Authority ordered TripAdvisor to delete all references on their site to the words "honest" or "trustworthy," including the phrase "reviews you can trust." [34] The Federal Trade Commission (FTC) is getting into the act of regulating user review sites, though they have been slow to target hotel review sites. In the past few years they have gone after several companies that hired people or used their employees to post positive reviews for products and services. [35]

TripAdvisor did get into hot water for the five-star reviews and a "Top 100" rating given to a homeless shelter in Glasgow, when some adventurous hackers gamed their system. The Bellgrove Hotel was inundated with 5-star reviews describing its outstanding service, spa, and pool facilities even though it is actually a shelter housing 150 homeless men.

Hotel did look a bit shabby on the outside however appearances can de deceitful. Luxurious rooms, spa and leisure facilities a real gem. [36]

The manager of the shelter contacted TripAdvisor asking them to take down the fake reviews.

A separate stream of research has investigated whether there are ways to separate fake from real reviews. Some of the work was commissioned after finding out that there were hotels in many countries that were bribing guests to write positive reviews on TripAdvisor and other sites in exchange for room discounts or money. [37] A small industry has sprung up advertising "astroturfers," who will write fake hotel, restaurant, and product reviews for a fee. [38]

Many people feel confident that they can spot fake reviews. Researchers at Cornell University asked freelance writers to produce 400 fake reviews of Chicago hotels and post them to a review site. They mixed the fake reviews with real ones and asked "judges" to try to tell apart the reviews. They were unable to do so.[39] In writing about decision making and judgment, Thaler and Sunstein discuss the "above average" effect that occurs because people tend to be unrealistically optimistic about their own abilities even when they know what their odds are statistically. For example, most people greatly overestimate their own driving abilities or the chances their own start-up will succeed, even when they have a realistic understanding of the actual odds.[40] Recently Cornell developed software to spot fake reviews 90 percent of the time, but this fix may be short-lived as writers get more adroit at writing fake reviews once they figure out what types of phrases the software is flagging.[41]

One extensive study was able to compare TripAdvisor (where anyone can write a review) with Expedia (where reviewers must prove they have stayed at a hotel to write a review). They were able to demonstrate that those hotels with close competitors nearby were much more likely to engage in both negative and positive fake reviews on TripAdvisor, where it is easier to post fake reviews, than on Expedia. Similar studies have been done at MIT that document that at least 5 percent of product reviews were likely faked and tended to be extremely negative. The researchers also showed how this relatively small number of negative reviews had a snowball effect and influenced subsequent reviewers, thereby plunging the aggregated star ratings and sales for these products.[42] Other researchers estimate that between 10 and 30 percent of online reviews are fake.[43]

In addition to fake reviews, there is also the problem that people writing reviews are an unrepresentative and small sample of the population as a whole. Duncan Simester at MIT says:

> *We worry that to the extent that customers are using these reviews, they're not making good decisions.*[44]

While it can feel like everybody is writing reviews, research has shown that only a small percentage of people provide reviews.[45] But other research indicates participation rates are climbing, though they remain a significant minority of the total number of people using a review site.[46] There is also evidence that these sites make careful editorial decisions about how to display comments and that they bury or delete negative comments. It is important to remember that the real customer of TripAdvisor is *not* the tourist seeking information, it is the booking agencies and hotels that are paying the bills.

I was wary given all that I knew about TripAdvisor and similar sites, but I was still drawn to using it to find a hotel in Nova Scotia. Travel writers and researchers indicate that despite all its problems, TripAdvisor and other sites like it are still valuable, it you use the following strategies to evaluate the reviews:

1. Read the reviews, don't rely on the aggregated star ratings. Research by Susan Mudambi found that there is a 41 percent misalignment between star ratings and the reviews, and it is especially high with the five-star reviews. The problem is that a simple star rating system cannot capture all the nuances involved in a review. For low-starred reviews the alignment is much higher, people rate the item low and then list negative experiences. But for hotels with five stars it is important to read through the reviews to get an accurate picture, and also keep in mind that some percentage of them are fake. [47]

2. Check the number of reviews. Researchers found that people were more apt to focus on the rank of a hotel, such as one that came in first or second, but did not attend to the number of total reviews. It is safer to choose a hotel ranked several places down but has many reviews. The more reviews about a hotel the less effective astroturfers will be. [48]

3. Look for trends. Try to spot information that appears multiple times, both positive and negative. Also, look for specific information such as someone mentioning that the sheets were not clean or the beds were uncomfortable. Specificity combined with items mentioned by a number of people can give reviews more credibility.

4. Ignore the extremists. Extremists are more likely to either be fake reviews or people who tend to get overly passionate and might exaggerate. Stick to the reviews that are a mix of positive and negative information.

5. Check the date of the review. If the review is more than a year or two old, things might have changed. TripAdvisor tends to have many recent reviews, as of this writing Google reviews has far fewer and many are dated.

6. Check the track record of the reviewer. Some review sites such as TripAdvisor allow you to see other reviews by that reviewer and to email them. Also, some reviewers tend to rate everything negatively so by looking at a few of their other reviews you can determine if you should take their reviews with a grain of salt.

7. See if the reviewer has similar tastes to yours. This is largely a gut reaction, but also varies site to site. If you are under forty-five years old, TripAdvisor may not be for you. The majority of TripAdvisor readers are between forty-five and seventy-five; this may not be your travel tribe. [49]

8. Compare and Corroborate! Check more than one review site or corroborate with another source of travel information.

For the Antigonish Evergreen Inn, I put it through all its paces: read reviews, checked number of reviews, and so on. I even corroborated the information with Expedia.com. Everything checked out, but it turned out I was wrong to choose it. I still had much to learn about travel planning.

COUCH VS. AIR MATTRESS?

Feeling I was limiting my world by hanging with a tribe of elders at TripAdvisor, I decided to jump in at the other end of the tribal spectrum. The sharing economy has generated some exciting and creative new ways of using technology to effectively facilitate the exchange of goods and services. I was thinking Couchsurfer.com and Airbnb.com would be similar types of sites catering to a younger, trendier, and more budget-conscious crowd. It turned out that the two sites could not have been more different. While both purported to be part of the sharing economy—peer-to-peer sharing—they were both struggling in different ways and experiencing troubling growing pains.

Couchsurfing.com has 7 million registered users living in 97,000 cities across 207 countries, though it still maintains some of its original informal warm and fuzzy community feel.[50] Founded in 1999 as a nonprofit, the site facilitates sharing by offering travelers a free place to stay, often a couch or spare bedroom. Hosts are expected to "share their life, their world, their journey." Hosts and guests write reviews about each other to promote safety and copacetic matching, and the site charges $25 to verify names and addresses.

After my experiences with BlaBlaCar and TripAdvisor, I was not shocked to learn that user reviews were overwhelmingly positive on Couchsurfing.com, but unlike many other review sites there have been few fake postings because there is no financial incentive to do so. While there have been a handful of concerning criminal activities connected to the site, with a community of this size these do not seem to be above the norm. Research on Couchsurfing.com has shown that the site has invoked a high degree of reciprocity with between 12 and 18 percent of Couchsurfing stays directly reciprocated. Often couchsurfers have formed long-term friendships.[51]

While many members assumed Couchsurfing.com was solely volunteer run and owned, the actual founders and owners accepted 7.6 million in venture funding and transformed from a .org to a .com in 2010, later accepting additional venture capital.[52] The culture and membership of the site began to shift, and when members complained about the changes their comments were deleted from the site's forum. The complaints then went viral and Couchsurfing.com is now experiencing a rapid decline with 40 percent of the staff laid off, the CEO stepping down, and the business model switching over to focus on mobile.[53]

Some former members say that the profit motive changed the culture of a site that was one of the best examples of the new sharing economy, others complain that men in search of dates now dominate the site and that it is morphing into a hookup site.[54] As one user lamented:

> *giving and sharing is just much more appropriate when it's organized by a non-profit. I feel awkward [now] hosting people through CouchSurfing, knowing that that's creating value for shareholders who will want to see some return on their investment.*[55]

David Bollier, a consultant and professor who works to promote "the commons" online, agrees:

> *When the new corporate owners and investors came on board, all of the accumulated social equity and goodwill created by Couchsurfers was essentially monetized. A great opportunity to create a new organizational form on a vast scale was lost.*[56]

People with years of experience in the sharing economy are saddened as one by one the more successful of these community models are taken over by corporate models. Sue Gardner, former executive director of the WikiMedia Foundation, says that the new Web is now hostile to self-organized collaborative efforts. She likens it to a city that has lost its public parks. "Our time is spent on an increasingly small number of increasingly large corporate sites," she says. "We need more public space online."[57]

While I was wary of the tectonic change occurring on Couchsurfer, I decided to become a member to see what the possibilities were for Nova Scotia. It didn't seem likely that my entire family would end up on someone's couch, but I was curious to see what turned up.

Well, Wayne B. is what turned up as my first suggested host in Nova Scotia! He had been verified and authenticated and had glowing reviews from dozens of guests. There was a friendly image of Wayne B., a balding man well north of the fifty-year mark, holding a lobster. Reading his profile I come to the following:

> *OKAY I HAVE EXPERIMENTED OVER THE LAST FEW YEARS ABOUT LIVING MY NUDIST LIFE AND ALSO TAKING IN COUCHSURFERS. . . . IT SEEMS I STILL GET LARGE AMOUNTS OF REQUEST EVEN THO I AM A NUDIST, SO STARTING IN 2014 . I WILL ONLY ECEPT PEOPLE WHO DO NOT MIND STAYING OR BEING AROUND A NUDIST.*[58]

Ok, Wayne was certainly friendly, but maybe not family friendly. I think I had wandered a little too far from my travel tribe.

As Couchsurfing.com started bleeding members, Airbnb was ramping up. Founded by three young men in 2007 when they started renting out air mattresses in their living room to help pay rent, the site now has over 800,000 listings in 33,000 cities and 192 countries.[59] While focusing originally on young people in need of an inexpensive place to stay, the site now advertises millions of vacation properties and the company is currently valued at $13 billion.[60]

Airbnb is a beautifully designed site with an equally well-designed business model. They add a 6 to 12 percent booking fee for the customer and a 3 percent charge to hosts, but they provide protection from scammers by not releasing the guest's money to the host until after the guest has arrived. Following a recent trend in online booking and review sites, Airbnb is also now linked to Facebook accounts so that customers can get recommendations from "real" friends and acquaintances and see if they have friends in common with their hosts.

While Airbnb evokes the feel of a sharing community, it is what researchers have labeled: "pseudo-sharing," defined as "commodity exchanges wrapped in a vocabulary of sharing." Professor Russell Belk calls sites like Airbnb "a wolf in sheep's clothing phenomenon whereby commodity exchange and potential exploitation of consumer cocreators present themselves in the guise of sharing."[61]

Airbnb is a site that is now predominantly involved in renting out entire apartments or providing listings for B&Bs.[62] When I hop on and look up Nova Scotia my results echo the current research: my 699 entries break down into 443 entire house rentals, 248 private rooms in B&Bs and houses, and 8 shared rooms. Only five of the 669 places available are under $100, not including the Airbnb fee.

Not surprisingly, the star ratings and reviews on Airbnb are again, you guessed it, abundantly positive. James Fallows, writing for the *Atlantic,* decided to spot-check VRBO, a similar site, when a reader told him that all the listings were five-star reviews with a few four-star reviews thrown in for plausibility. Fallows checked a random sample of listings and found similar results. He said:

> *I realize that I was naive even to have thought that "listing" sites would run critical reviews.*[63]

I look through the first thirty places listed for Nova Scotia on Airbnb and find similar results. Ratings are meaningless if they are all the same. To its credit, Airbnb will not let anyone post a review unless they have stayed at the listing to avoid the fake review activity that goes on at sites like TripAdvisor. Unfortunately, there is a downside to this as some people report booking a rental only to show up and find that it has been rented to someone else and they are unable to complain about it.[64]

While Airbnb, VRBO, HomeAway, FlipKey, and other travel review sites foster a sharing-economy culture and encourage people to contribute reviews, at the same time they have not lost sight of their paying customer. The property owner who lists a place is their customer, not the guest who reviews and thus helps advertise properties. While I did not seek proof that Airbnb deletes negative reviews like TripAdvisor does, it seems likely.

In late 2014 Airbnb was dealt a serious blow to its business model when the New York Attorney General's office found that nearly three-quarters of Airbnb rentals in New York City were illegal. The Attorney General's report states that commercial operators, not residents renting out rooms, supply more than a third of the revenue and a third of the units on Airbnb, and that some landlords are running what are essentially illegal hostels. The report issued by the Attorney General, *Airbnb in the City*, paints a picture of a company that has strayed far from its sharing-economy roots.[65]

Echoing New York's findings, the *San Francisco Chronicle* conducted an analysis of Airbnb, finding two-thirds of listings involved entire houses or apartments, not couches.[66] Senator Dianne Feinstein spoke out against sites like Airbnb, voicing concern that speculators will buy up houses in the city to rent them out for daily rates that avoid tax laws and hotel regulations. Other cities, states, condominium associations, and regulatory bodies are beginning to institute fines, taxes, fees, and adherence to regulations for sharing-economy sites that are taking a massive chunk of money away from more traditional hotel and B&B businesses.[67]

Despite its flaws, Airbnb is working hard to play by the rules by beefing up security, flagging sites that use words like "wire transfer" to crack down on scams, and sending takedown notices to huge landlords like "NY Furnished Rentals" that was advertising eighty separate furnished sites. The site has a lot at stake in maintaining its sharing-economy image of people helping each other out. But as Emily Badger writes for the *Washington Post*: "are you really 'sharing' something if you are charging money for it?"[68]

While Airbnb and Couchsurfer.com were the giants of the sharing-economy model, many smaller sharing-economy sites are humming along quietly and staying true to their roots. The big differences are that these more congenial sites tend to be small and cater to specific populations. For example, www.warmshowers.org—notice the ".org"—is a true volunteer-run sharing-economy site with 50,000 members and 32,000 hosts. They have worked out a system for connecting hosts and bikers, with hosts simply providing a warm shower, a couch, or even a place in their yard to camp. Sometimes they provide much more, such as breakfast and touring advice. Reviews on the site are "really just thank-you letters," but they encourage people to post a heads-up if a host or guest was inappropriate.[69] One key to success might be if they maintain their nonprofit status and do not get too big. One larger site, WikiVoyage.org, an exception to the rule of smaller is better, also seems to have managed to avoid the corporate onramp that could have destroyed their sharing-economy model.

Getting back to Airbnb, despite its many flaws it still has value for travelers, but maybe in the long run it is not so healthy for New York, San Francisco, and maybe Nova Scotia. While it is suffering from growing pains, a meaningless rating system, and the likelihood that negative reviews were being quashed, I think that places with more than a dozen reviews and photographs provide some meaningful though limited information. Nonetheless, I wondered if there was a better tribal match out there for me.

PARACHUTE ARTISTS

So, I haven't left my house and I am already experiencing travel fatigue. There are an overwhelming number of travel sites online and I'm just looking for a place to stay and haven't touched on sightseeing activities and restaurants in Nova Scotia. I decide to switch gears and resort to old media: travel guidebooks with their newer online counterparts.

While free travel websites and user-generated reviews seem to have some clear advantages because they are constantly updated, contain vast amounts of information, and are free, using a selective expertly curated guide is enticing. I am hoping that travel writers will be like experienced burglars: able to quickly and accurately select the most important cues. Sometimes called "parachute artists," experienced travel writers are said to have the ability to drop into a place and quickly assimilate and zero in on the best choices and experiences.[70]

I pop on to my public library website and log in to this year's edition of *Lonely Planet Nova Scotia* to investigate. The world of guidebook writing is small: there are only a handful of major publishers. Sales of printed guides had been in decline, though sales in 2013 have now stabilized and seen a slight upward bump. This appears to be due to a shakeout in the industry combined with a few of these old media dogs ramping up their new media tricks.[71] Despite all of the free user-review sites and piles of travel advice and information online, travel guidebooks, in print or ebook format, remain popular.[72]

Most guidebooks have origin stories involving homegrown labors of love such as Arthur Frommer's self-published *The GI's Guide to Traveling in Europe* in 1955 or Tony and Maureen Wheeler, who "with a beat-up old car, a few dollars in the pocket and a sense of adventure," started Lonely Planet in 1972. Just as Eugene Fodor, in 1936, provided an antidote to the dull collections of facts in previous guidebooks by publishing *On the Continent: The Entertaining Travel Annual*, Tony and Maureen Wheeler provided a creative alternative to the more staid guides started in the 1950s. Where Fodor's and Frommer's focused on historical sites and museums, Lonely Planet focused on the needs of backpackers and provided an informal tone. In their early editions they gave quirky advice customized for their readers such as where to score pot and advice on wearing a short-hair wig when going through customs.[73] After stapling together their first guidebook at the kitchen table in 1973, Lonely Planet's *Across Asia on the Cheap* immediately sold out.[74]

While many guidebooks start out as labors of love, the business side eventually takes over and the unique quirky authorial voice of early editions often transforms into a more uniform encyclopedic collection of facts and recommendations. As travel writer Jason Cochran laments:

> *Gradually, carefully pruned and opinionated advice was replaced by bland subject-verb descriptors more akin to a reference book's. Guides became almanacs that risked only timid, ginger hints at supplying context amidst the profusion of information. Hoping to be all things to all readers—a committee marketing decision, not an editorial or ethical one—they present every detail of a place on a heaping plate rather than suggesting to the reader which bite to take.*[75]

Dr. Ana Alacovska, who studies intercultural communication, has noted the shift in style, tone, and creativity in travel guide writing as the author role transitioned from being at the heart of a guidebook to that of a contract writer. Needing to cut costs, publishers discovered there was always a pool of new talent willing to step in and work for little pay.[76] Todd Friend, a staff writer for the *New Yorker,* bemoans the loss of the old quirky Lonely Planet guidebooks that had a unique authorial tone:

> *I learned to stuff my gear into one knapsack; never to ask a local where I should eat but, rather, where he ate; never to judge a country by its capital city; never to stay near a mosque (the muezzin wakes you); how to haggle; and, crucially, when I later went to Mongolia, to shout "Nokhoi khor!"— "Hold the dog!"—before entering a yurt. When you spend months with a guidebook that speaks to you in an intimate, conversational tone, it becomes a bosom companion.*

Alacovska writes that "parachute artists" were turned into an interchangeable corporate voice, and writers were pushed to be generalists hired to update facts, rather than allowing repeat writers to accumulate expertise and develop unique voices.[77] Today the books cater to wealthier travelers and the original "shoestring" series created by Lonely Planet for backpackers makes up only 3 percent of sales.[78] As these cottage-industry guidebooks morphed into major corporations many were then swallowed up in the last two decades by enormous media conglomerates such as Random House and Penguin/Pearson.

While guidebook writers were less experienced than I had hoped and often a little bland, spending months traveling still suggests a depth of experience far greater than the average TripAdvisor customer review of a one-night stay. There was also real appeal to using a source for which I could find no evidence of shady reviews, biased choices, or deletions. Guidebook writers adhere to careful standards when making recommendations because, unlike TripAdvisor and Airbnb, *I* am the customer, not the hotel industry. They are also more concise, no more slogging through bottomless websites. In an hour I could skim a book and plan an entire trip.

I ended up skimming through several additional guidebooks, looking through the curated content that included: a brief history, local culture, major sites and activities, an overview of important regions, best transportation options, and best places to stay and to eat arranged by town. They also include a survival guide with encyclopedic information about everything from electricity to discount cards and public holidays.

I check to see if the Antigonish Evergreen Inn is mentioned in any of the books. Surely the number one inn in all of Nova Scotia according to TripAdvisor has made the cut? In fact, none of the guides mention the inn and they barely touch on the town of Antigonish while devoting dozens of pages to the more exciting areas of the peninsula. It's easy to get led astray when you start on a massive site like TripAdvisor. Many in the travel industry agree that while TripAdvisor may be somewhat useful for hotel advice, it has not reached a point where it can give advice in choosing destinations and points of interest. For example, Robert Reid, a prolific author of Lonely Planet guides and now a travel writer for *National Geographic* talked with me about looking up New York City:

> According to TripAdvisor, eight of the top ten attractions in New York City are Broadway shows. The first one that isn't is number four, the New York City skyline. Are you telling me the Carole King musical is the top destination? And the Empire State building is number 80. Really? [79]

I abandon Antigonish, worried I might be incurring a repeat of our family Memphremagog fiasco. After reading a few concise overviews of areas in *Lonely Planet Nova Scotia*, I settle on Peggy's Cove and then choose Peggy's Cove Bed and Breakfast, one of the recommended places to stay. I corroborate the information from Lonely Planet by checking Fodor's: they confirm the choice. Not surprisingly, advance reservations are needed. Of course, this is the downside to travel guides. Because guides like Lonely Planet choose the "best" couple of places to stay at several price ranges, these places become overrun with tourists and it is difficult to book them. Some cities go one step further:

> Lonely Planet is the bible in places like India . . . If they recommend the Resthouse Bangalore, then half the guesthouses there rename themselves Resthouse Bangalore. [80]

I was drawn to travel guides because I knew they were reliable and concise, but also full of information that I wouldn't think to look for on a website, such as watching out for popular tourist scams or the likelihood of coming across a poisonous snake. As Alison Bing, a writer for Lonely Planet, says about guidebooks:

> *pay attention to the shortest phrases in there because when Celeste says don't swim in the river or I say watch your wallet, it's probably because we found out the hard way. So we're not being alarmist. It's our job to help you avoid vacation horror stories.* [81]

Guides are still struggling in their transition to digital, but they are starting to turn the corner. Sites like Frommer's put most of their guidebook content online, whereas Lonely Planet puts most of its content in its print guidebooks or eBooks, while hosting a spectrum of digital articles and a community forum online.

Travel writer Robert Reid helps solidify my feelings about guidebooks in two ways. According to Reid I had made the classic newbie mistake: starting my travel planning with a massive user-generated review site such as TripAdvisor to figure out where to go. *Wrong.* Big sites like these are not the right place to begin travel planning, but guides are very good at this.

Second, I was fighting with the idea that guidebooks were not cool. Reid writes that everyone uses phrases like "I'm going somewhere that is not found in a guidebook" to suggest a more authentic travel adventure, but that in fact most of these places *do* appear in guidebooks. Many travel writers agree that guidebooks remain an essential part of the travel-planning process, especially in the early stages of planning. As Reid says, they are: "your friend, perhaps your only friend, in a place you've never been before" and have the "eyes and ears of a handful of travel experts that have, over a generation or two, combed the place you're going." [82] The huge takeaways seem to be that guidebooks are reliable, they work for the traveler and not the industry, and they can sometimes be a little boring.

In the past guidebooks used to actually *guide* with a stronger, more opinionated voice on everything from avoiding venereal diseases to watching out for some local cuisine. Guidebooks don't give that kind of advice anymore. But who does? Where could I find that level of intimacy and reliable advice?

HOLD THE DOG!

In guidebooks I had found my reliable source, but the passion, the unique and quirky advice was missing. Where was my new Tony Wheeler? Who was going to tell me how to say, or even that I *should* say—*Nokhoi khor! Hold the dog!*—before entering a yurt? While I realize Nova Scotia is not exactly exotic travel, I still want advice on whether to order la poutine râpée. So where was my parachute artist?

If you have ever travelled to a developing country and entered the central market area you find yourself quickly surrounded by a cacophony of voices—dozens of sellers clamoring for attention. This is *exactly* what it feels like when you hop online to find travel information. To rely on a Google search was to be handed off to TripAdvisor or Expedia, or be buried in the latest trendy sites clawing their way up the search result ladder: Localeur.com, Tripexpert.com, or Oyster.com. But entering the world of travel blogging and websites was completely overwhelming: so many voices with *such* uneven quality.

Because I cannot find an obvious place to look for the best travel content, the next step is to locate a good curator. Content curation involves sorting through the enormous amounts of content available on a topic and selecting and organizing the best choices. A good content curator is a human with a discerning eye, not an automated search engine that can be gamed, or a commercial travel site that points to sponsored content. Unfortunately, the only curated lists I can find for travel sites are quickly compiled by content writers trying to generate traffic to commercial sites: *Top 10 Travel Websites Today!*

I am an expert at finding curated sites on any topic, so I'm embarrassed to say that the whole travel scene completely stumps me. I conduct multiple false starts by scanning massive numbers of professional travel writers, websites, blogs, Twitter feeds, Instagram collections, Pinterest sites, and travel forums and come up more confused than when I started. While I do come across a handful of intriguing and unique voices, they are few and far between and are buried by the thousands of bloggers that either want to report on their fabulous vacation or need to pump out lots of advertising copy to feed their sponsors. The most gifted amateur bloggers are buried because there are so many bloggers; the expert travel writers are buried because many write for media with restricted subscription access and this buries their content from appearing high in the list of Google search results.

In the past few years travel blogging has exploded and some travel bloggers are now successful marketing arms for tourism boards and travel businesses. The TBEX (Travel Bloggers Exchange) conference has gone from just over 100 attendees in 2009 to more than 1,000 in 2014. Programs at the conference are on how to attract readers and commercial sponsors. At a recent TBEX there were 3,629 speed-dating interactions between tourism sponsors and bloggers.[83] A related service provides the travel industry with a search engine for locating types of travel bloggers and indicating their social media influence.[84] Many bloggers hope for either sponsored travel gigs or to become brand ambassadors. While I enjoy reading a few of these bloggers, I'm not sure I can trust them to be unbiased.

Researchers have found that readers of blogs have trouble discerning if the content is reliable or simply advertising.[85] One of the main challenges with gauging the credibility of travel blogs is that bloggers are not always transparent about sponsored content, or if they do divulge sponsorship they bury it at the end of a post. Researcher Ric Jensen writes:

> *When I read a "Mommy blogger" describing how her children loved their most recent vacation to Disneyworld, it's nearly impossible to determine if the writing is an accurate account of what the author experienced or if the writer is instead merely repeating key marketing messages from Disney as part of a bribe to earn a free trip to a resort.*[86]

The FTC agrees that blogs and other digital communications are blurring the line between editorial and advertising, and in 2013 issued a document to clarify how writers must openly disclose sponsored trips and free goods and services.[87] The FTC recognizes the power of these personal blogs to influence consumer purchases, as does the travel industry.

People trust personal blogs and purchase goods and services based on what they read, even when they are aware that the blogger is accepting money to write what are essentially advertisements.[88] Research shows that consumers trust other consumers much more than they trust corporations.[89] But, research has also shown that on sponsored blog posts credibility is questionable at best, and most likely biased.[90] On the other hand, new media researchers have pointed out that there is a paradigm shift occurring in how we define credibility in relationship to blogs. Single-voice blogs have shifted the notion of credibility away from the realm of expertise, accuracy, and absence of bias and supplanted it with interactivity, transparency, and identification. Readers prefer the "real voices" of bloggers and maintain that when bloggers provide transparency (acknowledgment of sponsored travel arrangements), provide interactivity (readers can comment and provide corrections), and when they have a personal voice that people identify with, some bloggers are able to build audience trust. All three of these factors—interactivity, transparency, and identification—are now starting to be adopted by more traditional journalists, but how this will evolve is still in play.

The larger problem for me remains how to find the excellent travel bloggers that I know are out there. I end up interviewing a handful of professional travel writers and also locate and use the award pages posted on the Society of American Travel Writers and the North America Travel Journalists Association. These organizations are committed to improving travel journalism by rewarding excellence in the field. Because single-voice bloggers are not well represented on these award lists I also pick off keynote speakers from the TBEX bloggers conference. As I skim the work of what I consider professional travel writers—whether bloggers or those with more professional credentials—I realize what I have been missing. These writers differ dramatically from most of what I had spent the last few weeks slogging through.

Just as experienced burglars were great at casing a neighborhood and choosing a suitable target, true parachute artists were able to drop into a new place and spot what was important. Robert Reid talks about travel experts being able to recognize patterns: they can quickly spot the "fudge shops" or the inauthentic food trucks that are trying to capitalize on a recent trend and instead make a beeline for the rich and authentic travel experiences and communicate these back to their readers. [91]

While I can't completely put my finger on why I find these expert voices I have just read valuable, Reid explains a small study he did two years ago:

> *I looked at some "*New York Times*" articles, some magazine articles, and some blog articles and I picked a random destination and color-coded the content of each article. I used green for words expressing something you see or feel in a place—the benefit of being there, blue was a fact that could be fact-checked before or after that adds to your knowledge about being there, red is a quote, and yellow is something about the writer. Blogs were almost overwhelmingly fields of yellow, whereas something like the "*New York Times*" was a rainbow of colors.* [92]

Catharine Hamm, an award-winning longtime editor of the *Los Angeles Times* Travel section, concurs that what distinguishes professional travel writing from an amateur is that:

> *Travel journalism in its highest form is a combination of news reporting and consumer reporting. First and foremost, you need facts—travel reporting isn't just what we call the "rosy fingers of dawn"—that is, watching the sunrise over (fill in the blank) place. It's history, culture, people, and world events; it's the attractions we want to visit and those that are lesser known. Couple that with the consumer aspect of reporting. You are essentially telling people how to spend their time and money so you must become—very quickly—an expert. Ultimately, you need to cast an objective eye on a place and its components and convey that in a way that serves the reader. As travel author Arthur Frommer has taught me: it's not about your trip; it's about their trip.* [93]

Reid adds:

> *Travel experts try to add to the conversation, if you are not adding to the conversation of that place you are just adding noise. Unfortunately for that person that is trying to find the right blog or right source of information, there is a lot of noise.* [94]

While Reid is clear that some sponsorship for travel is ok, because many trips wouldn't be possible otherwise, he notes that travel writers need to be careful about getting too comfortable with always having a smiling sponsor greet them at the airport and customize their trip. Experts are able to look past the immediate itinerary and remain independent. If you go on hosted trips all the time, you are losing the view of the reader and forfeiting your ability to continue to develop your expertise and spot patterns and subtle cues that a onetime tourist would miss.[95]

Researchers have spent years studying how an expert differs from an amateur in many domains, although travel writing per se has not been well researched.[96] In chess it is easy to separate expert from novice—the expert is the one who consistently wins. For domains such as travel it is less clear. Researchers remain uncertain about all the components of expertise, but there is widespread agreement that experts differ from novices in that they "see" situations in their domain of expertise differently because they tend to process relational elements of a scene in parallel whereas novices see things serially, just like in the burglar study. Experts also differ in that they construct large and well-organized knowledge bases they can draw on, and that they spend many hours in deliberate practice. Deliberate practice is practice that is consciously intended to improve one's skills.[97] It is seen as the key ingredient in becoming successful in most vocations.

One additional item that seems to separate some expert travel writers from novices is a code of ethics. Most newspaper travel sections and some travel magazines have strict policies against taking sponsored travel, and most professionals travel anonymously and do not announce they are coming ahead of time so they are not beholden to anyone.[98]

ARE WE ALMOST THERE?

I decide to combine the information I get from several travel guides, uncool as they may be, with the words of a few of my favorite, newfound, expert travel writers and websites. I choose a handful of the latter and combine key words with Nova Scotia, for example:

> Google: *New York Times Nova Scotia*
> Google: *National Geographic Traveler Nova Scotia*
> Google: *Christopher Reynolds L.A. Times Nova Scotia*

I find great advice about destinations, food, and places to stay. I also follow the advice of several experts and consult the U.S. State Department website for reliable information on visa requirements, inoculations, common tourist scams, and dangerous political activities—though Canada is not exactly a bastion of terrorist activity.[99] And I look at the official tourism site for Nova Scotia. These official sites are highly biased but also have useful basic information.

There was just one thing left to do: go a little deeper. While all of the travel writers I interviewed mentioned this, Robert Reid articulated it best when he talked about how to travel like a travel writer, namely: deep research. Research can come from anywhere—a film, a book, a poem, a YouTube video. For Reid, a *New Yorker* article on Turkish soccer got him excited about going to Turkey. He calls his research "pre-absorbing" into the culture of a place.[100]

For Nova Scotia I use one simple comprehensive source: WorldCat. Called the "mother of all databases," WorldCat combines all the resources in most of the libraries in the United States. While Amazon and Google Books can be helpful, WorldCat has advanced search features that let you zero in on specific topics. I use advanced search in WorldCat looking for Nova Scotia and travel and limit by fiction and in a later search by nonfiction published in the last decade. I find some intriguing novels by Alastair MacLeod and also a biography about why the victims of the *Titanic* ended up buried in Nova Scotia. I also search for films about or shot in Nova Scotia and find that Wikipedia, for a factual question like this, does an excellent job.

Peggy's Cove in Nova Scotia and the B&B I found there turn out to be excellent. My next trip will involve a more streamlined process, and the six strategies would help me focus on what was important for spotting reliable information:

1. Start at the Source

Rather than a lot of Google searching, in the future if I was planning a significant trip I would start with a trusted guidebook such as Fodor's or Lonely Planet—on or off line.

2. Pay Attention to the "Psychology of Search"

Though I would use crowdsourced review sites, I would consult them with some trepidation knowing how easy it is to get sucked into the assumption of "What You See Is All There Is." Many review sites are working for the travel industry and negative reviews might be buried or deleted. I also want to hold on to how easy it is to be lured in by the personal voice of a reviewer or blogger, remembering that some reviews are fake and some bloggers are overly influenced by travel industry sponsorship.

3. Expert, Amateur, Crowd?

Clearly it was fine to use some combination of sources for travel information, but there were certain benefits to seeking out some professional travel reviewers and also using the more closely vetted traditional travel guides.

4. Context, Motivation, and Bias

There are a lot of issues with bias in travel reporting. Professional travel writers follow a code of ethics and are careful about adhering to it. Some bloggers also are transparent about their sponsors, but many are not. Single-voice bloggers are a powerful tool for the travel industry and their ranks will continue to grow. It is important to view many of them, though not all, as advertisements. They still may convey valuable information, but sometimes it might be prudent to consult other sources.

5. Comparison and Corroboration

Never use a single source for travel information. The degree of comparison and corroboration needs to be proportionally related to how big the trip is: going to a nearby city, not so much, but going halfway around the globe requires some digging.

6. Go Deep or Not

Clearly a personal preference with travel. If you are pretty easygoing and have experience in self-defense you can get away with a shallow dive. If you are more picky, spend at least a few hours researching and corroborating information.

NOTES

1. Aadapted from Rocio Garcia Retamero and Mandeep K. Dhami, "Take-the-Best in Expert-Novice Decision Strategies for Residential Burglary," *Journal of Psychonomic Bulletin & Review* 16, no. 1 (February 2009). Used with permission from Springer Publishing.

2. Andre Didierjean and Gobet Fernand, "Sherlock Holmes: An Expert's View of Expertise," *British Journal of Psychology* 99 (2008).

3. Rocio Garcia-Retamero and Mandeep K. Dhami, "Take-the-Best in Expert-Novice Decision Strategies for Residential Burglary," *Journal of Psychonomic Bulletin & Review* 16, no. 1 (February 2009).

4. Ibid.

5. Visit us at www.wongbakerFACES.org. Used with permission. Originally published in Whaley & Wong's Nursing Care of Infants and Children. © Elsevier Inc.

6. Susan Mudambi and David Schuff, "What Makes a Helpful Online Review? A Study of Customer Reviews on Amazon.com," *MIS Quarterly* 34, no. 1 (March 2010).

7. Email to author dated October 8, 2014, from Melisasandy, owners of Melisasandy Amazon Marketplace.

8. James Suroweiki, *The Wisdom of Crowds: Why the Many Are Smarter Than the Few and How Collective Wisdom Shapes Business, Economies, Societies and Nations* (New York: Little, Brown, 2004).

9. Ibid.

10. Lev Muchnik, Sinan Aral, and Sean J. Taylor, "Social Influence Bias: A Randomized Experiment," *Science* 341, no. 6146 (August 2013).

11. Dalvi Nilesh, Kumar Ravi, and Bo Pang, "Para 'Normal' Activity: On the Distribution of Average Ratings," in Proceedings of the Seventh International AAAI Conference on We-

blogs and Social Media, 2013, https://www.aaai.org/ocs/index.php/ICWSM/ICWSM13/paper/view/6117; Carolyn Y. Johnson, "Study Finds That Herd Mentality Can Overinflate Online Ratings," *Boston Globe,* August 9, 2013, http://www.bostonglobe.com/news/science/2013/08/08/the-pitfalls-crowdsourcing-online-ratings-vulnerable-bias/pw6HhJrZ3ZkP6oG6XYM2wO/story.html; Michael Luca, "Reviews, Reputation, and Revenue: The Case of Yelp.com," Harvard Business School Working Paper, September 6, 2011, http://www.hbs.edu/faculty/Publication%20Files/12-016.pdf.

12. Matthew B.Welsh, "Expertise and the Wisdom of Crowds: Whose Judgments to Trust and When," Building Bridges Across Cognitive Sciences Around the World: Proceedings of the 34th Annual Meeting of the Cognitive Science Society, Sapporo, Japan, August 1–4, 2012, ed. N. Miyake, D. Peeble, and R.P. Cooper, http://digital.library.adelaide.edu.au/dspace/bitstream/2440/74412/1/hdl_74412.pdf.

13. Mudambi and Schuff, "What Makes a Helpful Online Review?"

14. Tom Slee, "Some Obvious Things About Internet Reputation Systems," September 29, 2013, http://tomslee.net/2013/09/some-obvious-things-about-internet-reputation-systems.html.

15. Tom Slee, "Some Obvious Things About Internet Reputation Systems," September 29, 2013, http://tomslee.net/2013/09/some-obvious-things-aboutinternet-reputation-systems.html.

16. Tom Slee, "Some Obvious Things About Internet Reputation Systems," September 29, 2013, http://tomslee.net/2013/09/some-obvious-things-aboutinternet-reputation-systems.html.

17. Petya Eckler and Paul Bolls, "Spreading the Virus: Emotional Tone of Viral Advertising and Its Effect on Forwarding Intentions and Attitudes," *Journal of Interactive Advertising* 11, no. 2 (Spring 2011), http://jiad.org/article142.html.

18. Stephanie Rosenbloom, "Finding Your Travel Tribe," *New York Times,* October 1, 2014, http://www.nytimes.com/2014/10/05/travel/finding-your-travel-tribe.html.

19. Holly Goodier, "BBC Online Briefing Spring 2012: The Participation Choice," May 4, 2012, http://www.bbc.co.uk/blogs/legacy/bbcinternet/2012/05/bbc_online_briefing_spring_201_1.html.

20. Megan Geuss, "Google Mines Frommer's Travel for Social Data, Then Sells the Name Back," ArsTechnica, April 9, 2013, http://arstechnica.com/business/2013/04/google-mines-frommers-travel-for-social-data-then-sells-the-name-back/.

21. Alistair Barr, "Was Expedia Targeted by 'Negative SEO' Campaign?" *USA Today*, January 22, 2014, http://www.usatoday.com/story/tech/2014/01/22/expedia-negative-seo-google/4778359/.

22. Colin Fernandez, "Hotels 'Bribe Guests for Online Reviews' on Tripadvisor Website with Free Rooms and Meals," *Daily Mail,* October 8, 2014, http://www.dailymail.co.uk/news/article-2013291/Hotels-bribe-guests-online-reviews-Tripadvisor-website-free-rooms-meals.html.

23. R. Fillieri and F. McLeay, "The Effects of Social Influence and Cognitive Dissonance on Travel Purchase Decisions," *Journal of Travel Research* (April 4, 2014).

24. "David vs. Two Goliaths: Tripadvisor Could Challenge the Big Two Providers of Online Travel Services," *Economist*, August 9, 2014, http://www.economist.com/news/business/21611100-tripadvisor-could-challenge-big-two-providers-online-travel-services-david-vs-two.

25. E. Fenn, E.J. Newman, K. Pezdek, and M. Garry, "The Effect of Nonprobative Photographs on Truthiness Persists Over Time," *Acta Psychologica* 144, no. 1 (2013), doi:10.1016/j.actpsy.2013.06.004.

26. See. http://www.cs.dartmouth.edu/farid/.

27. "Photo Fakeouts," http://www.oyster.com/hotels/photo-fakeouts/.

28. Cyndy K. "TripAdvisor review of Park Hotel," http://www.tripadvisor.com/ShowUserReviews-g60713-d563989-r132549823-Park_Hotel-San_Francisco_California.html#CHECK_RATES_CONT.

29. Stephen W. Litvin, Ronald E. Roldsmith, and Bing Pan, "Electronic Word-of-Mouth in Hospitality and Tourism Management," *Tourism Management* 29, no. 3 (June 2008).

30. Myles Anderson, "2013 Study: 79% Of Consumers Trust Online Reviews as much as Personal Recommendations," Search Engine Land Blog, June 26, 2013, http://searchengineland.com/2013-study-79-of-consumers-trust-online-reviews-as-much-as-personal-recommendations-164565.

31. Pei-Yu Chen, Samita Dhanasobhon, and Michael D. Smith, "All Reviews Are Not Created Equal: The Disaggregate Impact of Reviews and Reviewers at Amazon.com," SSRN Prepublication, May 2008, http://dx.doi.org/10.2139/ssrn.918083; Judith Chevalier and Dina Mayzlin, "The Effect of Word of Mouth on Sales: Online Book Reviews," *Journal of Marketing Research* (August 2006); E.K. Clemons, Gao Guodong, and L.M. Hitt, "When Online Reviews Meet Hyperdifferentiation: A Study of Craft Beer Industry," *System Sciences,* 2006, HICSS '06, Proceedings of the 39th Annual Hawaii International Conference, 6 (January 2006), doi: 10.1109/HICSS.2006.534.

32. H. Xie, L. Miao, P.J. Kuo, and B.Y. Lee, "Consumers' Responses to Ambivalent Online Hotel Reviews: The Role of Perceived Source Credibility and Pre-Decisional Disposition," *International Journal of Hospitality Management* 30, no. 1 (2011).

33. Chuck Klosterman, "Tourist Retractions," *New York Times,* October 10, 2014, http://www.nytimes.com/2014/10/12/magazine/tourist-retractions.html.

34. Julian K. Ayeh, Norman Au, and Rob Law, "'Do We Believe in TripAdvisor?' Examining Credibility Perceptions and Online Travelers' Attitude Toward Using User-Generated Content," *Journal of Travel Research* 52, no. 4 (July 2013), doi:10.1177/0047287512475217.

35. Jayne O'Donnell, "Watch Out for Fake Online Reviews and Review Sites," *USA Today,* November 4, 2011, http://usatoday30.usatoday.com/money/industries/retail/story/2011-11-01/deceptive-product-review-sites/51033028/1.

36. Steve Robson, "'Hotel heaven': Hostel for the Homeless Soars to Top 100 Of Tripadvisor's Best Places to Stay After Jokers Give It a Five-Star Rating." *Mail Online,* April 25, 2013, http://www.dailymail.co.uk/news/article-2314546/Jokers-Glasgow-hostel-homeless-5-star-reviews-TripAdvisor-sending-countrys-100.html.

37. Fernandez, "Hotels 'Bribe Guests for Online Reviews.'"

38. Daniel Bates, "How to Tell If a TripAdvisor Review Is Fake . . . Researchers Reveal How to Spot Bogus Comments Which Hotels Pay For," *Mail Online,* August 22, 2011,http://www.dailymail.co.uk/news/article-2028561/TripAdvisor-How-tell-review-fake.html#ixzz3F0uqyOiZ.

39. Ott Myle, Yejin Choi, Claire Cardie, and Jeffrey T. Hancock, "Finding Deceptive Opinion Spam by Any Stretch of the Imagination," in Proceedings of the 49th Annual Meeting of the Association for Computational Linguistics: Human Language Technologies, June 2011, http://aclweb.org/anthology/P/P11/P11-1032.pdf.

40. Richard Thaler and Cass R. Sunstein, *Nudge: Improving Decisions about Health, Wealth, and Happiness* (New York: Penguin, 2008).

41. Ott et al., "Finding Deceptive Opinion Spam."

42. Eric Andreson and Duncan Simester, "Reviews Without a Purchase: Low Ratings, Loyal Customers and Deception," *Journal of Marketing Research* 51, no. 3 (2014), http://journals.ama.org/doi/abs/10.1509/jmr.13.0209.

43. Arjun Mukherjee, Bing Liu, and Natalie Glance, "Spotting Fake Reviewer Groups in Consumer Reviewers," in Proceedings of the 21st International World Wide Web Conference, doi: 10.1145/2187836.2187863; Luca, "Reviews, Reputation, and Revenue"; "The Consequences of Fake Fans, 'Likes' and Reviews on Social Networks," Gartner Report, 2012, http://www.gartner.com/newsroom/id/2161315.

44. Josephine Wolff, "One Percenters Control Online Reviews," *Nautilus Quarterly,* April 24, 2014, http://techupdates.com/go/924739#.

45. Anderson and Simester, "Reviews Without a Purchase."

46. Goodier, "BBC Online Briefing Spring 2012."

47. Pradeep Racheria, "Exploring the Patterns Underlying Online Reviews: The Study of a Travel Advisory Website," *Social Science Research Network,* December 5, 2011, http://dx.doi.org/10.2139/ssrn.2196885.

48. Raffaele Filieri and Fraser McLeay, "E-WOM and Accommodation: An Analysis of the Factors That Influence Travelers' Adoption of Information," *Journal of Travel Research* 53, no. 44 (March 2013), doi: 10.1177/0047287513481274.

49. Marc Courtenay, "TripAdvisor Trumps Yelp for Now," TheStreet, January 13, 2014, http://www.thestreet.com/story/12222752/1/tripadvisor-trumps-yelp-for-now.html.

50. Nancy Folbre, "Trading More and Sharing Nicely," Economix New York Times Blog, February 25, 2013, http://economix.blogs.nytimes.com/2013/02/25/trading-more-and-sharing-nicely/; Julianne Zigos, "Couchsurfing's Sex Secret: It's the Greatest Hookup App Ever Devised," *Business Insider,* December 7, 2013, http://www.businessinsider.com/couchsurfing-the-best-hook-up-app-2013-12.

51. Russell Belk, "Sharing vs. Pseudo-Sharing in Web 2.0," *Anthropologist* 18, no. 1 (2014), http://www.krepublishers.com/02-Journals/T-Anth/Anth-18-0-000-14-Web/Anth-18-1000-14-Abst-PDF/T-ANTH-18-1-007-14-1106-Belk-Russ/T-ANTH-18-1-007-14-1106-Belk-Russ-Tx[2].pdf.

52. Nicole Perlroth, "Non-Profit CouchSurfing Raises Millions in Funding," *Forbes,* August 24, 2011, http://www.forbes.com/sites/nicoleperlroth/2011/08/24/non-profit-couchsurfing-raises-millions-in-funding/.

53. Ingrid Lunden, "Tony Espinoza Steps Down as CEO of Couchsurfing, Jennifer Billock Steps up as Interim as Startup Lays Off Staff, 'Doubles Down' on Mobile," TechCrunch Blog, October 10, 2013, http://techcrunch.com/2013/10/10/tony-espinoza-steps-down-as-ceo-of-couchsurfing-jen-billock-steps-up-as-interim-as-startup-lays-off-staff-doubles-down-on-mobile/.

54. Zigos, "Couchsurfing's Sex Secret."

55. Belk, "Sharing Versus Pseudo-Sharing."

56. Anders Fremstad, "Democratizing the Sharing Economy," Center for Popular Economics Blog, June 24, 2014, http://www.populareconomics.org/democratizing-the-sharing-economy/.

57. Tom Simonite, "The Decline of Wikipedia," *MIT Technology Review,* October 22, 2013, http://www.technologyreview.com/featuredstory/520446/the-decline-of-wikipedia/.

58. See https://www.couchsurfing.com/users/252614/profile (log-in required).

59. Sarah Perez, "Airbnb CFO Andrew Swain Has Left the Company," Techcrunch Blog, September 18, 2014, http://techcrunch.com/2014/09/18/airbnb-cfo-andrew-swain-has-left-the-company/.

60. David Streitfeld, "Airbnb Listings Mostly Illegal, New York State Contends," *New York Times*, October 14, 2014, http://www.nytimes.com/2014/10/16/business/airbnb-listings-mostly-illegal-state-contends.html; Douglas MacMillan, Mike Spector, and Evelyn M. Rusli, "Airbnb Weighs Employee Stock Sale at $13 Billion Valuation," *Wall Street Journal*, October 23, 2014, http://online.wsj.com/articles/airbnb-mulls-employee-stock-sale-at-13-billion-valuation-1414100930.

61. Belk, "Sharing Versus Pseudo-Sharing."

62. Vikas Bajaj, "Who's Profiting from Airbnb?" Taking Note Blog, *New York Times,* October 7, 2014, http://takingnote.blogs.nytimes.com/2014/10/17/whos-profiting-from-airbnb/?_php=true&_type=blogs&_r=0.

63. James Fallows, "More on Yelp, Airbnb, and VRBO, Including Why I Was Naïve," *Atlantic*, January 1, 2012,http://www.theatlantic.com/business/archive/2012/01/more-on-yelp-airbnb-and-vrbo-including-why-i-was-naive/250737/.

64. Ibid.

65. Streitfeld, "Airbnb Listings Mostly Illegal."

66. Carolyn Said, "Window into Airbnb's Hidden Impact on S.F.," *San Francisco Chronicle*, June 15, 2014, http://www.sfchronicle.com/business/item/window-into-airbnb-s-hidden-impact-on-s-f-30110.php.

67. Jonathan Horn, "Man Who Rented Out Condo Fined $106K," U~T San Diego, October 24, 2014, http://www.utsandiego.com/news/2014/oct/24/airbnb-vrbo-mark-rent-steelers-gaslamp-condos/.

68. Emily Badger, "Why We Can't Figure Out How to Regulate Airbnb," *Washington Post,* April 23, 2014, http://www.washingtonpost.com/blogs/wonkblog/wp/2014/04/23/why-we-cant-figure-out-how-to-regulate-airbnb/.

69. See https://www.warmshowers.org/faq/account-features.

70. Tad Friend, "The Parachute Artist: Have Tony Wheeler's Guidebooks Travelled Too Far?" *New Yorker,* April 18, 2005, http://www.newyorker.com/magazine/2005/04/18/the-parachute-artist.

71. Sarah Robbins, "Travel Directions: Travel Books 2014. After Several Grim Years, Signs of (Cautious) Hope," *Publisher's Weekly*, February 14, 2014, http://www.publishersweekly.com/pw/print/20140217/61056-travel-directions-travel-books-2014.html.

72. Ibid.

73. Tad Friend, "The Parachute Artist," *New Yorker*, April 18, 2005, http://www.newyorker.com/magazine/2005/04/18/the-parachute-artist.

74. See Lonelyplant.com/About.

75. Jason Cochran, "The Internet Is a Directory, but a Good Guidebook Guides," Jason-Cochran.com Blog, August 14, 2013, http://jasoncochran.com/blog/the-internet-is-a-directory-but-a-good-guidebook-guides/.

76. Ana Alacovska, "'Parachute Artists' or 'Tourists with Typewriters': Creative and Co-creative Labor in Travel Guidebook Production," *Communication, Culture, and Critique* 6, no. 1 (March 2013).

77. Ibid.

78. Friend, "The Parachute Artist."

79. Robert Reid—writer for *National Geographic Traveler*—in discussion with the author, November 6, 2014.

80. Friend, "The Parachute Artist."

81. Robert Siegel, "Vacation Horror Stories: Even Travel Writers Make Mistakes," All Things Considered, radio show transcript, September 2, 2013, http://www.npr.org/templates/story/story.php?storyId=218288990.

82. Reid, discussion with the author.

83. Dan Saltzstein, "Travel Blogging Today: It's Complicated," *New York Times,* July 26, 2013, http://www.nytimes.com/2013/07/28/travel/travel-blogging-today-its-complicated.html?_r=0.

84. See http://travelbloggersassociation.com.

85. Bruce E. Drushel and Kathleen German, eds., *The Ethics of Emerging Media: Information, Social Norms, and New Media* (New York: Continuum, 2011).

86. Ric Jensen, "Blogola, Sponsored Posts, and the Ethics of Blogging," in *The Ethics of Emerging Media: Information, Social Norms, and New Media* ed. Bruce E. Drushel and Kathleen German (New York: Continuum, 2011).

87. Federal Trade Commission, ".com Disclosures: How to Make Effective Disclosures in Digital Advertising," March 2013, http://www.ftc.gov/sites/default/files/attachments/press-releases/ftc-staff-revises-online-advertising-disclosure-guidelines/130312dotcomdisclosures.pdf.

88. Long-Chuan Lu, Wen-Pin Chang, and Hsiu-Hua Chang, "Consumer Attitudes Toward Blogger's Sponsored Recommendations and Purchase Intention: The Effect of Sponsorship Type, Product Type, and Brand Awareness," *Computers in Human Behavior* 34 (May 2014).

89. K.T. Lee and D.M. Koo, "Effects of Attribute and Valance of e-WOM on Message Adoption: Moderating Roles of Subjective Knowledge and Regulatory Focus," *Computers in Human Behavior* 28 (2012).

90. Lu et al., "Consumer Attitudes Toward Blogger's Sponsored Recommendations"; Lisa Chow, "Top Reviewers on Amazon Get Tons of Free Stuff," NPR Planet Money Blog, October 29, 2013, http://www.npr.org/blogs/money/2013/10/29/241372607/top-reviewers-on-amazon-get-tons-of-free-stuff.

91. Reid, discussion with the author.

92. Reid, discussion with the author.

93. Catharine Hamm—writer for *LA Times*—in discussion with the author, October 27, 2014.

94. Reid, discussion with the author.

95. Ibid.

96. For a summary of the research on particular types of experts, see Andre Didierjean and Gobet Fernand, "Sherlock Holmes—An Expert's View of Expertise," *British Journal of Psychology* 99 (2008): 109.

97. Fernard Gobet, "Deliberate Practice Is Practice That Is Consciously Intended to Improve One's Skills," *Encyclopedia of the Sciences of Learning*, 2012, http://link.springer.com/referenceworkentry/10.1007%2F978-1-4419-1428-6_104.

98. Hamm, discussion with the author.

99. See http://travel.state.gov.

100. Reid, discussion with the author.

Chapter Five

The Dog Effect

Finding Reliable Science Information Online

Increasingly, as the abundance of information overwhelms us all, we need not simply more information, but people to assimilate, understand, and make sense of it.
—John Seely Brown and Paul Duguid, *The Social Life of Information* (2000)

Three days after his wife died from cyanide poisoning, medical researcher Robert Ferrante typed a search into Yahoo! Answers:

How would a coroner detect when someone is killed by cyanide? [1]

Several months before his wife was poisoned, Ferrante also searched for information on divorce laws, how to tell if a woman was having an affair, and the legal definition of "malice of forethought," an apparent reference to the legal term "malice aforethought," meaning premeditation.

During his trial, the prosecutor used Ferrante's online searches against him. Ferrante claimed that he was just doing "research" related to his work. In closing arguments the prosecutor noted that:

one article was titled, "Illinois man wins the lottery, poisoned by cyanide," and she asked the jury, "Does that sound like research to you?" [2]

Ferrante was later sentenced to life in prison without parole for first-degree murder.

Ferrante's choice to use Yahoo! Answers is a little like choosing to play the lottery: it's alluring and it occasionally provides good reliable information, but often it doesn't. For a question about cyanide detection in the body, there are a number of reliable sources that surface easily by doing a Google search. If you can manage to pass by the first few hits from companies selling products to detect cyanide, just a few sites down are reputable sites from the National Institute of Health, state poison centers, and scholarly medical articles about cyanide detection and poisoning. These are much more reliable then the random and anonymous person that might answer a Yahoo! Answers question.

Unlike searching for facts, questions like: "Is my wife having an affair?" can be dicey to throw out there on Google or Yahoo! Answers. Suddenly all the vultures pop up to "help." Affaircare.com, Savemysexlessmarriage.com, and beyondaffairs.com pop to the top of a Google search, but WikiHow snags first billing on my Google search with the enticing click-bait of:

How to Tell If Your Wife Is Cheating (With Pictures) [3]

The pictures are disappointing, but WikiHow also cites sources, probably to boost its ranking and get the number one slot in Google. The citations are not to research articles or even marriage counselor advice columns, but to other sites trying to boost their own traffic with quickly thrown together "articles." One of the four citations is to Matchmove.com. It provides a brief useless article in poorly written English on how to determine if your wife is cheating, and then suggests you might want to blow off steam by gaming on, you guessed it, Matchmove.com, their social media gaming platform based in Singapore.

In the same way that Ferrante ended up sidetracked and viewing the site on the lottery winner who died of cyanide poisoning, I find myself quickly sucked into investigating Matchmove.com. Why would WikiHow cite such a shoddy website? I jump on Wikipedia and the article on Matchmove.com screams:

> *This article has multiple issues . . . appears to be written by a contributor with a close connection to the subject . . . is an orphan—has no links to it or from it.* [4]

I hear the little voice in my head mimicking the prosecutor in the Ferrante case: *Does that sound like research to you?* I decide to conduct more strategic research and dive into the Deep Web to search huge databases of newspapers and magazine articles via my library. I find only one mention of Matchmove.com: A press release they wrote themselves. Almost all the Google searches point back to their own website. OK, time to stop, but it is clear they are not the premiere site for marriage counseling or even affair detection.

ARRR!

Questions are important: how you ask them and how you translate them into online searches. My friend Daniel and I are having a *discussion* about Johnny Depp. I say in passing that I read that Depp modeled his drunken speech in the *Pirates of the Caribbean* movies on Dudley Moore, the actor who played a drunk in the original *Arthur* movie. But Dan, who seems to know everything about everything, says no, that Depp modeled it after the drug-addled speech of Keith Richards of the Rolling Stones. We both whip out our smartphones to find the answer, but of course we front-load our search terms. Daniel searches:

Google: **Keith Richards** *Johnny Depp Pirates Caribbean Jack Sparrow*

And sure enough he points to stories from NPR, the *Guardian*, *DailyMail*, ABC Eyewitness News, and many other sources that prove his point.

I search:

Google: **Dudley Moore Arthur** *Johnny Depp Pirates Caribbean Jack Sparrow*

And here is the problem: I'm able to turn up a reference from Answers.com that provides me with information that Depp modeled his character's voice on Dudley Moore's Arthur in addition to Keith Richards. Daniel and I both engaged in what psychologists refer to as *biased information searching,* also referred to as the confirmation heuristic. We both sought evidence that confirms our existing beliefs. And I almost went one step further by using what is called *biased assimilation:* I wanted to give extra weight to information that supported my goals, despite finding a shoddy source, and I tried to ignore anything that signaled my theory was incorrect.

But as I hunt around I can't match Dan's findings of fact-checked news sites. I *want* to believe the handsome young man Mr. Y. on Answers.com who claims that Depp spoke of modeling his accent on both Dudley Moore and Keith Richards in a long-ago interview.[5] Mr. Y.'s image on Answers.com looks remarkably like Justin Timberlake standing on the beach, and he is using what appears to be his real name. I verify this with his LinkedIn account. Mr. Y. is also a "Gold Member" on Answers.com and has contributed 41,000 answers since 2008. He has earned 500 trust points. I look up trust points and Answers.com explains:

Trust Points enable you to vote for a WikiAnswers member whose contributions you think are worthwhile and legitimate. It is important to note that Trust Points are not a good measurement of how much you can trust the answer to a question.[6]

So Mr. Y. is a trusted member of the community, but that doesn't mean he gives accurate answers. My friend Daniel wins, *again.* Or does he?

Now we come to the embarrassing part of the story. I decide that Mr. Y.'s statement had to have come from *somewhere* since it matches my own understanding. And so, as if I had nothing better to do, I spend hours searching through online magazines, newspapers, film reviews, interviews with Depp, and every piece of information on the shallow web (Google searching) and the Deep Web (enormous databases of articles via my library) to get to the bottom of this extremely trite story in order to prove Daniel wrong, or at least to prove that I am partially correct. I'm not proud of this.

After more hours than I care to admit, I finally trace Mr. Y.'s comments, and probably my memory of the story as well, to some articles that came out at the time that the first two *Pirates* movies were released. In the *Atlanta Journal and Constitution*, Bob Longino reports:

> His Sparrow will make you think of Dudley Moore's ever-drunk man-child in
> "Arthur."[7]

And, in the *Charleston Gazette*, Roger Moore references Depp slurring the words:

> "And izza rum?" in his best Dudley Moore-as-"Arthur" accent.[8]

While it is almost impossible to definitively prove I am wrong, other than a phone call to Johnny Depp, all signs point to it. Over time the "makes you think of" and "in his best Dudley Moore accent" evolved into the assumption that Depp had said this in an interview or that he was consciously imitating Dudley Moore. This does not appear to be the case.

I KNOW A SHORTCUT

We search daily for big and little pieces of information online: celebrity gossip and medical treatment options. Some questions are so easy: *What's a polynomial?* Or have such low stakes: *Does Miley Cyrus really have two belly buttons?* Other questions are more challenging: *Why is the population of codfish declining in New England?* Questions related to science research can pose unique challenges, partly related to how we search for science information, but also due to the complexity of science and the challenges of conveying scientific research in understandable terms for laypeople.

We often use heuristics—mental shortcuts that help us process and evaluate information we find. These shortcuts allow us to ignore less important aspects of information to reduce cognitive load in order to make decisions quickly, accurately, and with less effort.[9] Researchers have found that heuristics are a double-edged sword: on the one hand they can reduce the amount of cognitive effort used in decision making, but using heuristics can also lead to systematic biases or errors in judgment. [10]

When we evaluate information we tend to not invest our full mental capacity. For my Johnny Depp search, because it was such a low-stakes question, I might have just settled for the Answers.com answer. If I had settled, I would have been engaging in satisficing. Sometimes satisficing is fine, it provides a "good enough" answer. For me, I couldn't justify using an Answers.com answer against Dan's findings on NPR.org, ABC, and *The Guardian*. In this case, had I satisficed I would have settled for false information.

In fact, my initial search on Johnny Depp illustrates just how many ways a search can go wrong. While the Web presents us with incredible opportunities for learning new things, it also presents us with an enormous amount of information to sift through with few easy markers of quality. Researchers who study how people evaluate information note that it is not so much that online resources have changed the cognitive skills needed to judge credibility, it is simply that the proliferation of so much information online means people need to call on these skills much more frequently. [11]

One of the biggest challenges to evaluating information is disintermediation—meaning the source of the information is often separated from the information itself. Often information is rebroadcast and it is difficult to trace it back to the original producer. It can be hard to tell not only who originally wrote a piece of information, but it is also difficult to evaluate qualifications. My Mr. Y. is a prime example. Yahoo! Answers vouches for his good behavior on the site, but that doesn't mean he has provided credible information or abides by certain standards such as citing sources. Researcher Paul Daguid notes that:

> *Oddly enough, information is one of the things that in the end needs brands almost more than anything else. . . . It needs a recommendation, a seal of approval, something that says this is reliable or true or whatever. And so journalists, but also the institutions of journalism as one aspect of this, become very important.* [12]

If we *can* locate the source of the information, this allows us to use the "reputation heuristic" as a shortcut for judging credibility. By recognizing a name or a publication and having some knowledge about it we are able to make a speedy judgment about the quality of the information. For example, Daniel and I barely read the NPR article; we assume the sentence about Keith Richards is true because of our familiarity with the source. Research shows that people attribute greater value to information from sources they recognize and this familiarity, even just with a source name, influences people's credibility judgments more strongly than the actual content or the credentials of the writer.[13]

The reputation heuristic is related to our tendency to overly rely on famous people or famous publications, because we believe they cannot be wrong. But in fact, even heavily fact-checked sites such as the *New York Times* occasionally post articles that turn out to be fabricated, though this is rare. In most cases we can trust publications that have solid track records and adhere to strong fact checking, knowing that occasional mistakes will be corrected.

The bandwagon heuristic is another shortcut we frequently use.[14] Research indicates that people are more likely to believe in, and rate highly, information that others have recommended, "liked," or ranked highly. Social endorsement is extremely powerful in influencing people's decisions about whether to trust information. In fact, people place more value on social endorsements even when their own firsthand information runs counter to what they are reading. When people feel skeptical about a particular website, high numbers of endorsements overcome this initial skepticism.[15] The bandwagon heuristic is especially prevalent on Twitter, where the more someone is followed the more people join in and follow and even trust the person posting.

Another heuristic is the consistency heuristic. Daniel used this by finding the same information on a handful of news sites. It can be effective: it is just a form of corroboration, but sometimes on the Web a quick check of several sites is really looking at the same information that has simply been rebroadcast on multiple sites, which fails to corroborate anything. It is important to review the content of the articles to ensure that it is new original reporting and not just a rebroadcast.

Many of the heuristics we use work well at least some of the time, we just need to be aware we are employing them and be careful about how we employ them. For example, one heuristic we use is assuming that the first few hits in a Google search are credible.[16] Sometimes they are accurate, but often they are not. Google ranks pages on dozens of items and aims for quality, but there are so many factors that feed the algorithm, so much information to plow through, and so many ways to game the system that Google's ability to surface the most reliable information is uneven at best.

For science information in particular, there is concern that crowdsourcing and click rates are influencing what people find when they use a search engine, and this in turn shapes how we make sense of a topic. Brossard calls this a self-reinforcing informational spiral, meaning *how* people search for a topic then influences how a search engine like Google weighs and retrieves content. Brossard questions whether we are really making science more accessible to laypeople online or if we are moving to a science communication process in which knowledge is greatly influenced by what links search engines pull up: In effect narrowing our options.[17] Moving forward, as many people are fed news, through Facebook, Twitter, or other social media sites, this phenomenon will likely accelerate.[18] It may be that your friend who keeps "liking" cat videos is also choosing the science news you read.

More research is needed on the heuristics we use and the ways they interact with each other, as well as how we can more effectively use shortcuts to find reliable information. We are only in the early stages of investigations. Researchers know that people vary greatly in which heuristics they rely on: heavy social media users rely more on the social endorsement heuristic and may be more easily influenced by the "crowd," whereas users who are more familiar with traditional media may have a tendency to overly rely on the reputation heuristic when judging sources. People also rely on certain heuristics for some information needs but not for others. Many people are less likely to take shortcuts when the piece of information sought is highly important to them.

So by now you are thinking: *Yes, yes, but there was a dog mentioned in the title of this chapter. What about the dog?*

EVERYONE LOVES A DOG STORY

Several days after our Johnny Depp discussion, I meet my friend Daniel for dinner. He mentions that he read an article recently that dogs actually experience empathy for humans. He's not convinced, but he said he is a good judge of research articles, and this article seemed to be credible and cited several scholarly studies.

I can feel myself instantly lured in. Bait taken. I'm not *exactly* a competitive person, but this feels almost too easy: Dogs feeling empathy? Much as this would be wonderful to believe—I love dogs—I'm guessing Daniel has not looked too closely at whatever article he found, and I'm guessing I can prove him wrong. I nonchalantly ask where he saw the article. "Just Google it," he says, "it was in some magazine like *National Geographic*—a good science source that referenced some recent studies." I change the subject, knowing that the second I get home I'll research dogs and empathy and be able to correct Daniel and gently point out his flawed research abilities.

Daniel and I have had many "discussions" over the years, but there is a reason I'm writing about this one. Journalists and writers have known intuitively for some time that a story related to a dog sells better than a story without a dog. I'm not just talking about cute dogs doing funny tricks, but newsworthy stories that happen to include a dog, such as a dog involved in a rescue or a working dog detecting narcotics. Now there is cleverly designed research to back this up. Researchers tracked articles from the *New York Times* to identify which ones were picked up by regional news outlets. Regional news outlets tend to grab the front-page stories from the *Times* while often disregarding most back-page, less important stories. The researchers were able to unequivocally prove that there is a "Dog Effect."

Vastly oversimplifying, there are two factors required for events to get into the news: they are important and they can capture the audience's attention. Dogs are able to do the latter. Regional newspapers were much more likely to report on stories from the *Times* if they had a dog in the story, and the dog effect was nearly as strong as the "front page" effect. In other words, dog stories on the back page were almost as likely to be picked up as front-page stories, over other nondog back-page stories.[19]

So there are many stories I could tell you about disagreements and bets Daniel and I have had, and they're not pretty, but the dog and empathy story was one of the more intriguing, and it turns out that this was not *just* because of the dog effect.

SIDETRACKED BY CHACHA

The story of dogs and empathy is largely a science story. If you search the massive scholarly database Web of Science (WOS)[20] available in some academic libraries for articles on dogs and empathy the research breaks down like this:

Web of Science Categories	Record Count	% of 72	Bar Chart
Veterinary Sciences	25	34.722%	
Sociology	23	31.944%	
Environmental Studies	17	23.611%	
Anthropology	17	23.611%	
Zoology	8	11.111%	
Psychology Multidisciplinary	7	9.722%	
Behavioral Sciences	7	9.722%	
Psychology Clinical	4	5.556%	
Multidisciplinary Sciences	4	5.556%	
Evolutionary Biology	4	5.556%	

Subject category breakdown for the study of dogs and empathy analyzed by Web of Science.[21]

If you omit articles on the effect dogs have on helping humans develop empathy, then you wipe out many of the social science articles. I use WOS and analyze the results to get a feel for the size of the topic and how much research has been done. It's a small field of study, about seventy-two articles, but these studies also connect to other areas such as the study of empathy in humans or other research about dogs.

But rather than jumping into the deep scholarly research, I decide to first trace Dan's footsteps by searching Google and seeing what turns up.

Google: *Dogs Empathy*

Google returns the typical one million plus results with some blogs and magazine articles rising to the top. Knowing it is unlikely that there would be any articles stating: "Dogs do *not* feel Empathy," not very exciting news, I glance down the list of candidates. I try to avoid ones like this from Answers.com that comes up near the top of my search results:

> *Yes, dogs feel all kinds of emotions, just like you do. They may not be able to talk about them but that does not mean they don't have them.*[22]

I feel myself being sucked in, even though it's likely a waste of time. I can't resist and I peak at the credentials of the poster. He is a graphic artist who has answered 13,000 questions on Answers.com. His "answer usefulness" score is zero, so that makes me hopeful that perhaps people are weeding out these kind of unsubstantiated answers, but then I notice three people have voted this particular answer as "useful." Jumping in I start hunting for what a "usefulness score" means. After twenty minutes I give up. I decide instead to go to the scholarly literature about Q&A sites generally, and Answers.com in particular, to see what the experts are saying about reliability and Q&A sites. I search Google Scholar and one of the most promising articles is out of Butler University College of Business. It is titled:

Q&A Platforms Evaluated Using Butler University Q&A Intelligence Index.[23]

The article looks like a research article and has three authors, though none have degrees listed after their names. The article is on topic: The credibility of Q&A sites. In it the authors describe a study they did in 2012 evaluating all the major Q&A sites. The research looks reasonable: they ran a large number of questions through the different Q&A sites available via smartphones to see which ones gave the most accurate answers. They then used two students working independently to judge if an answer was accurate and then combined their responses and reviewed any disagreements between the two evaluators.

Apparently the site ChaCha did extremely well in accuracy of answers at 73 percent with an "intelligence index" of 72, pretty much head and shoulders above the rest. Answers.com comes in at 65 percent, but with an intelligence index of a paltry 46 percent. The intelligence index is a combination of coverage and accuracy.

Rank Provider	Type	Coverage	Accuracy *	Intelligence Index
ChaCha	Human-assisted	99.4%	73.2	72.8
Ask	Crowdsourcing	100%	63.9	63.9
bing	Algorithm-only	100%	55.1	55.1
YAHOO!	Crowdsourcing	100%	54.5	54.5
Iris²	Virtual Assistant	98.2%	52.9	51.9
Google	Algorithm-only	100%	50.1	50.1
Answers.com	Crowdsourcing	70.8%	65.2	46.2
speaktoit	Virtual Assistant	78.6%	43.8	34.4
WolframAlpha	Structured Data	86.9%	35.9	31.2
Siri.	Virtual Assistant	43.5%	37.5	16.3
Quora	Crowdsourcing	23.8%	55.4	13.2

Coverage, accuracy, and intelligence index to ChaCha and other Q&A providers. [24]

But here's the rub: lightly shaded at the top of the "article" are the words "White Paper." This should raise a red flag because a White Paper is typically designed to market a product. There are different types of White Papers: Some summarize research and then draw a straight line between the research and the product they want to sell, and others do original research and with the findings highlight a particular product as being superior to others. If the original research fails to point to the "right" product, the White Paper is often deep-sixed. This White Paper was clearly a plug for ChaCha, but searching through the paper I find no mention of the fact that ChaCha sponsored the research. Digging around the Web I turn up the following in an article about Siri being interested in acquiring ChaCha:

> *Siri's intelligence ranked second to last out of 11 of the most popular Q&A programs, according to a January study by Butler University, which ChaCha commissioned.* [25]

Does ChaCha paying Butler to write the White Paper guarantee that the research is biased? This is tricky and the answer may vary from White Paper to White Paper. Suffice it to say that the information presented in a White Paper can be useful and informative, but may not be more reliable than the information in any advertisement. [26]

In evaluating this paper the "persuasive intent heuristic" had kicked in for me. This is a shortcut to information evaluation that involves the tendency to feel that information that might have a bias is not credible. Many types of commercial information can trigger this heuristic, especially when the advertising is unexpected or if people feel they are being manipulated.[27] What is tricky about White Papers is that they often resemble scholarly research papers and the persuasive intent heuristic won't kick in for people unfamiliar with the goals of a White Paper. On the other hand, some information in White Papers can be useful: a double-edged sword.

I dig a little deeper into Q&A site reliability and confirm my suspicions: research shows that the credibility of answers on these sites is all over the map. Research also indicates that accuracy does not improve when multiple answers are provided, nor does popularity correlate with answer quality in terms of accuracy, completeness, and verifiability.[28] Some researchers hold out hope that over time answer quality will increase as more people respond to questions, but so far the jury is out.[29] Other researchers discuss the different motivations people have for participating on Q&A sites, noting that there is a strong appeal in the social connections made via these networks and that reliability may not be the top motivation for using these sites.[30]

While this whole tangent has been interesting, it seems that Q&A sites might be fun for finding answers for trivia questions or getting advice about whether to grow out my hair, but they don't provide accurate information even for the derivation of a movie star's accent, let alone credible science information. I've wandered far afield and it's time to get back on track if I'm to do better research than Daniel did about dogs and empathy.

THE BIG DISCONNECT

I switch gears, sidestepping the Q&A sites and instead, using the reputation heuristic, I choose some of the reputable names I recognize listed in my search results: *Science, Discovery, National Geographic*, and a few others. They are likely the ones Daniel was referencing.

The *Science* article is titled: *Dogs Feel Your Pain*. It states:

> *Yawn next to your dog, and she may do the same. Though it seems simple, this contagious behavior is actually quite remarkable: Only a few animals do it, and only dogs cross the species barrier. Now a new study finds that dogs yawn even when they only hear the sound of us yawning, the strongest evidence yet that canines may be able to empathize with us.*[31]

A *Scientific American* article chimes in with:

Contagious yawning is related to empathy scores in adults. It looks like some dogs also contagiously yawn. The yawn test is just the owner yawning and seeing if their dog yawns back! It's a really simple test but it can tell you a lot about your dog.[32]

My Labrador retriever Zoe is lying next to my desk. I turn, make eye contact, and yawn loudly. Zoe yawns back immediately. *Could Daniel be right?* But of course this is what scientists call anecdotal evidence. People mistakenly use anecdotal evidence as proof when, in fact, one isolated example proves nothing: That's why scientific studies often use large numbers of subjects.

I read several articles and see references to a study by Dr. Silva and another by Dr. Custance. All the articles hold out a promise:

Canine Empathy: Your Dog Really Does Care If You Are Unhappy.[33]
Can Dogs Feel Our Emotions? Yawn Study Suggests Yes.[34]

I use Google Scholar to quickly look up Dr. Custance's research article that these articles are based on. Custance states:

In conclusion, we in no way claim that the present study provides definitive answers to the question of empathy in dogs.[35]

That pretty much encapsulates much of what is wrong with science journalism.

There is a tremendous disconnect between what journalists report on: *Your Dog Really Does Care . . .* and the work of scientists: *We in no way claim. . . .* The media reports on the latest scientific study as if it represents a major breakthrough, when a new piece of research is actually an incremental contribution to a long and complex scholarly discussion that has been going on for years.

Scientific breakthroughs are quite rare. More typically a study suggests something *might* be true and other studies try to move knowledge slowly forward by replicating it or refuting it. Science blogger Travis Saunders suggests that science journalists should instead report on systematic reviews that pull together the findings of many studies because this would better reflect the current state of science on a particular subject.[36]

The flip side is that for science journalists their bread and butter is based on attracting as many readers as possible, and this is much harder if they have to explain all the nooks and crannies of a collection of studies. Journalists excel at what Andrew Revkin calls "Single-Study Syndrome."[37] Journalists typically focus on a single person or a particular project, whereas science is more about the long game and a community working together—and sometimes competing with each other—to confirm or refute working hypotheses.

Sabine Hossenfelder writes that scientists and journalist are "locked in an eternal tug of war."[38] While it is the job of the journalist to educate the public about the latest findings, they are also charged with quickly writing a short entertaining story. Journalists try to translate complex research into meaningful "explainers." Scientists then grumble that the resulting knowledge transfer to the public is extremely low.[39] This tug-of-war is by no means a new phenomenon.[40] Journalists rely on a narrative strategy—the who, what, when, where, and why—to make the science easier to follow, but it can turn a complex topic into an oversimplified research story. That is what turns this:

we in no way claim that the present study provides definitive answers to the question of empathy in dogs.[41]

Into this:

Canine Empathy: Your Dog Really Does Care If You Are Unhappy![42]

All this is nontrivial because scientific findings impact our daily lives. We need to make medical choices, help our elected officials make good policy decisions, and weigh in on complex issues such as climate change. To do this we need help understanding the current science research and to not be swayed by interest groups or unreliable websites. Many people feel that journalists are failing us. Though the dog and empathy story isn't that important in the scheme of things, I had hoped a journalist might have done a better job translating the dog research within the context of the seventy-two studies I had seen evidence of, and tell me which way the research was currently leaning.

Unfortunately journalists are not the only ones generating hype. Scientists and university press offices are also making research findings appear exciting in order to attract funding.[43] Researchers studying how science is communicated find that "hyping" science is now the norm, and this hype has led to public distrust of science and science journalists.[44] Scientists have started to join journalists in turning science into enhanced storytelling to better "sell" their science to boost publicity and encourage funders, even though storytelling often distorts a finding.[45] Science has become so caught up in the media game that some researchers worry it is impacting the nature of scientific study itself, that scientists are getting too involved in politics, power plays, and marketing, and that this impacts their ability to be objective and trustworthy.[46]

All this goes to explain that when I look up articles about dog empathy on Google, it's as if a giant breakthrough occurred around 2012. But did it? There is a "herding phenomenon" that occurs in journalism: Everyone races to cover the same "big" story and they tend to do so in the same way at the same time.[47] For example, the research on dogs and empathy, a very tiny branch of scientific knowledge, has been going on for roughly fifteen years. According to WOS it breaks down like this:

Publication Year	Record Count	% of 72	Bar Chart
2014	9	12.500%	
2011	9	12.500%	
2013	8	11.111%	
2012	8	11.111%	
2010	8	11.111%	
2009	7	9.722%	
2006	4	5. 556%	
2008	3	4.167%	
2003	3	4.167%	
2000	3	4.167%	

Publication-year breakdown of articles on dogs and empathy from Web of Science.[48]

I look back at my Google search results. It's as if a parallel universe exists: on one side are dozens of *National Geographic*–type articles that spout the findings of a couple of studies done in 2012, on the other side are seventy-two scholarly articles spread out over fifteen years, most of which are not easy to access unless you are connected to a research library. This is one more piece of the big disconnect between scientists, journalists, and the public. While more studies are being published in an "open access" format—free and easily linked to—most science articles are still barricaded behind paywalls. This lack of open access generates multiple problems: journalists sometimes can't access studies they are reporting on and readers can't review for themselves the study a journalist is referencing.

These access issues also cause the distortion of science reporting, with gatekeepers such as university press officers, journalists, and social media deciding what science stories we end up seeing. Not a new phenomenon, just an exacerbated one. With seventy-two studies researching dogs and empathy, why are the articles I find via Google all reporting on two or three research studies from 2012? Were these the only studies that indicated that dogs might be empathic?

Researchers at the Public Library of Science (PLOS) investigated how journalists reported on ADHD during the 1990s. They found that ten ADHD studies indicating positive treatment options were heavily reported on in the press, while many others were ignored. They traced these ten studies and found that in subsequent research seven of the ten studies could not be replicated, an eighth study was flawed, and two held up. That is often how the scientific process works: One step forward, several steps back. Unfortunately the press failed to report that many of the earlier findings had not been replicated and failed to tie new findings back to the original studies. Instead the press reported each study as an isolated finding, misrepresenting the big research picture. [49]

Researchers have also investigated how science journalists select from the hundreds of studies that cross their desks daily. They found that fourteen news factors had the highest impact on the selection of science news, including: astonishment, controversy, economic relevance, personalization, reference to elite persons, unexpectedness, and so on. These factors were often found to weigh more heavily in the selection process than the actual importance that a scientist might rate a particular finding. [50] Add in the "dog effect" and it's no wonder that the dog and empathy studies, at least a few of them, made the news. For me, trying to get to the bottom of the dog story and prove Daniel wrong is going to take more than just a handful of Google searches and wading around in the shallow web.

FINDING A SUPERHERO JOURNALIST

Most people don't see any quick fixes to the challenges associated with science journalism and the "medialization" of science generally, though some people advocate for greater transparency and an investment in in-depth science reporting and critical analysis rather than just skimming the surface. A recent policy brief from the Organization for Economic Cooperation and Development calls for making science more transparent and for "extended peer review," allowing nonscientific peers to engage in reviewing science research in order to generate greater public trust of science. [51]

Journalism professor Sharon Dunwoody argues that journalists need to be more invested in finding the truth and not just rebroadcasting news releases. Dunwoody states that journalists need to follow the "weight of evidence" and take a stand. While many science journalists try to present "both sides" to avoid the appearance of bias, Dunwoody argues that what would be more useful to the public is for journalists to interview different scientists, dig deeply, and then inform their readers as to where most scientists "land" on a particular issue. [52]

Rob Morrison agrees and pushes for journalists to cover complex scientific matters and not feel the overriding need to provide balanced coverage. Morrison points out that by trying to be fair, sometimes this leads to absurd coverage where huge numbers of scientists with peer-reviewed evidence to back them up are "balanced" out by providing equal time to one zealot that has drawn the opposite conclusions. [53] Morrison suggests that while some journalists provide opposing views to make the story more exciting, that's valid only if it's a topic where the research really does fall somewhat equally on both sides.[54] Professor Jalees Rehman also calls for science journalists to take a more active role in the critical analysis of science reporting to convey the contextual nature of science: how does a study relate to the others that have been done, has it been replicated, are there design flaws, and were there any "negative studies" that failed to show an anticipated effect?

This journalist superhero may already be in development. Some publications are now sponsoring long-form journalism, gauging that there is an audience for deeper stories and that science cannot be explained accurately in less than 800 words.[55] Unfortunately, no one has done a long-form article on dogs and empathy yet, so I am going to have to find my answer elsewhere. I was reluctant to read through seventy-two lengthy dog research studies to get my answer. I wondered if science bloggers might help shed some light on this topic.

SCIENCE BLOG AS VIRTUAL WATERCOOLER

After my experiences with travel and food blogs, I approached science blogging with some trepidation. While I wanted analysis on the dog research beyond what I was getting from mainstream journalists, I wasn't sure of two issues: the credibility of science blogs and how best to locate one on my topic.[56]

Science bloggers are a diverse species. They run the gamut from avid high school science geek to serious researcher. Also, there are tens of thousands of them.[57] I was hoping that a great science blogger could bridge the thick line between news article melodrama and long dense scholarly article. Perhaps if I found the right blog I could get a more accurate analysis of the dog research, rather than a dummied down: "Dogs Feel Your Pain"![58]

When science blogging became widespread more than a decade ago, it developed organically with all kinds of people jumping in feet first with no single plan as to purpose and goals. Alice Bell, who studies science bloggers, suggests that there may be three main types of science bloggers:

1. "Bad Science" bloggers whose purpose is to correct many of the problems the mainstream media creates in trying to communicate science to the public. They are especially vocal in debunking what they see as media-created science myths, and they often write about controversial science topics that connect to public policy decisions. They have varying credentials and experience.
2. Outreach bloggers whose purpose is to educate the public about science and translate science into understandable prose. If that sounds a

lot like science journalism that is because it is, though with a lot less editorial control. These bloggers also have varying credentials ranging from hobbyists to those with advanced degrees. They differ in their goals: many write for themselves or other hobbyists, whereas others have a strong interest in scientific literacy for the public, often in a particular area.

3. Research bloggers who are faculty or graduate students and use their blogs to communicate to a select group of other researchers or students, to "think aloud," and to create a virtual watercooler to chat about and test out ideas and promote their work. These research blogs walk the line between verbal and written communication: They are informal and resemble the way scientists might talk to each other at a conference, but they cover meaty and often cutting-edge science topics. Their main purpose is not usually citizen science literacy. [59]

Science bloggers tend to be closely networked online, and there is often a great deal of sturm and drang surrounding these connections. While the "Bad Science" bloggers take the prize for the most mudslinging and tempestuousness, they are also the more visible and open to participation from anyone. They embrace their mission of debunking science myths and democratizing science communication with great passion.

ScienceBlogs.com was one of the first large networks of science bloggers. Started in 2006, it included "Bad Science" bloggers and outreach bloggers, whereas most academic research bloggers rely on institutional websites, professional societies, or scholarly journal websites. Like many networks, ScienceBlogs has gone through several iterations, including a huge revolt when one-quarter of the bloggers jumped ship when site administrators decided to host a blog by PepsiCo staff about nutrition. Succumbing to commercial pressures is viewed as abandoning what many science bloggers hold dear.

ScienceBlogs was later purchased by National Geographic in 2011, but seems to run independently. I do a quick search on dogs and empathy on ScienceBlogs, but turn up nothing of interest. The collection of blogs includes only thirty active ones and hundreds that are archived. Most are fun and chatty: such as The Angry Toxologist and Guilty Planet, but their reliability appears uneven.

What happened at ScienceBlogs was not an isolated event. It represents the natural life cycle of many science blogging communities, including the Nature Network, which shuttered its doors in 2013. The life cycle starts with the initial excitement of dedicated and passionate volunteer contributors attracting increasing numbers of readers, then comes the need for better infrastructure and support, and ultimately there is an increasing need for money and the view that with so many readers there must be a way to generate revenue. Then the tension between the original mission that attracted the bloggers in the first place, and the views of those running the network, starts to fester. Eventually there may be a revolt, mean-spirited remarks on all sides, and then the mainstream media siphons off some of the better writers who are willing to go while the remaining players tootle along or are archived.[60]

Bloggers that transition to the mainstream media are paid minimal if any wages, and they replace the more expensive and experienced but now laid-off science journalists. Although this varies by site, the bloggers typically lose some of their freedom and are subject to some degree of editorial control, and the public gets talented writers who lack formal training in journalistic standards such as verification and completeness. Essentially these blogs morph into traditional opinion columns, not strong, reliable science writing. David Crotty, a senior editor at Oxford University Press, sums up the situation:

> That's how most of us encounter science blogs these days, as the occasional article appearing via a major publication's website, with all the trappings of a formal opinion column.[61]

The popularity of opinion writing is accelerating. Many readers seek and trust this "news with a view."[62] While we used to value expertise, objectivity, and perceived lack of bias, and while we continue to believe that unbiased sources are more credible than those that lack balance, at the same time we tend to seek out opinion pieces. Researchers have found that readers seek out "attitude consistent" information over less biased sources.[63] People recognize bias in writing when it goes against what they believe, but they don't recognize bias when it supports their beliefs. Ironically, people actually believe that information they read that is congruent with their beliefs is *more* credible than neutral or balanced information, and they have a strong tendency to seek out this congruent information.

At the same time, the journalism gatekeepers—namely editors—that used to select what science topics we learn about are being replaced by "likes," popularity votes, and the Google search algorithm. While many people objected to editors having so much power over what science topics we see in the news, I'm not sure I like my news curated by the crowd. It explains today's top science article in Buzzfeed:

> Scientists Got Some Birds Drunk to see if it has any Effect on their Singing. "Should auld acquaintance be (hiccup)." —A bird.[64]

Recent research indicates that when people read traditional news articles online they select them based on the reputation of the source, but when they read blogs they pay attention to ratings.[65] Scholars have expressed concern over using audience metrics in the selection of news, and they point out that market forces end up controlling data-driven news selection because media that want page views end up pandering to their audience, giving them the dog and drunk bird stories, and this can have a detrimental effect on our long-term media diet.[66]

Researchers are also concerned that as we repeatedly select attitude congruent information to read, over time this might breed extreme intolerance for other points of view. As early as 2007, legal scholar Cass Sunstein wrote that our self-selected exposure to information could result in the "Daily Me" of personalized news stories that filter out anything that disagrees with our beliefs.[67] In 2010 a Pew study indicated that 31 percent of Americans admit to a clear preference to *only* read sources that share their point of view and research suggests this is increasing.[68]

On the other hand, perhaps what we lose in journalistic standards we make up for in the checks and balances that derive from the interactive nature of blogging. Most bloggers find that the second they pop anything out there, mistakes are quickly caught and corrected by readers. This interactive open-ended journalism is becoming standard fare in the mainstream media now also, a gift from the blogosphere. While this can be a valuable way of catching errors, it can also incur a lot of spam and ranting if there are no editorial filters. While annoying in some news situations, comments on science articles can detrimentally influence people's understanding of a science topic.[69]

Researchblogging.org and PLOS-sponsored blogs seem to be two of the better collections of science bloggers I come across. Researchblogging.org contains more than a thousand bloggers who go through a registration system and must cite scholarly sources if they want to be included. This mild editorial control bumps up the quality of the blogs and provides a good enough filter that I find a lot of the writing on par with the better science journalists. Also, more than half of the bloggers are tied to academic institutions as graduate students or researchers, which provides an additional marker of quality, as does the ".org" address.

While much smaller, only sixteen, the PLOS bloggers also adhere to a strong sense of professionalism similar to that of science journalists. Some of the PLOS writers are currently academic researchers. While they resemble science journalists, they use a more informal tone, are unpaid, and unlike traditional journalists, they wear more hats, including researcher, writer, publisher, editor, teacher, discussion moderator, and comment editor, with the power to delete comments they feel are unproductive.[70]

Though recognizing that these are casual discussions on the level of informed opinion, rather than peer-reviewed science, I pop on Researchblogging.org to search for dogs and empathy. There are two potentially promising articles by one author, but when I click on them I am informed that the "author has deleted the site." In fact the author seems to have evaporated from the universe. Science bloggers sometimes write under pseudonyms, and I'm not sure who this blogger is or why he or she chose to delete what looked like interesting articles, but unlike archived news articles, bloggers sometimes just disappear. I search the PLOS collection as well, but it is too small and has nothing on my topic.

So my foray into blogging in search of more reliable information about dogs and empathy so far has been a bust. While some of the better bloggers are migrating into traditional media, their opinion columns are not the hard evidence I want.[71] I decide to turn to the third category of blogger: the academic researcher.

The watercooler set turns out to write for a completely different audience. Academics have participated for centuries in what is called the invisible college: A networked group of researchers who share and discuss highly granular research topics. These researchers go to the same conferences, read, write, and peer review for the same journals, and all know, or know of, each other. Blogs, as well as Wikis, are just new devices that have stepped in to help researchers more effectively communicate with each other, get feedback on their work, increase their visibility, and sometimes discuss areas outside of research such as grant proposals, lab work, and journal submission processes.[72]

While many academics do not write blogs because there is not yet a serious recognition of blog writing within the academy, others see it as a useful way to informally discuss or think aloud about research interests. But they call these bloggers part of the *invisible* college for a reason: they are small bunches of researchers talking to each other, and while brilliant for supporting science research, these types of blogs do little to enhance public understanding of science. This isn't where I'm going to find an analysis of the research on dogs and empathy.

I feel like I am running around in a circle with one foot nailed to the ground. If I look for blogs through some of the large blogging platforms I turn up articles similar to the fluff I've already viewed via Google: the ones from *Discovery*, *National Geographic*, and *the Guardian* collection of science blogs. The *Guardian* blogs appear incessantly, because while they host some high-quality blogs they also let almost anyone blog for them. Many media companies use this strategy: the more content, the more hits, the more advertisements viewed, the higher the Google ranking: wash, rinse, repeat.[73] All these cute yawning-dog stories are not going to win my bet with Daniel or get to the bottom of the research on dogs and empathy. It was time *to start at the source.*

START AT THE SOURCE

Google searches, Q&A sites, news sites, and blogs can be good for many types of information—sports scores, factual questions, current events—but to get a deep understanding of a science topic involves deeper searching. It was time to bite the bullet and go into the actual research literature: The primary sources that provide the research results on dogs and empathy. I return to both WOS and Google Scholar and pull together a list of articles from the past decade that directly relate to my topic: seventy-two.

The next step is to apply three filters to narrow my list of candidates:

1. **Recent review articles available?** By searching WOS and filtering by "review" I can find out if there have been any recent literature reviews that would sum up the current state of the research on the topic, similar to what I used in chapter 3. For this topic there are no literature reviews, probably because the topic is small. I double-check on Google Scholar using the advanced search pull-down box and looking for the words Dogs, Empathy, and Review in the title field. Nothing.

2. **You *can* judge an article by its title, and abstract.** I glance through the titles of the seventy-two articles. More than half I can eliminate as they are about empathy in people and how dogs can promote this, or they are off topic in some other way. For the remaining few dozen articles I skim abstracts and realize that a few more are off topic, and I narrow my pool of articles to a reasonable fifteen.

3. **Organize and locate strays.** Next I capture the remaining articles in a bibliographic tool. I use Mendeley, which is free; other popular tools are Zotero, RefWorks, and EndNote. Mendeley takes PDF articles and enables annotations and note taking in addition to automatically for-matting footnotes. If this is a onetime endeavor, even a simple spread-sheet like Excel can help in tracking articles. Once I have the articles housed in Mendeley, I glance at the beginning of each article. Science articles begin with a mini literature review: what's been happening in this area of study, who are the major players, what have they been saying, and where does this new piece of the research puzzle fit. This mini literature review lets me pick up any important stray articles that I may have missed. I also glance at each article's bibliography. I find a few items to add to my pile.

Now it is actually time to read through what is now seventeen articles: a hefty bunch. Science research articles can run from four to forty pages, but, as many academics know, you don't really have to *read* an entire article to know what it says. Instead:

1. Glance over the structure and features of the article.
2. Make a note of the author's main points—often in the abstract and discussion. Abstracts typically include: the purpose (the why), the methodology (the how), the results (the what), and the conclusion (what it means).
3. If you are a visual learner look over the graphs and charts that tell the key pieces of the research story.
4. As you skim, ask questions: What are they saying? What are they trying to prove? Did they prove it?
5. Skim the introduction. A good introduction will tell you what is already known about a topic, what is not known, and what specific question this little piece of research seeks to answer.
6. As you skim the article look for words like: "we hypothesize," "unexpected," "in contrast to previous work," "the data suggest."[74]

In reading these science articles I try to tell myself the story of the research: just like the science journalist turns science into a narrative. There is drama, a plot, often some twist or climax, and then a denouement with a "what's next?" What does future research need to address? I also like to think of science research as a collaborative *and* competitive sport: a little like ultimate Frisbee. Often there is a healthy competition going on where researchers try to build out research further or where they sometimes disprove or poke holes in other researchers' work.

THE STORY OF DOGS AND EMPATHY

So here is my narrative. Once upon a time . . . there was a researcher named Joly-Mascheroni. (Note: To simplify I am using the last name of the first author of each study. All studies were from peer-reviewed journals and were conducted by multiple authors.) Joly-Mascheroni's research was the first to document that human yawns might be contagious to dogs. The study used twenty-nine dogs and subjected them to both yawns and mouth movements that were similar to yawns.[75] Though Joly-Mascheroni was the first to show contagious yawning in dogs, like all good science his study was not done in isolation. There had been a substantial amount of research on several fronts that led the way to this study, including:

1. Research suggesting a link between contagious yawning and measures of empathy in humans and a lack of contagious yawning in very young children who have not yet developed empathy, and in children with autism who lack the ability to empathize.

2. Several studies documenting contagious yawning in chimpanzees, but not in other primates.
3. A number of studies that suggest dogs are unusually skilled at reading human social cues. [76]

Based on this, Joly-Mascheroni hypothesizes that dogs may have the capacity for some form of rudimentary empathy and that proof of contagious yawning may help document this. Joly-Mascheroni found that 72 percent of dogs had contagious yawning, which is higher than the 60 percent found in humans. He goes on to say that the dog yawning could be empathy, but could also be a stress response and further studies with physiological measures of stress would be needed to rule this out.

Ok, next up comes Yoon. Yoon doesn't report on research, but instead writes a thought piece in which she notes that Joly-Mascheroni's research findings are exciting, but it is hard to parse out what might be empathy, simple mimicry, or a hard-wired contagion response. [77] With mimicry, many studies show that humans imitate other human behaviors without awareness or intent and that this mimicry serves to smooth social interactions. Could dogs be doing that? Yoon also mentions new research by Harr, that shows that dogs watching videos of humans yawning do not "catch" yawns, but that humans watching videos of humans yawning do catch yawns. [78] In fact, just reading this text now you are likely to be yawning if you are one of the 60 percent of humans that are particularly prone. Are you yawning yet?

Harr takes and runs with the ball, pointing out that her study not only fails to show dogs catching yawns, but that there is only a tiny amount of research connecting contagious yawning and empathy anyway. Harr does lament the fact that her study included videos, and that perhaps if she had used more "live" humans she would have confirmed Joly-Mascheroni's findings that dogs actually "catch" yawns. [79]

Next up is Silva, who writes an "opinion piece" to sort through the research on dogs and empathy and propose further research directions. She states that there may be some level of empathy beyond simple emotional contagion, given the yawn effect from Joly-Mascheroni's study, and she reviews many studies that have tried to sort out various emotional connections between dogs and humans. [80]

O'Hara steps up to the plate to report on her strong research study that used family dogs and shelter dogs to see if there is a familiarity link that is found between humans, because humans are more empathic with humans that they know. O'Hara also tries to control for stress in the environment to rule out a "stress" yawn in dogs, as well as using real people rather than videos. This is important: O'Hara noted the problems the previous researchers reported and corrected for these. Essentially O'Hara found "little support for empathy-related yawning contagion in dogs" and questions the validity of the Joly-Mascheroni study given that both Harr and O'Hara cannot replicate even the finding of yawn "catching." While O'Hara did find a tiny amount of yawn contagion he agrees with Yoon: Some of the dogs might yawn to mimic humans to smooth interactions with them or for some unknown biological reason.[81] Not exactly empathy.

And, just when the empathy researchers are thinking of throwing in the towel, along comes Silva again, a year after her opinion piece, to report on her research showing unexpected findings: not only did dogs catch yawns, but they did it more when they were familiar with the people yawning. While not conclusive, Silva says this opens the door for the potential for empathy. Silva mentions problems with some of the studies that found negative effects (no contagion or no potential for empathy), and, of course mentions that more research is needed.[82]

Meanwhile, on the sidelines, the plot thickens. Custance takes a separate approach from the yawning studies and adapts a protocol used with infants and finds that when dogs approach a human who is pretending to cry they do so for reasons such as mimicry or previous rewards, rather than any type of possible empathy.[83] But then along comes Romero, back on track, with the aim of replicating the successful yawn studies. She finds results similar to Silva's while attempting to control for stress, and agrees that this may open the door for the potential for some rudimentary form of empathy in dogs.[84]

Interestingly, this is when the dog studies hit the media fan and are blown around the Web: "Dogs Feel Your Pain!" This is around 2012 that the research by Custance, Silva, and Romero are reported on. Silva and Romero have reported optimistically about a link, but Custance is clear that her research negates the link, though she is quoted as saying:

> *On the surface, it certainly seemed as if the dogs were demonstrating empathy.*[85]

Now for the intrigue: Madsen comes along in 2013 with a study that carefully avoids any of the challenges earlier studies had encountered and that shows that dogs catch yawns, but the emotional connection with the human yawner (stranger or owner) has no impact on which dogs catch yawns. Madsen also shows some evidence that yawning has other purposes, but that there appears to be no connection to empathy.[86]

And then along comes Moyaho, taking a different approach. He finds that many vertebrates actually yawn contagiously, including the rats he studies. In fact, his study finds that rats most likely show contagious yawning in order to communicate possible greater physiological capacity as a precursor to a possible conflict with a fellow rat. At the same time as Moyaho's study, further research on dogs and yawns also suggests that while yawn contagion occurs, it may be explained by stress, contrary to what other studies suggested, as higher cortisol levels were found in dogs that caught human yawns. [87]

Other books and studies have come out recently suggesting that even experienced science researchers can sometimes be anthropocentric in studying dogs: they forget to take into account how the dog experiences the world. For example, dogs view the world much more from their acute sense of smell than through the use of their eyes, so research on dogs watching people yawn may not be the best measure of communication from a dog point of view. [88]

And to add fuel, a separate line of inquiry about why humans catch yawns seems to indicate that yawning promotes vigilance and alertness that overrides a drive to sleep, rather than empathy, though there might be different reasons people "catch" yawns. [89] Another large study looking just at humans and yawn catching found no indication that catching yawns suggested greater levels of empathy, but that contagious yawning was genetic and remained consistent over time for a certain percentage of the human population. [90] So if you haven't been yawning throughout this passage, according to the latest research don't worry, your propensity for empathy remains intact.

LESSONS LEARNED

And so it goes. Boring? Maybe, except to the researchers trying to parse this out. Is it any wonder that science journalists struggle to tell a more exciting version? At the same time, should science journalists and bloggers have reported on the couple of studies that suggested an empathy connection? Yes, but they should have provided follow-up as more research failed to confirm the initial studies. They should also have reported on them with more context and nuance. The story about dogs and empathy on the shallow web right now tells a story that is not just superficial: It is not true. And that is the story that Daniel read.

Perhaps science reporters should report less frequently and in long form with a contextual review, not just a single study report that is often meaningless. Easy for me to say. Would anyone read it? Maybe, but only people who really wanted to know. And of course by not producing scads of content it would go against generating a strong revenue stream.

While diving deep and reading longer studies may seem like more work, in fact I had spent twice as much time wading through the shallow web of magazine articles and blogs. The searches on WOS and Google Scholar, the quick review and narrowing down of titles, and the skimming of just over a dozen articles took about three hours. But my dog topic was less complex than many science topics: Your mileage may vary. Getting to the best current research on a science topic takes time if you want accurate and reliable information.

For science information in particular, given its complexity, it is important to keep in mind the following:

1. Start at the Source

It's always tempting to rely on Google, but when Google continually churned up fluff pieces I finally went to the scientific literature. I relied on two large aggregated collections: Google Scholar and Web of Science. For some science topics there are better choices to help narrow your topic: for example PubMed for health-related information or BIOSIS for coverage of biology journals. Using a more filtered database will help weed out off-topic articles. Three quick tricks for getting directly at scholarship within a particular discipline:

  a. Combine the discipline name with the word "database" to locate the name of databases that cover journals in a specific area. Often these databases cost money but can be used for free if you have access to an academic library or larger public library.
  b. Search the discipline name with the word *LibGuides*. The Library Guide will then give you a list of the best resources to use when searching for information within that area. This can be a little confusing because LibGuides are designed by librarians for specific libraries, which means you will not have access to all of the resources listed. If you are connected to an academic institution, use their LibGuides on their website to search by discipline for links to the best sources they own.
  c. Many scholars also provide pre-prints to articles that have not yet gone through peer review but are headed that way. For a comprehensive list of pre-print repositories by discipline, see http://oad.simmons.edu/oadwiki/Disciplinary_repositories or http://www.osti.gov/eprints/.

2. Pay Attention to the "Psychology of Search"

Be aware of the heuristics or shortcuts you use to approach searching for and evaluating information. Heuristics are not in and of themselves wrong, but it is important to be mindful that you are using them. In particular, satisficing is always going to jeopardize the quality of information you retrieve, but if it is a low-stakes piece of information it may be ok to do a quick search. For seeking information that is important to you, follow Kahneman's advice by thinking slow, doubting, hesitating, and qualifying. [91]

3. Expert, Amateur, Crowd?

There are science journalists and bloggers out there—they are few and far between—that provide critical science journalism and are worth reading. Are they experts or amateurs? While they are not scientists, they are experts at reporting on science. But many science journalists and bloggers fail to push past the hype and simply write "explainer" pieces that provide little content or accuracy. As for the crowd, in science there are many places where crowd wisdom has been tapped—projects like Galaxy Zoo and bird counts by Project FeederWatch—that have been tremendously valuable. For getting information on a science topic, crowd-sourced information such as that found on Q&A sites and Wikipedia can be unreliable.

4. Context, Motivation, and Bias

These are tricky concepts in science research. For science journalists and bloggers sometimes the motivation to pull in readers outweighs the accuracy of the reporting. And even for expert researchers some bias comes in to play. To a large degree, peer-review and editorial filters assist in keeping this to a minimum. Context is the most important piece to keep in mind when researching a science topic: one study will not give an answer, only by looking at reviews of the literature or reading a handful of recent key studies can one arrive at a fair take on the current state of scientific knowledge about a topic. If anyone says the science is settled on a topic, don't believe them. This goes for me too: When I report back to Daniel I'm only reporting on our present understanding of dogs and empathy. We just don't know, but we know which way the research is currently leaning.

5. Comparison and Corroboration

This is how science works: It is a series of studies that are later confirmed or refuted, or sometimes a mix of both. By reading several key articles and by paying attention to the mini literature reviews at the beginning of scholarly articles, comparison and corroboration is built into the research process.

6. Go Deep, or Not

Did I really need to go deep for the dogs and empathy story? That's a question only I can answer. Daniel is not happy that I did.

NOTES

1. Joseph Mandak II, "Cyanide Searches Found on Poison Suspect's Laptop," *Boston Globe,* October 28, 2014, http://www.bostonglobe.com/news/nation/2014/10/28/cyanide-searches-found-poison-suspect-laptop/bGf880zbkGr3kllSWqa9II/story.html.

2. Paula Reed Ward, "The Ferrante Trial: A Look Inside the Cyanide Poisoning Case," *Pittsburgh Post Gazette,* October 19, 2014, http://www.post-gazette.com/local/city/2014/10/19/The-Ferrante-trial-Inside-the-Autumn-Marie-Klein-cyanide-poisoning-case-in-Pittsburgh/stories/201410190091.

3. See http://www.wikihow.com/Tell-if-Your-Wife-Is-Cheating.

4. See https://en.wikipedia.org/wiki/MatchMove.

5. D.Y. are the initials of a member on Answers.com.

6. See Answers.com help section at http://wiki.answers.com/help/trust_points.

7. Bob Longino, "Pirate Depp Is Summer's Real Treasure," *Atlanta Journal-Constitution,* July 9, 2003.

8. Roger Moore, "Yo, ho, ha!: Gladly Returning to a Depp-Charged Sea," *Charleston Gazette,* July 6, 2006.

9. Gerd Gigerenzer and Wolfgang Gaissmaier, "Heuristic Decision Making," *Annual Review of Psychology* 62 (January 2011), doi:10.1146/annurev-psych-120709-145346.

10. Katarzyna Materska, "Information Heuristics of Information Literate People," 2014 pre-print, http://eprints.rclis.org/23919/.

11. Miriam J. Metzger and Andrew J. Flanagin, "Credibility and Trust of Information in Online Environments: The Use of Cognitive Heuristics," *Journal of Pragmatics* 59 (July 16, 2013), http://www.comm.ucsb.edu/faculty/flanagin/CV/Metzger&Flanagin,2013%28JoP%29.pdf.

12. Bree Nordensen, "Overload! Journalism's Battle for Relevance in an Age of Too Much Information," *Columbia Journalism* Review, November 30, 2008, http://www.cjr.org/feature/overload_1.php?page=all&print=true#sthash.yoaFpa6t.dpuf.

13. D.J. O'Keefe, *Persuasion: Theory and Research* (Newbury Park, CA: Sage, 1990).

14. M.J. Metzger, A.J. Flanagin, and R. Medders, "Social and Heuristic Approaches to Credibility Evaluation Online," *Journal of Communication* 60, no. 3 (2010); S. Sundar, "The MAIN Model: A Heuristic Approach to Understanding Technology Effects on Credibility," in *Digital Media, Youth, and Credibility,* ed. M. Metzger and A. Flanagin (Cambridge, MA: MIT Press, 2008).

15. Ibid.

16. E. Hargittai, F. Fullerton, E. Menchen-Trevino, and K. Y. Thomas, "Trust Online: Young Adults' Evaluation of Web Content," *International Journal of Communication* 4 (2010), http://webuse.org/pdf/HargittaiEtAlTrustOnlineIJoC10.pdf.

17. Dominique Brossard and Dietram A. Scheufele, "Science, New Media, and the Public," *Science* 339 (2013), doi: 10.1126/science.1232329.

18. Amy Mitchell, "State of the News Media 2014," Pew Research Journalism Project State of the Media, March 26, 2014, http://www.journalism.org/2014/03/26/state-of-the-news-media-2014-overview; Claire Cain Miller, "Why BuzzFeed Is Trying to Shift Its Strategy," *New York Times,* August 12, 2014, http://www.nytimes.com/2014/08/13/upshot/why-buzzfeed-is-trying-to-shift-its-strategy.html?action=click&contentCollection=Media&region=Footer&module=MoreInSection&pgtype=article; Vindu Goel and Ravi Somaiya, "With New App, Facebook Aims to Make Its Users' Feeds Newsier," *New York Times,* February 4, 2014, http://www.nytimes.com/2014/02/04/technology/with-new-app-facebook-aims-to-make-its-users-feeds-newsier.html.

19. Matthew D. Atkinson, Maria Deam, and Joseph E. Uscinski, "What's a Dog Story Worth?" *PS: Political Science & Politics* 47 (2014), doi:10.1017/S1049096514001103.

20. Web of Science is one of two "comprehensive" databases to the scholarly literature that is available in some academic libraries. Scopus has similar coverage and search features.

21. Reproduced under a license from Thomson Reuters. You may not copy or redistribute this material in whole or in part without the prior written consent of Thomson Reuters.

22. See https://wiki.answers.com/Q/User:Mediatech.

23. Trent Ritzenthaler, "Q&A Platforms Evaluated Using Butler University Q&A Intelligence Index," White Paper, January 31, 2013, http://www.butler.edu/media/3109221/bba-qa_study.pdf.

24. Trent Ritzenthaler, "Q&A Platforms Evaluated Using Butler University Q&A Intelligence Index," White Paper, January 31, 2013, http://www.butler.edu/media/3109221/bba-qa_study.pdf.

25. Dan Human, "Apple Buyout in ChaCha's Future," *Indianapolis Business Journal*, November 30, 2013, http://www.ibj.com/articles/print/44847-apple-buyout-in-chacha-s-future.

26. Sachiko Sakamuro, Karl Stolley, and Charlotte Hyde, "White Paper Purpose and Audience," Purdue OWL, https://owl.english.purdue.edu/owl/owlprint/546/.

27. Metzger et al., "Social and Heuristic Approaches."

28. Pnina Fishman, "A Comparative Assessment of Answer Quality on Four Question Answering Sites," *Journal of Information Science* 37, no. 5 (October 2011), doi: 10.1177/0165551511415584; Alton Y.K. Chua and Banerjee Snehasish, "So Fast So Good: An Analysis of Answer Quality and Answer Speed in Community Question-Answering Sites," *Journal of the Association for Information Science and Technology* 64 (2013), doi: 10.1002/asi.22902.

29. Chua Snehasish, "So Fast So Good."

30. Erik Choi and Chirag Shah, "User Motivation for Asking a Question in Online Q&A Services," *Journal of Association for Information Science & Technology* (in press); C. Shah, Vanessa Kitzie, and Erik Choi, "Modalities, Motivations, and Materials—Investigating Traditional and Social Online Q&A Services," *Journal of Information Science* (2014).

31. Zuberoa Marcos, "Dogs Feel Your Pain," *Science* (May 7, 2012), http://news.sciencemag.org/2012/05/dogs-feel-your-pain.

32. Gareth Cook, "The Brilliance of the Dog Mind," *Scientific American*, February 5, 2013, http://www.scientificamerican.com/article/brilliance-of-dog-mind/.

33. Stanley Coren, "Canine Empathy: Your Dog Really Does Care If You Are Unhappy," *Psychology Today*, June 7, 2012, http://www.psychologytoday.com/blog/canine-corner/201206/canine-empathy-your-dog-really-does-care-if-you-are-unhappy.

34. Christine Dell'Amore, "Can Dogs Feel Our Emotions? Yawn Study Suggests Yes," *National Geographic*, August 8, 2013, http://news.nationalgeographic.com/news/2013/08/130808-yawning-dogs-contagious-animals-empathy-science.

35. Deborah Custance and Jennifer Mayer, "Empathic-Like Responding by Domestic Dogs (Canis Familiaris) to Distress in Humans: An Exploratory Study," *Animal Cognition* 15, no. 5. (September 2012), doi: 10.1007/s10071-012-0510-1.

36. Travis Saunders, "Dear Newspapers: Individual Studies do not Exist in a Vacuum," PLOS Blogs, December 8, 2011, http://blogs.plos.org/obesitypanacea/2011/12/08/dear-newspapers-individual-studies-do-not-exist-in-a-vacuum/.

37. Andrew C. Revkin, "Single-Study Syndrome and the G.M.O. Food Fight," *New York Times*, September 20, 2012, http://dotearth.blogs.nytimes.com/2012/09/20/the-gmo-food-fight-rats-cancer-and-single-study-syndrome/?_r=0.

38. Sabine Hossenfelder, "The Eternal Tug of War Between Science Journalists and Scientists. A Graphical Story," BackReaction Blog, February 2014, http://backreaction.blogspot.com/2014/02/the-eternal-tug-of-war-between-science.html.

39. "Public Praises Science; Scientists Fault Public, Media," Pew Research Center for the People & the Press, July 9, 2009, http://www.people-press.org/2009/07/09/public-praises-science-scientists-fault-public-media/.

40. Jim Hartz and Rick Chappell, *Worlds Apart: How the Distance Between Science and Journalism Threatens America's Future* (Nashville, TN: First Amendment Center, 1997).

41. Custance and Mayer, "Empathic-Like Responding by Domestic Dogs."

42. Coren, "Canine Empathy."

43. Charlotte Autzen, "Press Releases: The New Trend in Science Communication," *JCOM Journal of Science Communication* 13 no. 3 (September 22, 2014); "Nature. Media Studies for Scientists," *Nature* 416 (April 4, 2002), doi: 10.1038/416461a.

44. T. Bubela, "Science Communication in Transition: Genomics Hype, Public Engagement, Education and Commercialization Pressures," *Clinical Genetics* 70, no. 5 (November 2006); Brigitte Nerlich, "Moderation Impossible? On Hype, Honesty and Trust in the Context

of Modern Academic Life," *Sociological Review* 61 (December 3, 2013), doi: 10.1111/1467-954X.12099.

45. Simone Rodder, Martina Franzen, and Peter Weingart, eds., "The Sciences' Media Connection: Public Communication and its Repercussions," *Sociology of the Sciences Yearbook* 28 (2012); B. Drescher, "Science and Spin Are Very Bad Bedfellows," ICBS Everywhere Blog, 2012, http://icbseverywhere.com/blog/2012/05/science-and-spin-are-very-bad-bedfellows.

46. Martin Carrier and Peter Weingart, "The Politicization of Science: The Esf-zif-bielefeld Conference on Science and Values," *Journal for General Philosophy of Science* 40, no. 2 (2009); Marin Bauer and Massimiano Bucchi, eds., *Journalism, Science and Society: Science Communication Between News and Public Relations* (London: Routledge, 2007).

47. Martin Robbins, "Why I Spoofed Science Journalism, and How to Fix It," *Guardian,* September 28, 2010, http://www.theguardian.com/science/the-lay-scientist/2010/sep/28/science-journalism-spoof.

48. This material is reproduced under a license from Thomson Reuters. You may not copy or redistribute this material in whole or in part without the prior written consent of Thomson Reuters.

49. F. Gonon, J.P. Konsman, D. Cohen, and T. Boraud, "Why Most Biomedical Findings Echoed by Newspapers Turn Out to Be False: The Case of Attention Deficit Hyperactivity Disorder," PLoSONE 7, no. 9 (2012), doi:10.1371/journal.pone.0044275; Curtis Brainard, "The Value of Skepticism—Why Science Reporters Should Question Research," *Columbia Journalism Review,* (October 9, 2012), http://www.cjr.org/the_observatory/medical_research_spin_media_pr.php?page=all.

50. III Franziska Badenschier and Holger Wormer, "Issue Selection in Science Journalism: Towards a Special Theory of News Values for Science News?" in *The Science's Media Connection and Communication to the Public and Its Repercussions*, ed. Simone Roedder, Martina Franzen, and Peter Weingart (Dodrecht, The Netherlands: Springer, 2012); David Murray, Joel Schwartz, and S. Robert Lichter, *It Ain't Necessarily So: How Media Make and Unmake the Scientific Picture of Reality* (Lanham, MD: Rowman & Littlefield, 2001).

51. OECD Innovation Policy Platform, Issue Brief Peer Review, June 2011, http://www.oecd.org/innovation/policyplatform/48136766.pdf.

52. Sharon Dunwoody, "Weight-of-Evidence Reporting: What Is It? Why Use It?" Nieman Reports, December 15, 2005, http://niemanreports.org/articles/weight-of-evidence-reporting-what-is-it-why-use-it/.

53. Rob Morrison, "A Catalyst for Better Science Journalism," *Austraasian Science* 35, no. 1 (January/February 2014).

54. Ibid. See also "Science Journalism: A Delicate Balancing Act," *Lancet,* (July 30, 2011), doi: http://dx.doi.org/10.1016/S0140-6736(11)61192-6.

55. Slate and Medium.com both have programs supporting long-form journalism. Jill Abramson, former editor of the *New York Times*, and Steven Brill have recently started a long-form journalism project. See Kelly McBride, "Jill Abramson Startup to Advance Writers up to $100k for Longform Work," *Poynter Media Wire,* November 2, 2014, http://www.poynter.org/news/mediawire/278851/jill-abramson-startup-to-advance-writers-up-to-100k-for-longform-work/.

56. A Google search combining "LibGuides" (librarian-curated resource guides) and "science blogs" turns up a handful of big science blog collections, but my search results on dogs and empathy were disappointing. No different than what I had already uncovered through a regular Google search. Many of the large blog search engines are defunct or ineffective. Google's blog search engine went belly up in 2013 and Technorati, famous for tracking the blogosphere, has shifted over into social media generally. Sites such as Networkedblogs.com tend to deal with light content on music, parenting, weddings, and so on. They do not even have a science category for searching.

57. S. Fausto, "Research Blogging: Indexing and Registering the Change in Science 2.0," *PLOS One* 7, no. 12 (2012), http://www.plosone.org/article/info%3Adoi%2F10.1371%2Fjournal.pone.0050109.

58. Zuberoa Marcos, "Dogs Feel Your Pain," *Science* (May 7, 2012), http://news.sciencemag.org/2012/05/dogs-feel-your-pain.

59. J. Priem, H. Piwowar, and B. Hemminger, "Altmetrics in the Wild: Using Social Media to Explore Scholarly Impact," ArXiv, March 20, 2012, http://arxiv.org/abs/1203.4745; Alice Bell, "'ScienceBlogs Is a High School Clique, Nature Network Is a Private Club': Imagining the Communities of Online Science," *CJMS Special issue* (Fall 2012); Merja Mahrt and Cornelius Puschmann, "Science Blogging—An Exploratory Study of Motives, Styles, and Audience Reactions," *SISSA International School for Advanced Studies* (July 22, 2014), http://jcom.sissa.it/archive/13/03/JCOM_1303_2014_A05/JCOM_1303_2014_A05.pdf; C. Puschmann, "(Micro)Blogging Science? Notes on Potentials and Constraints of New Forms of Scholarly Communication," *Opening Science*, ed. S. Friesike and S. Bartling (New York: Springer, 2014); I. Kouper, "Science Blogs and Public Engagement with Science: Practices, Challenges, and Opportunities," *Journal of Communication* 9, no. 1 (2010).

60. David Crotty, "A New Science Blogging Scandal: Deja Vu All Over Again," Scholarly Kitchen Blog Post, October 17, 2013, http://scholarlykitchen.sspnet.org/2013/10/17/a-recent-science-blogging-scandal-deja-vu-all-over-again/; David Crotty, "The Nature Network Implosion—Hmmm, This All Seems Awfully Familiar," (December 13, 2010), Scholarly Kitchen Blog Post, http://scholarlykitchen.sspnet.org/2010/12/13/the-nature-network-implosion-hmmm-this-all-seems-awfully-familiar/.

61. Crotty, "A New Science Blogging Scandal."

62. Burton St. John III and Kirsten A. Johnson, eds., *News with a View: Essays on the Eclipse of Objectivity in Modern Journalism* (Jefferson, NC: McFarland, 2012).

63. Ethan Hartsell, Miriam Metzger, and Andrew J. Flanagin, "Contemporary News Production and Consumption: Implications for Selective Exposure, Group Polarization, and Credibility," in St. John III and Johnson, *News with a View*.

64. Monica Galazka, "Scientists Got Some Birds Drunk to See If It Has any Effect on Their Singing," BuzzFeed, December 29, 2014, http://www.buzzfeed.com/kasiagalazka/drunk-birds-slur-when-they-sing#.nynaWe4o9.

65. Stephen Winter and Nicole Krrämer, "A Question of Credibility—Effects Of Source Cues and Recommendations on Information Selection on News Sites and Blogs," *Communications* 39, no. 4 (November 2014).

66. Edson C. Tandoc Jr. and Ryan J. Thomas, "The Ethics of Web Analytics: Implications of Using Audience Metrics in News Construction," *Digital Journalism,* May 1, 2014, doi: 10.1080/21670811.2014.909122.

67. Cass Sunstein, *Worst-Case Scenarios* (Cambridge: Harvard University Press, 2007).

68. Hartsell et al., "Contemporary News Production and Consumption."

69. A.A. Anderson, D. Brossard, D.A. Scheufele, M.A. Xenos, and P. Ladwig, "The 'Nasty Effect': Online Incivility and Risk Perceptions of Emerging Technologies," *Journal of Computer-Mediated Communication* 19 (2014), doi: 10.1111/jcc4.12009; Chris Mooney, "The Science of Why Comment Trolls Suck: The Online Peanut Gallery Can Get You so Riled Up That Your Ability to Reason Goes Out the Window, a New Study Finds," *Mother Jones*, January 10, 2013, http://www.motherjones.com/environment/2013/01/you-idiot-course-trolls-comments-make-you-believe-science-less.

70. Camille L. Rogers, "A Community of (Hybrid) Practice: Identifying the Cultural Influences of Journalism, Academic Extension and Blogging Within the External PLOS Blogs Network," University of Wisconsin–Madison, ProQuest, UMI Dissertations Publishing, 2014.

71. Dominique Brossard, "New Media Landscapes and the Science Information Consumer," in Proceedings of the National Academy of Science of the United States of America, June 26, 2013, http://www.pnas.org/content/110/Supplement_3/14096.full.

72. Melissa Gregg, "Banal Bohemia: Blogging from the Ivory Tower Hot-Desk," *Convergence* 15 (2009), http://www.academia.edu/694900/Banal_Bohemia_Blogging_from_the_Ivory_Tower_Hot-Desk; Arthur Charpentier, "Academic Blogging, A Personal Experience," Freakonomics Blog, February 18 2014, http://freakonometrics.hypotheses.org/12660; Paige Brown Jarreau, "A Network of Blogs, Read by Science Bloggers," SciLogs Blog, December 28, 2014, http://www.scilogs.com/from_the_lab_bench/a-network-of-blogs-read-by-science-bloggers/.

73. Crotty, "A New Science Blogging Scandal."

74. This list was adapted from Mary Purugganan and Jan Hewitt, "How to Read a Scientific Article," Cain Project in Engineering and Professional Communication, Rice University, http://www.owlnet.rice.edu/~cainproj/courses/HowToReadSciArticle.pdf.

75. Ramiro M. Joly-Mascheroni, Atsushi Senju, and Alex J. Shepherd, "Dogs Catch Human Yawns," *Biology Letters,* October 23, 2008, doi: 10.1098/rsbl.2008.0333.

76. Ibid.

77. Jennifer Yoon and Claudio Tennie, "Contagious Yawning: A Reflection of Empathy, Mimicry, or Contagion," *Animal Behavior* 79 (March 17, 2010), doi: 10.1016/j.anbehav.2010.02.011.

78. Aimee L. Harr, Valerie R. Gilbert, and Kimberley A. Phillips, "Do Dogs (Canis Familiaris) Show Contagious Yawning?" *Animal Cognition,* (May 19, 2009), doi: 10.1007/s10071-0090233-0.

79. Ibid.

80. Karine Silva and Liliana de Sousa, "'*Canis Empathicus*'? A Proposal on Dogs' Capacity to Empathize with Humans," *Biology Letters,* February 16, 2011, doi: 10.1098/rsbl.2011.0083.

81. Sean J. O'Hara and Amy V. Reeve, "A Test of the Yawning Contagion and Emotional Connectedness Hypothesis in Dogs, Canis Familiaris," *Animal Behavior* 81, no. 1 (January 2011), doi: 10.1016/j.anbehav.2010.11.005.

82. Karine Silva, Joana Bessa, and Liliana de Sousa, "Auditory Contagious Yawning in Domestic Dogs (Canis Familiaris): First Evidence for Social Modulation," *Animal Cognition* 15, no. 4 (July 2012), doi: 10.1007/s10071-012-0473-2.

83. Custance and Mayer, "Empathic-Like Responding by Domestic Dogs."

84. Teresa Romero, Akitsugu Konno, and Toshikazu Hasegawa, "Familiarity Bias and Physiological Responses in Contagious Yawning by Dogs Support Link to Empathy," *PLOS One* (August 7, 2013), doi: 10.1371/journal.pone.0071365.

85. Leslie Garrett, "New Scientific Studies Ask: Can Dogs Feel Empathy?" Ceasars-Way.com, January 30, 2014, http://www.cesarsway.com/dogbehavior/basics/Can-Dogs-Feel-Empathy#ixzz3NxdgW8Ju.

86. Elainie Alenkaer Madsen and Tomas Persson, "Contagious Yawning in Domestic Dog Puppies (Canis Lupus Familiaris): The Effect of Ontogeny and Emotional Closeness on Low-Level Imitation in Dogs," *Animal Cognition* 16, no. 2 (March 2013), doi: 10.1007/s10071-012-0568-9.

87. Alejandro Moyaho, Xaman Rivas-Zamudio, Araceli Ugarte, Jose R. Eguibar, and Jaime Valencia, "Smell Facilitates Auditory Contagious Yawning in Stranger Rats," *Animal Cognition* 17, no. 1 (January 2014), doi: 10.1007/s10071-014-0798-0.

88. Nicola Rooney and John Bradshaw, "Canine Welfare Science: An Antidote to Sentiment and Myth," in *Domestic Dog Cognition and Behavior,* ed. A. Horowitz (Berlin: Springer-Verlag, 2014); Alexandra Horowitz and Julie Hecht, "Looking at Dogs: Moving from Anthropocentrism to Canid Umwelt," in ibid.

89. Dmitry Arbuck, "Is Yawning a Tool for Wakefulness or for Sleep?" *OJPsych* 3, no. 1, (January 2013), doi: 10.4236/ojpsych.2013.31002.

90. Alex J. Bartholomew and Elizabeth T. Cirulli, "Individual Variation in Contagious Yawning Susceptibility is Highly Stable and Largely Unexplained by Empathy or Other Known Factors," *PLOS One* (March 14, 2014), doi: 10.1371/journal.pone.0091773.

91. Daniel Kahneman, *Thinking, Fast and Slow* (New York: Farrar, Straus & Giroux, 2011).

Instructor Guide

Exercises for each chapter can be found at LeslieStebbins.com. Suggested activities and assignments are based on the *Framework for Information Literacy for Higher Education*[1] as well as the six strategies discussed in this book.

Each collection of exercises connects to a specific chapter and provides a menu of options to pursue depending on time and resources. Most can be done either during classroom time or as homework. Most important, the exercises are being updated and improved in real time based on feedback from instructors like you! Please feel free to connect with me at LeslieFStebbins.com for suggested changes or additions.

The six threshold concepts that anchor the Framework are:

1. **Authority Is Constructed and Contextual.** Information resources reflect their creators' expertise and credibility, and are evaluated based on the information need and the context in which the information will be used. Authority is constructed in that various communities may recognize different types of authority. It is contextual in that the information need may help to determine the level of authority required.
2. **Information Creation as a Process.** Information in any format is produced to convey a message and is shared via a selected delivery method. The iterative processes of researching, creating, revising, and disseminating information vary, and the resulting product reflects these differences.
3. **Information Has Value.** Information possesses several dimensions of value, including as a commodity, as a means of education, as a means to influence, and as a means of negotiating and understanding the world. Legal and socioeconomic interests influence information production and dissemination.

4. **Research as Inquiry.** Research is iterative and depends upon asking increasingly complex or new questions whose answers in turn develop additional questions or lines of inquiry in any field.

5. **Scholarship as Conversation.** Communities of scholars, researchers, or professionals engage in sustained discourse with new insights and discoveries occurring over time as a result of varied perspectives and interpretations.

6. **Searching as Strategic Exploration.** Searching for information is often nonlinear and iterative, requiring the evaluation of a range of information sources and the mental flexibility to pursue alternate avenues as new understanding develops.

NOTE

1. "Framework for Information Literacy for Higher Education," Association of College and Research Libraries, February 2015, http://www.ala.org/acrl/standards/ilframework.

Glossary

Above Average Effect. People have a tendency to be unrealistically optimistic about their own abilities even when they have a realistic understanding of the actual odds of success for a given event. This is also referred to as over-optimism. A strong body of research notes this effect: that when asked about a specific skill—for example driving ability or business success—the vast majority of people believe they are above average.

Advergame. A downloadable or web-based computer game that advertises a brand-name product by featuring it as part of the game.

Association of Food Journalists Food Critics Guidelines. These guidelines issued by the Association of Food Journalists provide food journalists with ethical industry suggestions for reviewing restaurants. While recognizing that restaurant criticism is not an objective pursuit, goals such as fairness, honesty, and a deep understanding of the cuisine under review should be followed. The guidelines encourage reviewers to report on the whole of a restaurant and its intentions about creating a dining experience.

Astroturfing. The practice of masking the sponsors of an organization or company to make it appear that the content contributed originates from, and is supported by, individual people not connected with the organization or company. It often involves people using fake names to post positive or negative reviews. It is common and in most cases illegal.

Bad Science Bloggers. Bloggers whose purpose is to correct many of the problems the mainstream media create in communicating science information to the public. These bloggers try to debunk what they see as media-created science myths, and they often write about controversial science topics that connect to public policy decisions. Their credentials and experience varies.

Bandwagon Heuristic. A shortcut used when evaluating information that involves people assuming that if many others think something is correct, then it must be correct—and thus credible.

Biased Assimilation. This information evaluation strategy involves giving extra weight to information found that supports the searcher's goals.

Biased Information Search. This information search strategy involves seeking out evidence that is congruent with existing beliefs.

Black Hat Search Engine Optimization. Illegal strategies undertaken to maximize the number of visitors to a particular website by ensuring that the site appears high on the list of results returned by a search engine.

Blind Peer Review. During the journal peer-review process, authors submitting manuscripts do not know the identities of their reviewers in order to ensure more objective reviewing. *See also Double-Blind Peer Review.*

Bounce Rate. The percentage of people who view the home page of a website and then leave—that is bounce—without viewing any more web pages on the site.

Bot. A software program that visits websites and reads their pages and other information in order to create entries for a search engine index.

Citation. A reference to a published or unpublished source used to provide credit to the original source from which content is referenced or quoted and to assist the reader in tracking down the original information.

Click Rate. The percentage of people visiting a web page who click on a link to a particular site, typically a link to an advertisement.

Closure, Need for. In the context of searching for information, for some information needs there is a strong need to get a quick answer and have an issue settled. A strong need for closure results in sometimes settling on the first piece of information found, even if it is from an unreliable source.

Confirmation Bias. The tendency people have to view information as credible if it confirms to a preexisting belief, and not credible if it is counter to an existing belief.

Consistency Heuristic. A shortcut or strategy for evaluating information by checking to see if information across different sources is consistent. This is a shortcut to evaluating information because it is easier to check a few sources than to investigate source credentials, research methodology, or other markers of quality and reliability. Sometimes this shortcut provides an effective check to ensure the original piece of information is reliable, but other times searchers perform a superficial search using only one or two other sources, and this can result in an ineffective check on the reliability of the original piece of information.

Content Farm. A company that hires large numbers of contract workers to write large amounts of text-based content specifically designed to satisfy search engine algorithms and increase the likelihood of a site appearing as high as possible in the list of results retrieved by a search engine.

Content Writer. Content writers range from full-time staff journalists to contract employees who are paid pennies per paragraph. The commonality for content writers is that they are producing relevant content for websites with an eye toward a target audience and toward using keywords that will improve the odds that the website in which the writing appears will come up near the top of a search results list.

Couchsurfing. Staying for free or extremely cheaply in another person's home, usually while traveling. Typically this means sleeping on a living room couch or some other informal or improvised sleeping arrangement.

Crowdsourcing. The practice of compiling and using large amounts of user-generated online information, services, reviews, data, or other types of content. Often people are not reimbursed financially for their participation in creating content and the company or organization gathering content can use the crowd data rather than hiring paid staff.

Crowdturfing. A combination of crowdsourcing *(see entry above)* and astroturfing. Astroturfing involves using fake names to post positive or negative reviews for a specific company or organization. It is common and illegal.

Curation, Digital. Sorting through large amounts of content available on a specific topic and selecting and organizing the best of the content available. Some content or digital curation involves providing interpretation and commentary. Useful digital curation sites are invaluable, but many poor-quality collections exist as well. If the content is curated by crowdsourcing it is called social curation.

Data Mining. The analytic process of exploring large amounts of data in search of consistent patterns or systematic relationships between variables, and then validating the findings by applying the detected patterns to new subsets of data. The ultimate goal of data mining is prediction. Data mining has many business, education, and research applications.

Deep Web. The Deep Web consists of all the information on the Web that cannot be found by using a regular search engine such as Google or Bing. The vast bulk of the Deep Web includes scholarly articles and books that are behind paywalls or hidden within databases that traditional search engines cannot access. Pages buried several layers down in a site hierarchy are also part of the Deep Web, because search engines tend to skim the top and second-layer pages; they do not go more than a few layers down unless a page has multiple links to it from other websites. The Deep Web also includes *some* government information (billions of pages), white papers, special archives, some blogs and wikis, many social media sites, corporate intranets that are behind firewalls, and pornography sites. Also referred to as the Invisible Web. The size of the Deep Web has been estimated at between 5 and 500 times the size of the parts of the Web that are searched by Google.

Digital Forensics. A branch of forensic science encompassing the recovery and investigation of material found in digital devices, often in reference to computer crime. One section of digital forensics involves authenticating images on the Web and determining if they have been altered.

Disintermediated Information. Disintermediation refers to the elimination of an intermediary in the supply chain between the producer and the consumer. With regard to information, disintermediation has allowed people direct access to information while at the same time eliminating the value that is added by publishers, editors, librarians, doctors, educators, scholars, and others. Disintermediated information hands the job of selection and evaluation of information over to search engines and consumers.

Double-Blind Peer Review. During the journal peer-review process, authors submitting manuscripts do not know the identities of their reviewers and reviewers do not know the identities of the author(s) in order to ensure more objective reviewing.

Double-Blind Experiment. An experimental procedure in which the subjects of the experiment and the persons administering the experiment do not know the critical aspects of the experiment. It is used to attempt to prevent both experimenter bias and placebo effects.

Echo Chamber. A situation in which information, ideas, or beliefs are amplified or reinforced by transmission and repetition inside an enclosed system, where different or competing views are not provided. This effect usually pertains to media and can be greatly amplified online.

Electronic Word of Mouth (eWom). The passing of information between a consumer or other unpaid communicator and a receiver over social media or other online platform relating to a brand, product, or service. If the provider of information receives some type of reward this is referred to as electronic word-of-mouth marketing.

Fact Checking. The process of determining the veracity of a specific piece of information, usually before it is published.

Fast Thinking. Based on the work of Daniel Kahneman and others, Fast Thinking is intuitive thinking that is often relied on when we make decisions. Sometimes we derive greater benefit from using a slower, more deliberate, and effortful form of thinking called Slow Thinking.

Filter Bubble. The result of personalized search algorithms that search engines use to customize information for each individual searcher based on information about the user, including location, past click behavior, and search history. This personalization results in shielding users from information that disagrees with their viewpoints and isolates them within their own cultural or ideological bubbles, resulting in less exposure to viewpoints that differ from the user's beliefs. Writer Eli Pariser created the term.

Herding Behavior. In reference to information rating systems, such as online five-star rating systems, studies have demonstrated that people are easily influenced by the ratings of others, especially when those ratings are positive. There is a related snowball effect: the more positive ratings people see the more likely they will be influenced to also give a positive rating. This is one of the reasons many review sites are skewed toward overly favorable ratings.

Herding Phenomenon. In reference to journalism, as the number of journalists covering a story increases a herding phenomenon typically occurs consisting of individual reporters becoming likely to imitate the angle and approach previous reporters have developed. The individual journalist is dissuaded from taking an original or unique approach to a story because of the time involved in creating the story from scratch and the concern that a different take on a story might go against the perceived wisdom of a group of journalists. This herding phenomenon reduces the chances that each journalist will investigate and write a unique story. While more efficient for news organizations this effect can lead to a magnification of any errors made by the first reporters of an event.

Impressionistic Knowledge. Sometimes called intuition or instinct because it seems to come from gut feelings, these are highly informed gut feelings. Impressionistic knowledge develops after years of experience. Sometimes referred to as connoisseurship or professionalism.

Informal Knowledge. Knowledge that is acquired through personal experience, outside of formal learning environments such as schools and training.

Inter-Rater Reliability. The degree of agreement among raters. In social science this is used when tallying the results of a survey or study where there is some degree of subjectivity in user responses. Two or more judges, or raters, are used to independently categorize results. The more often the judges agree that an answer belongs in a certain category the higher the inter-rater reliability. If raters do not agree, either the scale is defective or the raters need to be re-trained to accurately interpret the scale.

Internet Water Army. A term used in China, also known as Wangluo shuijun, it refers to a large group of Internet ghostwriters paid to post online comments with particular content that is either positive or negative about a particular product or service.

Invisible College. This has various definitions, but in relationship to scholarly communication it refers to a loose-knit community of scholars who informally communicate with each other and form an unofficial network to connect researchers working on similar topics. The invisible college serves an important function in helping build knowledge and provides interpersonal connections and support among researchers as well as drawing in researchers from related disciplines in order to share ideas. Invisible colleges can influence research orientation and help constrain scientific work within a manageable framework. This can have both positive and negative effects on the development of knowledge.

Invisible Web. *See Deep Web.*

Journal Impact Factor (JIF). This is one measure of journal prestige and is based on the measure of the frequency with which the "average article" in a journal has been cited in a given period of time. A JIF is only one measure of prestige, and it can sometimes be manipulated by authors who cite their own work or play politics by heavily citing the specific work of peers to increase their research reputation.

Likert Scale. A psychometric scale or rating scale used in research often with questionnaires. It is also commonly used with rating and evaluation applications on the Web. Often a scale will use five to seven ordered responses, for example: 1) strongly agree, 2) disagree, 3) neither agree nor disagree, 4) agree, 5) strongly agree. On many review sites the rating scale is represented by stars, with one star indicating poor and five stars indicating excellent.

Long-Form Journalism. Also called long-form content, the definition varies, but there is general agreement that long-form journalism is writing pieces that are longer than 700 words and typically longer than 1,800 words.

Medialization. A concept used to describe the centrality of the media for communication in society and the orientation of social systems toward the media. In particular, this concept is focused on the increasing media attention placed on scientific issues and the increasing orientation of science toward the media, including using university press offices to create hype and thus increase funding opportunities for specific kinds of research.

Motivated Cognition. The unconscious tendency of individuals to fit their processing of information to conclusions that suit some end or goal. This concept can include biased information searching (seeking out evidence that is congruent with existing beliefs) and biased assimilation (giving extra weight to information found that supports the searcher's goals).

Native Advertising. Paid sponsored content that is designed to look almost identical to the other content offered by a media outlet.

Negative Search Engine Optimization. Performing an action that damages a competitor's organic search rankings. One common example of this is to build low-quality links which point at a competitor website. This results in Google or another search engine penalizing the competitor by pushing them down in the list of results.

Network Effect. A phenomenon whereby a good or service becomes more valuable when more people use it, and leads to an even greater number of people using it.

Observational Study. A study in which a researcher simply observes behavior in a systematic manner without influencing or interfering with the behavior. Observational studies can involve naturalistic observation (observing behaviors in the natural environment) or laboratory observation (observing behaviors in a research laboratory).

Open Access (OA). Literature that is digital, online, free of charge, and free of most copyright and licensing restrictions. OA removes price barriers such as subscriptions and licensing fees to provide free availability and unrestricted use, but it also remains compatible with copyright, peer review, revenue, and other features and support services associated with conventional scholarly literature. The primary difference from regularly published works is that the bills are not paid by readers and hence do not function as access barriers.

Outreach Science Bloggers. Bloggers whose goals include educating the public about science topics, similar to the goals of science journalists.

Peer Review. Peer review, in reference to journal articles, is the process of using predetermined reviewers or ad hoc reviewers who individually read a submitted manuscript and prepare a written review. In the vast majority of refereed journals, the identity of the reviewer(s) is not revealed to the author(s), to ensure more objective reviewing. This is termed single-blind reviewing. Double-blind peer review requires the author(s) and the reviewer(s) to remain anonymous.

Persuasive Intent Heuristic. This involves a tendency to feel that information that may be biased is not credible. This tendency typically involves people feeling negatively about the credibility of a piece of information when unexpected advertisements or commercial content is shown next to the information. People perceive the advertising as manipulative and this leads them to suspect the credibility of the information they are viewing.

Primary Research. Research that involves original data collection rather than an analysis of data collected by others. Examples include surveys, interviews, observations, and ethnographic research.

Procedural Knowledge. The type of knowledge or expertise that comes from skill development that is gained from formal education and reading.

Proof by Repeated Assertion. A phenomenon that occurs when a piece of information is repeated over and over again. The repetition reinforces the idea that because so many sources have reported it as true it therefore must be true.

Randomized Design. In a randomized experimental design, objects or individuals are randomly assigned to an experimental group. Using randomization is the most reliable method of creating homogeneous treatment groups, without involving any potential biases or judgments.

Refereed Journal. A refereed journal is a journal that is subjected to a detailed peer review following a defined formal process according to a uniform set of criteria and standards. Essentially this means that there is a formal review process in place so that articles are reviewed by peers or colleagues before they are accepted for publication and published.

Reliable Information. For the purposes of this book, reliable information refers to information that can be verified to be trustworthy, true, valid, authentic, and accurate to the degree that that is possible.

Reputation Heuristic. This shortcut in evaluating information involves relying on the reputation or name recognition of a source of information rather than seeking out other evaluative criteria. People tend to favor recognized alternatives over less familiar ones and they sometimes attribute greater value to these recognized sources of information. Even a vague familiarity with the name of a source can strongly influence credibility judgments.

Research Science Bloggers. Science faculty or graduate students who use their blogs to communicate to a select group of other researchers or students, to "think aloud," or to create a virtual watercooler to chat about and test out ideas and promote their work. These research blogs are often informal, but they cover meaty and often cutting-edge science topics.

Satisficing. A term developed in 1956 to explain why people often pull together a limited amount of resources in order to find "good enough" information. It is a practical coping technique, because everyone is bound by time limitations. Satisficing is used more frequently in making less important decisions.

Scholarly Database. A database that covers published academic content, including journal articles, reports, statistics, case studies, book chapters, books, and other materials. Scholarly databases provide access (citations or full text) to the Deep Web and many reliable resources found via scholarly databases do not appear in Google search results. Some scholarly databases cover multiple disciplines; others focus on one specific discipline.

Search Engine. A software program that searches for, and identifies, online items that correspond to keywords or characters specified by the user.

Search Engine Optimization (SEO). This involves a growing number of strategies undertaken to maximize the number of visitors to a particular website by ensuring that the site appears high on the list of results returned by a search engine.

Selective Exposure to Information. The tendency for people to prefer and seek exposure to information that agrees with their preexisting opinions.

Selection Bias. In reference to searching for information, this phenomenon occurs when people choose something they expect to like and their choice then influences their opinion in a positive direction.

Self-Regulated Knowledge. Knowledge about oneself that is needed in order to function effectively in a particular domain or field. It is not about *how* to be, for example, a wine expert. It is about how to manage oneself, with one's strengths and weaknesses, within that field.

Self-Reinforcing Information Spiral. More people see a shrinking, more similar set of news and opinion pieces on particular subjects when they do online searches because features such as suggested search terms and autocomplete come up based on a searcher's past behavior. The more people influenced by these interventions the more popular certain search approaches become. Researchers Dominique Brossard and Dietram Scheufele coined this term in talking about science information.

Shallow Web. Also referred to as the surface web or static web, this encompasses the collection of websites indexed by automated search engines such as Google that use bots or Web crawlers that follow URL links and index Web content and relay the results back to the search engine for consolidation and user query. Bots and crawlers are only able to access and index a small percentage of the entire Web, and this portion that they are able to access is called the shallow web. Its counterpart, the Deep Web, is estimated to be anywhere from 5 to 500 times as big.

Sharing Economy. Also called the peer-to-peer economy, it is an economic model in which individuals are able to borrow or rent assets owned by someone else. Often this model is facilitated by platforms on the Web.

Single-Study Syndrome. This phenomenon has been used to discuss how advocates for a particular issue seize on one study—no matter how tenuous its findings—in order to push a specific agenda. More broadly this phenomenon also refers to the habit of some journalists or writers to seize on the latest scientific finding as representing the truth. This is a problem because one study, no matter how well done, only represents one aspect of the world under one set of conditions. Scientific research needs to be presented in context and seen as a process rather than a single event. Multiple studies need to be conducted and understood before any conclusions can be drawn about a topic.

Slow Thinking. Based on the work of Daniel Kahneman and others, Slow Thinking involves deliberate and effortful thinking, as opposed to fast and intuitive thinking. We frequently rely on fast thinking when certain choices we make could benefit from slow thinking.

Snowball Effect. In reference to user rating systems, research has shown that if a number of positive ratings are given to a certain product or service early on that that effect quickly multiplies due to a social influence phenomenon that is less likely to occur with negative reviews. The power of social influence to impact choices made by others is not a new phenomenon, but social media greatly magnifies the effect.

Snowballing Strategy. In reference to tracking down information on a specific research topic, this involves tracing the citations at the end of a research article, looking up those articles, and then tracking the citations at the back of those articles. For a comprehensive literature review the snowball strategy is used until all the articles have been found that focus on a specific topic.

Source Amnesia. When an information searcher remembers a piece of information and treats that information as true, but forgets what the source of the information is, or whether it came from a reliable or unreliable source.

Spider. A program that visits websites and reads their pages and other information in order to create entries for a search engine index. The major search engines on the Web all have such a program. Also called a "bot" or "crawler."

Substitute an Easier Question. When faced with a difficult question people often answer an easier but related question instead, usually without noticing the substitution. This happens more frequently when someone has little expertise on a particular topic.

Take the Best Heuristic. This information shortcut involves choosing between two alternatives, by predicting which of the two will have the higher value with regard to some relevant criterion. It involves comparing the two alternative choices on a list of characteristics, with these characteristics listed in order of importance. Rather than going through the entire list of values, participants use a shortcut and decide based on the fist value in the list that differs from the competing alternative. They choose the better alternative based on that single value. This is often a superior method, and also more efficient, than going through and weighing each value that differs. It is a strategy that is typically used by experts in a particular domain.

Test Group. In the context of an experiment, this is a group of subjects closely resembling the treatment group in many demographic variables but not receiving the active medication or factor under study and thereby serving as a comparison group when treatment results are evaluated.

Triangulation. The mixing of data or methods so that diverse viewpoints cast light on a topic. In the social sciences, triangulation is used to validate data through cross verification from two or more sources that use different methodologies in studying the same phenomenon.

Trolls. People who post comments on social media or other websites that are specifically designed to stir up trouble.

Viral Marketing. Any marketing technique that uses social networking sites or other technologies to increase brand awareness or product sales. The implication is that information or "buzz" about the product can be spread among social networks like a virus. Viral marketing can be paid for or unpaid.

Weighted Additive Linear Model. A common decision-making strategy novices use by assigning each piece of information a positive or negative point and then adding up the points to make a decision. This decision making differs from a technique experts use called "Take the Best." *See also Take the Best Heuristic.*

What You See Is All There Is. A form of fast intuitive thinking where the decision maker assumes that the information at hand is all there is on a topic, without looking further or even considering that there might be more information on a topic.

White Hat Search Engine Optimization. This involves a growing number of legal strategies undertaken to maximize the number of visitors to a particular website by ensuring that the site appears high on the list of results returned by a search engine.

White Paper. A report that is not peer reviewed but has the appearance of research. There are different types of White Papers: Some summarize research and then draw a straight line between the research and the product they want to sell, and others do original research and with the findings highlight a particular product as beings superior to others or more effective. The product highlighted is typically from the company sponsoring the White Paper. Not all White Papers are marketing tools, and many can provide useful information despite their marketing orientation.

Wisdom of the Crowd. A frequently misused term, this is a well studied phenomenon that demonstrates that aggregating the answers to a specific question from a large crowd of individuals often provides as good and in some cases a superior answer to the answer given by any one individual in the group. The wisdom effect is dependent on answers being provided independently of knowing the answer given by any other individual, because the effect is easily undermined by social influence. Also, aggregated answers work best when they are responses to questions that have correct answers such as quantity estimates or factual knowledge.

Word of Mouth (WoM). The passing of information between a consumer or other unpaid communicator and a receiver relating to a brand, product, or service. If the provider of information receives a reward, this is referred to as word-of-mouth marketing; if the interaction takes place online, it is called Electronic Word of Mouth (eWom).

—

Index

About the Author

Leslie Stebbins has more than twenty years of experience in higher education with a background in library and information science, instructional design, research, and teaching. She has a Master's degree in Education from the Technology Innovation & Education Program at the Harvard Graduate School of Education and a Master's in Information Science from Simmons College. For twenty years she created and led library research instruction and information literacy programs at Brandeis University. Currently she is the director for research at Consulting Services for Education (CS4Ed). Her clients both at CS4Ed and as an independent consultant have included Harvard University, the California State University Chancellor's Office, the U.S. Department of Education, Facing History and Ourselves, Tufts University, and the Joan Ganz Cooney Center. She is the author of numerous articles and three books, including the popular *Student Guide to Research in the Digital Age*. She currently writes a review column for the *Journal of Academic Librarianship*. For more on Leslie Stebbins, see LeslieStebbins.com.